We Are Coming, Unafraid

We Are Coming, Unafraid

The Jewish Legions and the Promised Land in the First World War

Michael Keren and Shlomit Keren

ROWMAN & LITTLEFIELD PUBLISHERS, INC.
Lanham • Boulder • New York • Toronto • Plymouth, UK

Published by Rowman & Littlefield Publishers, Inc.
A wholly owned subsidiary of The Rowman & Littlefield Publishing Group, Inc.
4501 Forbes Boulevard, Suite 200, Lanham, Maryland 20706
http://www.rowmanlittlefield.com

Estover Road, Plymouth PL6 7PY, United Kingdom

British Library Cataloguing in Publication Information Available

Library of Congress Cataloging-in-Publication Data
Keren, Michael.
  We are coming, unafraid : the Jewish legions and the promised land in the first
world war / Michael Keren and Shlomit Keren.
      p. cm.
  Includes bibliographical references and index.
  ISBN 978-0-7425-5274-6 (cloth : alk. paper) — ISBN 978-1-4422-0550-5
(electronic)
  1. Great Britain. Army. Jewish Legion—History—20th century. 2. World
War, 1914–1918—Personal narratives, Jewish. 3. World War, 1914–1918—
Participation, Jewish—Anecdotes. 4. Jewish soldiers—Correspondence. I.
Keren, Shlomit. II. Title.
  D568.7.K47 2010
  940.4'1241—dc22   2010013668

Printed in the United States of America

Contents

Acknowledgments

We are grateful to the archives in which the life-writing material used in this study of Jewish Legionnaires in the First World War resides: the Legions House in Aviha'il, Israel; the Haganah Archive in Tel Aviv, Israel; the Archive of Australian Judaica in Sydney; the Jabotinsky Institute in Tel Aviv, Israel; and the IDF archive in Tel HaShomer, Israel. We are particularly grateful to Rachel Silko of the Legions House, Dorith Herman of the Haganah Archive, and Marianne Dacy of the Archive of Australian Judaica for their assistance.

We are indebted to Dr. Khane-Faygl (Anita) Turtletaub of Northwestern University for her translations of the material appearing in chapters 2, 3, 4, 6, and 10 from the original Yiddish and to Dr. Laurel Halladay of the Center for Military and Strategic Studies at the University of Calgary, who edited, formatted, and indexed the manuscript.

We thank Dr. Martin D. Herman for donating the Yiddish memoir of his granduncle Miguel Krel, published in Montevideo in 1938 by Y. Blekham. We thank Ira Jacob Liss's children Vickie Herzberg and Dr. Shelly Liss for their help in confirming Liss as the writer of the diary presented in chapter 6. We also thank Michael Falk of Sydney, Australia, for information on his grandfather, the Legions' chaplain, L. I. Falk.

This study was made possible by financial support from Canada's Social Sciences and Humanities Council and the faculties of Social Science and Communication and Culture at the University of Calgary.

We received inspiration and encouragement from conversations with professors Stewart Cohen of Bar-Ilan University, Richard Freadman of La Trobe University, Robert O. Freedman of Baltimore Hebrew University,

Craig Howes of the University of Hawaii at Mānoa, and Joel S. Migdal of Washington University in Seattle, as well as from our colleagues at the University of Calgary, professors David Bercuson, Stephen Randall, and David Taras. We received invaluable feedback in the first stages of this study during a workshop, "Place and Displacement in Jewish History and Memory," held at the Kaplan Center at the University of Cape Town in January 2005, and thank all participants in this successful workshop.

We thank the Taylor & Francis Group for permission to incorporate in this book material published in the following articles: Shlomit Keren and Michael Keren, "The Jewish Legions in the First World War as a Locus of Identity Formation," *Journal of Modern Jewish Studies* 6 (March 2007): 69–83; and Shlomit Keren and Michael Keren, "Chaplain with a Star of David: Reverent L. I. Falk and the Jewish Legions," *Israel Affairs* 14 (April 2008): 180–97.

We also thank the University of Hawaii Press for permission to incorporate material published in the following article: Michael Keren, "National Icons and Personal Identities in Three Israeli Autobiographies," *Biography* 27 (Spring 2004): 357–83.

Finally, we would like to acknowledge British poet Nina Davis Salaman's "Marching Song of the Judeans," from which the main title of this book has been drawn.

1

Introduction

In July 1918, during the First World War, Yitzhak Ben-Zvi, a Jewish labor leader, sailed on board a British warship that carried a contingent of Jewish volunteers from a recruit depot in Windsor, Nova Scotia, to Plymouth, England. Three years earlier, Ben-Zvi had been expelled from Palestine with his comrade David Ben-Gurion by the Ottoman authorities. While exiled in the United States, Ben-Zvi and Ben-Gurion joined the Jewish Legions formed within the British army in 1917 and helped recruit other volunteers among labor Zionists in America to take part in the Allies' Middle East campaign. Fighting to secure its oil installations in the Persian Gulf and control strategic routes and waterways such as the Dardanelles and the Suez Canal, Great Britain suffered repeated defeats in Gallipoli and in Gaza, and in 1917 had a severe shortage of manpower as a result of the transfer of troops to the Western Front. It thus relied in its war against the Ottoman Empire on a large multinational force which included four battalions, known as the Jewish Legions, recruited among Jews in England, the United States, Canada, Argentina, and Palestine. On July 5, Ben-Zvi wrote his wife, Rachel Yana'it, a letter in which he noted the heterogeneity of the Jewish recruits. There were men endowed with a strong national and social consciousness alongside recruits of dubious character. Ben-Zvi seemed perplexed over the diversity of social class, educational background, and personal motivation among the volunteers.[1]

The heterogeneity of the recruits has been noted in many memoirs. Roman Freulich wrote that "[m]ost were ardent Zionists, but among them were also men who were seeking adventure, running away from their wives or from their creditors. The caliber of men ranged from high to low: from gentle idealists who hated war, to men of violent passions who enjoyed the idea of combat and dangers."[2] The latter group included, for example, a Brooklyn gang whose leader "Mickey" said one day, "Boys, let's go to fight for the Jews," and fight they did: "Mickey was always spoiling for a fight, and gave a good account of himself, especially when the opponent happened to have insulted the Jewish people. Of the others, Tommy was a thief and a gambler, 'Tish' and 'Chick' were 'tough guys,' and the slogan of the group as a whole was, 'All for one and one for all.'"[3]

David Todis describes his own adventures as a sixteen-year-old boy from Riga, Latvia, who was studying in a yeshiva (a school for religious studies) in Palestine. When the First World War broke out, he was on a family visit to Riga and was forced to report to the Russian army. A band of smugglers helped him escape from Russia through Siberia, Manchuria, China, and Japan to finally land in his brother's home in Brooklyn. In 1917 he joined the Jewish Legions and fought in Palestine, where he was injured and contracted malaria. While in the hospital, he signed up for his next adventure—carrying gold to Arab sheikhs by camel in the Arabian Desert for Lawrence of Arabia.[4]

Baruch Gurevitz, a volunteer from Palestine, profiled in his notebook various characters he met in the course of his service in the Legions. One is described as "the Russian sergeant." His face was typically Slavic, his walk straight, and his body fit and strong. His father was a Russian general of aristocratic descent, and his mother was a Jew who hid her Jewish origins. At the beginning of the war, the father was killed in Galicia and the widow departed with her son for America, where her family lived. In America, the son revealed his Jewish origins and enlisted with the Jewish Legions.

Another and very different character profiled in the notebook is "the boy from Chicago," who at a young age had been sent from Russia to live with his Orthodox grandfather in Chicago. The grandfather tried, to no avail, to teach him religion. The boy dropped out of several schools and failed even to hold down a job as an apprentice; instead, he spent his days and nights in coffeehouses. One day, two recruitment officers came into the coffeehouse where he and his ne'er-do-well friends were playing cards and invited them to go and liberate the land of Israel. As he told Gurevitz, who met him in a detention center in Palestine:

> I asked them where actually is the land of Israel and what is it good for. They explained that the tyrannical, lazy Turks are in charge there now and are preventing the development of the land. The land is mainly uninhabited, with only some poor Arabs living there; the country is waiting for its redeemers, for the children of Israel to return to it. . . . They ended by saying to me: by enlisting you will be honored and glorified, your name will be written in the Golden Book. I then asked about the book which I had never heard of. They

explained that Baron Rothschild had a big and magnificent palace in Paris. And inside the palace was a special room where the Golden Book is kept; it is a large book made entirely of gold and covered with precious stones. Inside the book, the names of all the great men of our generation are listed; you can find there the Rothschilds, Roosevelt and the names of kings and knights, and among them [your] name will appear because [you] will honor America and the entire people of Israel. This appealed to me, I got up and called upon all the guys, let's go and enlist in the Hebrew legion of the Zionists, and kick the Turks out.[5]

Thus, side by side with Zionist leaders like Ben-Zvi (who would become Israel's second president) and Ben-Gurion (eventually Israel's first prime minister), professional soldiers like Colonel Eliezer Margolin (awarded the Distinguished Service Order for his command of Australian forces in Gallipoli and France), and noted artists like sculptor Jacob Epstein, a variety of less prominent characters had joined the Jewish Legions. This book is for the most part about the latter—Jews from the immigrant enclaves of London, New York, Montreal, and Buenos Aires who in 1917 answered the call to liberate the Promised Land.

One of the characteristics of the First World War was the formation of "citizen armies," at the center of which stood not the professional soldier but the civilian who "exchanged his private self and his individual self-interest for a public and communal identity represented in the uniform."[6] The recruitment of civilians was no smooth process. When the war broke out in 1914, only the German army was prepared for the massive fighting, with forty-four army corps divided into nine armies, while, in comparison, the British Army Expeditionary Force included roughly 160,000 troops.[7] Ian Beckett estimates that by 1918 over 65 million men were mobilized worldwide, including 4.9 million British, half of whom were volunteers and the other half of whom enlisted after the introduction of conscription in 1916. Becket emphasizes the unequal distribution of recruits in terms of profession and nationality; more British soldiers were taken away from professions like finance and commerce than from industry and agriculture, and Wales and Scotland had a larger percentage of males under arms than Ireland. He singles out Jews, especially immigrants from Russia, who, he claims, were automatically rejected by conscription boards as physically unfit as a result of "social prejudice."[8]

The question of the recruitment of Jews to the British army is, however, more complex and involves, as in the cases of other nationalities, factors of region and class. As Todd Endleman explains, when Britain went to war in 1914, acculturated, middle-class Jews responded to the call to arms with enthusiasm, partly as a result of their genuine patriotism and partly as a way to disprove the charges of disloyalty, cowardice, and unmanliness that were the stock-in-trade of anti-Semites. However, immigrant families from Eastern Europe, many of whom lived in London's East End, refused to send their sons to the army, where they would be forced to violate religious dietary laws and fight on the side of Britain's ally, the Russian czarist regime that they had just escaped. Speaking of twenty-five to thirty thousand Russian-born English Jews who avoided conscription by taking advantage of the exemption of "friendly aliens," Endleman notes that they were the only group of able-bodied men escaping military service, which reinforced the anti-Semitic image of Jews as "slackers."[9]

Similar dynamics existed elsewhere. Although Jews in many countries fought in the Great War in greater numbers than their respective populations would have dictated, Jews were largely stereotyped as being "disloyal, uncourageous, and constitutionally unfit as soldiers."[10] This posed a difficulty for nonenlisted Jews of military age, many of whom had not taken part in the war because they did not meet citizenship and naturalization requirements. The situation was especially acute in North America, where the failure of many young Jews to participate in the great experience of the age stood in contrast to their desire to integrate into the "New World," especially after the Selective Service Act was signed by American president Woodrow Wilson in May 1917 and the Military Service Act was passed in the Canadian parliament two months later.

In his study of Jewish immigrants in the United States on the eve of the Great War, Christopher Sterba describes their dilemma. Living in immigrant enclaves with practically no interference from federal and local governments, their engagement with the wider American environment was limited. Most immigrant Jews had not become naturalized before the war, and although the Military Service Act allowed nonnaturalized persons to enlist if they declared their intention to become citizens, and many did, there was still great resistance to the draft. According to Sterba, "fear of conscription stemmed from [experience of] military service in czarist Russia, which had meant abuse, hunger, and a high mortality rate even in peacetime. Many Jews from the Russian Pale fled to America specifically to evade conscription."[11]

North American Jews who did enlist could point to their military records "as proof of their feelings toward their adopted country."[12] As Michael Berkowitz explains, "the war offered the unique opportunity to testify to the Jews' mettle as able-bodied fighting men, and as a stock worthy of equal rights."[13] But those who did not enlist because they were either unnaturalized residents in Canada or "nondeclarants" for personal, economic, or religious reasons in the United States found they were lacking the preconditions for the process of conversion of "immigrants into Americans"[14] that wartime service would have provided. But in 1917, they were given a unique opportunity to join the war by enlisting with the British army.

When Lord Horatio Kitchener became Britain's war secretary in August 1914, committed to the effective formation of a citizen army, the War Office encouraged the recruitment of groups composed of the same ethnicities and social groupings. For example, Scotsmen and Irishmen were recruited into distinct military units, and regiments were composed of recruits belonging to the same social clubs, church groups, and professional organizations.[15] This sparked the idea, considered in the War Office in 1914, of recruiting an exclusively Jewish regiment, which would allow Russian Jewish immigrants to express their loyalty to the Empire without violating their religious beliefs.

Influential Jewish English leaders who objected to a distinct Jewish fighting force out of fear it would call into question their loyalty to the overall British war effort and hinder Jewish assimilation in English society managed to kill the idea in 1914,[16] but it continued to preoccupy the Jewish press and public in England.[17] When Turkey joined the war on the side of the Central Powers, Zionist leaders, notably Ze'ev (Vladimir) Jabotinsky and Joseph Trumpeldor, who realized the importance of active Jewish support of the Allies on that front as a means to gain national standing when the war ended, got permission to organize a "Zion Mules Corps," made up mainly of Jews exiled by the Ottomans from Palestine to Alexandria.

The corps participated in the fierce fighting on the Gallipoli Peninsula in 1915. Jabotinsky, who considered this too minor a role, made, from 1915 onward, relentless efforts to get permission from the British government to form a Jewish battalion in the British army. These one-man efforts were met with resistance by leaders of the World Zionist Organization, which declared neutrality in the war. They were also rejected by officials in the British War Office, who, while concerned over the thousands of Russian Jews who did not join the war effort, were reluctant to allow an all-Jewish unit formed for political purposes. Jabotinsky's efforts failed until 1917, when pro-Zionist attitudes prevailing in Lloyd George's government, combined with Britain's decision to launch a major campaign against the Ottomans in Palestine, paved the way for the War Cabinet's decision to recruit a Jewish regiment both in England and abroad.[18]

Three battalions were formed as part of the Royal Fusiliers: the 38th Battalion, composed of English Jews who were largely forced into service by the Military Service Convention between Britain and Russia of July 1917, calling upon Russian subjects of military age to choose between conscription and repatriation; the 39th Battalion, composed mainly of Jews from the United States (which allowed the recruitment of residents but not of citizens) and from Canada and Argentina; and the 40th Battalion, recruited in the summer of 1918 among Jews in Palestine. A fourth battalion, the 42nd, was a holding battalion stationed in Plymouth. About seven thousand soldiers served in these battalions during the war under the command of Colonel John Henry Patterson, an Irish Protestant.[19] The Jewish Legions, as they came to be known, were part of a multinational force composed of British soldiers, Australians, New Zealanders, Indians, South Africans, French, Italians, West Indians, Egyptians, and even some Polynesians.[20] While the War Office played down the uniqueness of the various components of the force (which was the reason for the inclusion of the Jewish battalions as part of the Royal Fusiliers), the Jewish Legionnaires were allowed to carry a Star of David insignia on their left sleeve, which was the symbol adopted by the World Zionist Congress. The three battalions were distinguished by the color of the Star of David, which came in purple, red, and blue.

The Legions were established too late to allow participation in the Gaza campaign launched on October 31, 1917, under the command of General Edmond Allenby, who replaced General Archibald Murray, the commander of the Egyptian Expeditionary Force, who failed to take the city in two former attempts. Both the 38th and the 39th Battalions, however, fought in Allenby's battles in the Jordan Valley in summer 1918.[21] Allenby, attaching more strategic importance to the region's Arabs than to Jewish aspirations, as he is reported to have told Patterson and Jabotinsky,[22] displayed continual hostility to the Jewish Legions, evidenced by his proposals that they become labor battalions or be amalgamated with West Indian Legions. While allowing the recruitment of the 40th Battalion, Allenby was suspicious of any initiative to turn the Legions into a Jewish brigade or to employ them as a major force in the occupation of Palestine. The Legionnaires were assigned such duties as guarding the bridges on the Jordan River and protecting Turkish prisoners of war. After the armistice, the Legions were further marginalized by Allenby's headquarters. Continuing ambiguity over their status led to two rebellions—one by American Legionnaires protesting delays in their demobilization, and another by the soldiers recruited in Palestine, who refused to serve outside the country's boundaries.

At the end of 1919, the shrinking Legions received some recognition with the granting of the title of "The First Judean Battalion," the badge of which was the Jewish symbol of the menorah (the seven-branched candelabrum used in the ancient temple). The London War Office's symbolic gesture, however, did not free the Legions from the restraints that prevented them from intervening in the skirmishes between Arabs and Jews in Palestine in 1920 and 1921, and the Legions were disbanded.

In his book *The Jews in America*, Arthur Hertzberg wrote that as a result of the Legions' experience, "American Jews received a glorious sense of their own power and of their participation in the renaissance of Jewish power in the land of their ancestors."[23] This assessment is understandable in light of the symbolic role of the Legions as the first military formation of Jews in the modern era, but it is also exaggerated in light of the small number of recruits to the Legions and their limited role in the massive battles of the First World War. Service in the Jewish Legions was mainly significant on the individual level, as we shall now explain.

The need to call millions of civilians to arms turned the First World War into an intense war of propaganda in which the press, the visual arts, the pamphlet, the motion picture, and other media were mobilized to invite the brave to join the war; bash the slackers and war profiteers; blame the enemy for causing the war, bringing to light atrocities it committed; and strengthen the morale of whole populations subjected to the destructive effects of the first total war in history. When the war, believed in August 1914 to be a short one, turned into a lengthy trench war in which millions of young men lost their lives for causes that became increasingly unclear, massive propaganda was used to give meaning to the meaningless slaughter of a whole generation. When one sees the photos of "Kitchener's Army," those thousands of young civilians in short jackets, ties, and beret hats assembled in London's recruitment centers to die soon in the fields of Flanders, one realizes how effective the call must have been to "stop the barbarous enemy" and "take up the sword of justice."[24]

Soon after the decision was made to form the Jewish battalions, it became clear that Jabotinsky's vision of a large Jewish force was all but unrealistic. His own attempts to speak in favor of joining the war in London's East End were met with violence. In December 1917, the month Allenby entered Jerusalem, the average number of Jewish recruits in England did not exceed forty per week.[25] Thus, the propaganda machine was set in motion, following the strategy applied to other nationalities. Just as the Irish were called upon to stop being bystanders and follow in the footsteps of Irish heroes like Sergeant Michael O'Leary, who took an enemy trench single-handedly, the Jews who failed to enlist were criticized, while those who were willing to swear allegiance to the king were portrayed as liberators of the Promised Land. For example, a poster colored blue and white (the colors of the Zionist flag) was published showing the image of the Daughter of Zion, who is referred to in the Old Testament's book of Lamentations as follows: "And from the daughter of Zion all her beauty is departed: her princes are become like harts that find no pasture, and they are gone without strength before the pursuer."[26] In the poster, the female figure points her finger forward, calling upon Jews in Yiddish to join the British army, as the time has come for her to regain her land.

Such religious symbols were common in the First World War and became part of the overall imagery of the war. In his study of literary works by Great War combatants, Paul Fussell shows, for example, the great impact of John Bunyan's *Pilgrim's Progress*, the seventeenth-century tale

of Christian's journey "From This World to That Which Is to Come."[27]
As Fussell puts it, "front-line experience seemed to become available for
interpretation when it was seen how closely parts of it resembled the action of *Pilgrim's Progress.*"[28] These parts included Christian's journey with
a great burden on his back, moving physically through a terrible topo-
graphical nightmare; his reaching "the Valley of the Shadow of Death"
where "lay blood, bones, ashes, and mangled bodies of men, even of Pil-
grims that had gone this way formerly"[29]; and the promise that the meaning of it all will be revealed at the end. The famous tale, Fussell writes,
allowed English soldiers to describe in familiar terms a war that was
otherwise utterly incredible and incommunicable in its own terms. He
agrees that Dante's *Inferno* may have been more appropriate to express
the reality of the new industrialized mass trench warfare, but Dante has
never been domesticated in Protestant England, which turned to Bunyan
when looking for traditional images of waste, horror, loss, and fear.

The Jewish recruits from England, the United States, Canada, and Argentina were exposed to a religious symbol that was clearly domesticated
in their culture: the Jews' journey to the Promised Land. This symbol not
only guided the recruitment efforts but became an important component
of the allies' propaganda in the Middle East campaign. Consider the following poem published in the *New York Evening Sun* on the eve of the
departure of one contingent of Jewish recruits from New York.

> Awaken O Jerusalem
> Thou city of the king:
> The Lord God of Israel
> Has wrought a wondrous thing;
> A byword and a mocking
> Through centuries of shame,
> He comes to raise thee from the dust
> And build again thy name.[30]

A Toronto newspaper reporting on the government's decision to allow
nonnaturalized Canadian Jews to enlist in the British army also used re-
demptive language when it stated that "[t]he Jews claim a better fight will
be put up this way as they will be fighting for ideals. In addition to fighting for [the] British Empire, they will be striving to restore Jerusalem to
its people, a fight which has been going on for 2000 years."[31] And a month
later, the same newspaper heralded the departure of Jewish recruits to the
training camp in Windsor, Nova Scotia.

Amid stirring scenes of enthusiasm and acclaim the second corps of young
Hebrews has left Toronto for the East to join the Jewish Legions for service
with the British armies in Palestine. It was a send-off in which citizens of all

creeds and classes participated, and bespoke the spirit of the whole Canadian people. The Jew has already distinguished himself in heroic war service on both battlefronts in Europe, and, with occupation of the Holy Land by the British and the ending of centuries of misrule by the Unspeakable Turk, has a new and national concern to the ultimate triumph of the cause of freedom and right. . . . Canada will follow with admiration and confidence the achievements of her Jewish citizen-soldiers on the fields of conflict.[32]

The *Canadian Jewish Chronicle* was particularly enthusiastic and declared that "Our Legionnaires are going, are going far away, to fight for Faith and freedom. . . . Our Legionnaires have answered, Have answered Freedom's call To buy by blood our home back. . . . For theirs is a goal of Honor, And theirs is a cause so high—And a Hebrew will fight for his honor, He'll fight—nor fear to die!"[33]

The image of the Legionnaires as liberators of the Promised Land was reinforced by the excitement they caused when seen in train stations and other locations along the way. Jews noticing the Legionnaires—a waiter in France, a Jewish German prisoner of war on the way to Italy, Jews on the streets of Alexandria—were exhilarated by the sight of the Star of David on the soldiers' sleeves. That image was also enhanced by emblematic gestures. One Legionnaire remembered, "The Sergeant-Major of the Legion marched in the first row, carrying the Torah scrolls of the Legion, accompanied by three of our members who carried the flags of the USA, of England and the Hebrew flag. We were applauded by all the residents of Halifax as we marched past them."[34]

The notion that they were fighting for the restoration of Jerusalem to its people, and the consistency of that notion with the overall aims of the Allies, had an enormous effect on the recruits' consciousness. Individuals who were often displaced immigrants or the children of such immigrants now had bestowed upon them the image of liberators of the Promised Land and turned that image into a building block of a new identity as Jewish soldiers. The development of that identity is our concern in this study. We follow personal diaries, memoirs, and letters of a handful of Legionnaires in an attempt to learn how they negotiated their identity in light of this new symbolism.

Service in the Legions provided an opportunity never before entertained by Jews: an opportunity to fight for a cause that combined parochial and universal goals, as symbolized by the Jewish and British flags they carried in military marches. This makes the life-writing material analyzed here particularly exciting; it tells a story that differs in important ways from the common tale of Jewish soldiers in military formations in their respective countries. For example, in *GI Jews*, a study of Jewish American soldiers in the Second World War, Deborah Dash Moore writes that donning an American uniform made Jews paradoxically both more

American and more Jewish. The perception that such a dual American-Jewish consciousness is paradoxical stems from the author's emphasis on anti-Semitism, which categorizes her description of Jewish service in the American military as a process of adaptation to a hostile environment.

> Trained to carry guns, Jews learned how to defend themselves not just as soldiers but as Jews. From brainy, smart-aleck, urban, talkative ethnic recruits, Jews became disciplined, physically fit, skilled in handling weapons. As assertive soldiers they would manage somehow to deal with antisemitism even as it caused them some anguish. They determined to prove themselves as soldiers and as men. Their Jewishness became integral to their individual identity.[35]

In other words, the encounter with anti-Semitism strengthened the Jewish recruits' identity as Jews, and partial success in overcoming its effects altered the terms of Jewish life in America. Whether or not one accepts this view of Jewish service in the American military as inherently problematic and of Jewish national identity as largely dependent on the amount of respect given by others, this is not the story of the Jewish Legions in the First World War. The life-writing material here reflects the emergence of a Jewish soldiering culture that may at times have been encouraged by a successful boxing match against Gentile units but that was not haunted by anti-Semitism or determined by encounters with the "other." While the consciousness of Moore's GIs as American Jews supposedly developed as a response to such factors as the army's nonkosher food that "challenged identities absorbed in their mother's kitchens,"[36] the First World War Legionnaires never abandoned their mother's kitchens. Not only were they living among Yiddish-speaking soldiers within a Jewish setting, which included a supply of kosher food, an ark with Torah scrolls, public celebrations of the Jewish holidays, musical performances of Jewish music, lectures on Jewish affairs, and the like, but they were also endowed with a mission that was consistent with their people's longtime traditions.

This consistency was not incidental, as it was, for instance, in the case of Jewish American soldiers whose fighting in the Second World War turned out to be consistent with their concern for their brethren in Europe. The Legions' aim was defined as the liberation of the Promised Land, a mission that was inherently part of the soldiers' upbringing. We are thus given a rare opportunity to observe the development of a Jewish military culture and national identity on an existential level rather than as a response to anti-Semitism. We learn about the ways in which men from a culture that lacked a national military tradition for two thousand years acquired the norms, ideas, and practices common among warriors in the First World War and adapted the war's rhetoric to a uniquely Jewish context. We follow the life writing of Legionnaires, whose evolving consciousness as soldiers and as Jews instructs us about a new phase in Jewish history.

Writings by individual soldiers have not traditionally served as a major source of historical insights but are receiving increasing attention by historians who appreciate the more subtle and complex understanding they provide, especially of the Great War.[37] Most of the material we discuss in this book was composed by simple soldiers who were not versed in the grand historical debates of the times, such as those taking place within the Zionist movement, but whose writings add, as we shall show, an element of subtlety and complexity to these debates.

The material, housed by veterans of the Jewish Legions in Israeli archives, was in bad shape when we found it, especially the diaries written in notebooks distributed by the British army, in which the handwriting has often faded beyond recognition. The diaries we discuss are those that were in good enough shape to be translated and saved from oblivion. Due to its historical importance, we decided to present the life-writing material almost in its entirety with little annotation.

The life-writing material reflects the rites of passage of Jews who, lacking a military tradition, turned into members of a community of First World War soldiers with unique Jewish features. Their accounts of the transformation they underwent in their experience in the Jewish Legions can be seen as travelogues. Scholarly and literary works on the impact of war on soldiers have often used the notion of the journey to represent the transition in the individual's life.[38] Eric Leed, in his study on the Great War as an initiation process in the life of soldiers, describes three stages of that journey: separation, transformation, and return.[39] The personal accounts here correspond quite closely to that typology.

For the North American recruits, the journey began literally at the British recruit depot in Windsor, Nova Scotia, from which they sailed to the Crown Hill training camp near Plymouth, where they joined the English recruits. From Crown Hill, the Legionnaires went by train and ship to Egypt and Palestine. The journey to the Promised Land, corresponding with the notion prevailing in Canada, which sent its young to fight for the British Empire overseas, and in the United States, which came in 1917 to the rescue of the free world, became a common motif in the diary entries written in the Atlantic Ocean during the submarine war, on the trains of Europe and Egypt, and in the battlefields of Palestine.

The departure ceremonies described in the writings are characteristic of fighting men anywhere going to war: the recruits noted the marching bands, the kisses good-bye from the girls, and so on. Whatever personal reasons might have led to their enlistment, the soldiers saw their departure for war as a noble mission, consistent with the prevalent view of the

Great War as one that would rescue nations from moral decay and bring people back to the basic truths from which they had wandered.[40]

The writings concerning Crown Hill depict the soldiers' intense process of adjustment to the bad food, the ill-fitting uniforms, the snoring comrades, the potato peeling in the kitchen, the drills, the discipline, and all other features of barracks life. The writers express a strong will to fulfill their duties and become "real" soldiers, which to many obviously does not come naturally. They often envied their Gentile comrades, who seemed to be far more disciplined. Gradually, however, a martial culture with unique Jewish themes developed. The writings express a prideful excitement over such experiences as a march in uniform to the synagogue on the Sabbath, the celebration of the Passover seder in the land of Israel, or lying in trenches across the Turkish lines during Yom Kippur, the Day of Atonement.

As was the case on all fronts of the First World War, the initial excitement of the journey to the battlefields was soon replaced by disenchantment. After the fighting on the Jordan River as part of the Megiddo front, the Legionnaires were preoccupied in building roads and fortifications, patrolling across Turkish lines, and guarding prisoner camps. At this point, the life-writing material takes a downward turn in tone and begins to express exhaustion over the widespread malaria, the unbearable summer heat, and the boredom. The Legionnaires describe the routine of guarding Turkish prisoners of war in the heat and sandstorms of southern Palestine or in the malaria-stricken Jordan Valley in a manner reminiscent of First World War novels like *A Farewell to Arms* or *All Quiet on the Western Front*.

A strong sense of ambiguity and of life on the brink develops. The end of the war seems near, but the dreams and expectations for personal or national redemption have not been fulfilled. The future seems insecure and the soldiers feel they have no control over their lives. This is where the role of the chaplain, Reverend Leib Isaac Falk, becomes central. In contrast to Patterson, the Irish Protestant commander of the Legions to whom the presence of Jewish soldiers in the Holy Land in itself meant the fulfillment of the Gospel's promise, the Jewish chaplain tried to invigorate the soldiers by characterizing the unpleasant soldiering experiences as a journey to a Promised Land that had not yet been completed.

The life-writing material reveals that despite disenchantment, and with the benefit of some reflection, the Legion experience endowed the Jewish soldiers with comradeship, bravery, endurance, commitment, and equality, all of which they acquired as a result of their sharing a common goal and continued to cherish for years to come. They wrote each other mementoes in which they idolized the hardships they encountered, indulged in the comradeship they found as a result, and expressed pride in having become Jewish soldiers continuing the tradition of ancient Hebrew heroes.

Our decision to present as much as possible of the original writings by the Legionnaires resulted, of course, in some repetitions, as the experiences recorded by the soldiers were sometimes similar. However, each of the following chapters represents a different dimension of the Legionnaires' journey to the Promised Land.

In chapter 2, we consider the memoir of Miguel Krel, a volunteer from Argentina who served in the 38th Fusiliers. This memoir, published in Yiddish in Montevideo in 1938, presents the first step in the Legionnaires' experience: leaving one's home, family, and former life for an unknown future. The memoirist makes a distinction between the tears shed by Jewish parents in the past, when their children were forced into the czar's army, and those shed by his parents when he went to war for his own people. He describes the banquets, parades, and other ceremonies arranged by local Jewish communities upon the soldiers' departure and some of the adventures they experienced on the way to Palestine, sailing the world's oceans during the submarine war, and landing in such spots as the British colony of Sierra Leone. Particularly instructive is the description of the Legionnaires' reaction to news about a pogrom in Poland in November 1918. The pogrom brought back hard memories from the time in which Jews were helpless while, holding British rifles in their hands, the soldiers considered commandeering a ship that would take them abroad to help their brethren.

In chapter 3, we examine the diary of a Russian Jew from Chicago who served in the 39th Fusiliers and whose name is unknown. The diary provides detailed and perceptive descriptions of the landscapes and sights of the world during the Great War. We accompany the unknown soldier on a warship carrying hundreds of men pressed together like sardines going down the St. Lawrence River, and accompany him as he sails into the turbulent Atlantic Ocean in a British convoy threatened by German submarines, goes by train through England, becomes part of an army-in-waiting in which endless drills are conducted and only the reminder that it is all part of a worthy cause keeps the soldiers sane, arrives in the Egyptian city of Port Said, and finally enters Palestine, which, covered by thousands of army tents and railroad tracks moving exhausted soldiers from place to place, hardly resembles its biblical image of "a land of milk and honey."

In chapter 4, we bring the wartime notes of Private Chaim Baruch Berezin of the 39th Fusiliers, who fought in the battle in the Jordan Valley. The notes are amusing at first, as when the Bronx Jew describes his reluctance to swear allegiance to His Majesty the King of England or tells of his adventures as a singer entertaining British officers decorated with medals and their young wives dressed in silk and diamonds. Then, the notes turn to the reality of war, with the long walks in the Palestine summer under a sun that is burning like hell, Turkish shelling on Yom Kippur, the sights and smells of dead men and horses, and an encounter with German and Turkish prisoners of war. The notes reflect the adoption of soldiering norms by a person who is strongly rooted in Jewish tradition and folklore, and explore the inspiration he gets in hard moments by realizing the fighting is taking place in biblical locations like the Judean Hills, Jerusalem, Jericho, and the Jordan River.

In chapter 5, we bring a memoir written by an English-born Legionnaire named Abraham Jacob Robinson, who fought with the 38th Fusiliers and received a Military Medal for bravery. In contrast to those who felt the English recruits lacked the Zionist idealism characterizing the North American volunteers, including the founder of the Legions, Jabotinsky, we show that although Robinson may not have been versed in the Zionist literature of the time, his self-consciousness as a Jewish soldier fighting for the British Empire contains a large degree of idealism. This memoir is a strong example of what we call existential Zionism—namely, Jewish national consciousness that stems from religious roots rather than from an imagined model formulated by political leaders and intellectuals.

In chapter 6, we review excerpts from a diary by Ira Jacob Liss of Detroit, who served in the 39th Fusiliers and recorded in thirteen lengthy notebooks the transformation he underwent from a displaced immigrant to a proud American Jew. A month after he was drafted, the young man, traveling on a warship in the Atlantic Ocean surrounded by eight British destroyers, already felt a dramatic change in his own fate and that of the Jewish people. The diary reflects on army life, war and peace, cruelty toward prisoners, and other issues familiar from soldiers' writings in the First World War, while pointing to the uniqueness of service in the first Jewish formation of modern times. Liss shows, for example, how the biblical tale of the Exodus served as a reference point for him in the foreign terrain of Egypt. He expresses his strong disenchantment after his arrival in the Promised Land when his unit was confined to the desert town of Rafa, on the outskirts of Palestine, where the summer heat, sandstorms, and mosquitoes became the soldiers' main preoccupations. The diary shows how difficult military routine became once the symbolism attributing to the soldiers the role of liberators of the Promised Land faded.

In chapter 7, we discuss the memoir of the Legions' chaplain, Rabbi L. I. Falk, who helped formulate the symbol of the Jewish Legions as a vanguard on the way to the Promised Land and consoled Legionnaires disenchanted by the encounter with reality in Palestine by explaining that the journey had not yet been completed. The memoirs, written in London in 1922, revisit the debates over the formation of the Jewish Legions and

Falk's stand in the debates, which stressed the consistency between the goals of British victory in the war and Jewish national revival, both of which he saw as providential. In line with his spiritual mentor, Rabbi Abraham Isaac Hacohen Kook, Falk promoted the notion of the Legionnaires as descendents of ancient Hebrew warriors who were given the opportunity to reassert their religious and national roots and thus gain a place in the community of enlightened nations. Falk's call to Jews to fight under both a British and a Jewish flag as a means to enhance their status in Great Britain put him in discord with Zionist leaders, including Jabotinsky, who saw Jewish participation in the war as a means to support Jewish presence in Palestine. His attempt to relate the soldiering experience to Jewish theology led to conflicts with Palestine's Zionists, who took a road to national revival devoid of religious faith and tradition.

In chapter 8, we present letters written by Major Henry D. Myer, veteran of the Western Front who served as second-in-command of the 40th Fusiliers, to his fiancée, Louie Solomon. The letters display the impressions of a young professional officer belonging to the Jewish British assimilatory elite who treats displaced Jewish immigrants from Russia with snobbery and applies the stereotype of "weakling" to them. The letters indicate, however, a change of attitude over time. While describing at length the football matches and other rituals conducted in British military barracks, as well as the lizards, mice, goats, tortoises, guinea pigs, and other creatures he and his fellow animal-loving officers adopted in the Egyptian desert, Myer increasingly becomes part of the crowd of Israelites walking the desert road to the Promised Land. Colonel Patterson, for one, becomes "a second Moses" to him. The letters Myer writes from Palestine provide interesting observations of the political situation in the country after the British occupation.

In chapter 9, we discuss a memoir composed half a century after the events by another veteran of the Jewish Legions, Benjamin Bronstein. Written by this active ex-Legionnaire in Lynn, Massachusetts, the memoir sheds light on how Bronstein's service in the Legions affected his later thoughts and experiences. One learns, for example, how service in the British army in Palestine made him feel a stronger tie with his ancestors. One also learns of the ambivalence felt by this devout Zionist toward the Palestinian Jews—for example, their demand that the Hebrew language be used exclusively in public performances in the military camp. Although Bronstein served in the 40th Fusiliers side by side with prominent figures like Labor leader Berl Katznelson, Israel's first chief of staff Yaakov Dori, and third prime minister Levi Eshkol, he was less impressed by his encounters with them than by events related to his Jewish heritage, such as the celebration of Jewish holidays during his service. The chasm between the volunteers from Palestine and the Legionnaires from abroad that comes to light in this memoir provides a partial explanation for the neglect of the latter in many of Israel's history books.

In chapter 10, we appraise some exciting letters written by Legionnaire B. Zilberman, who wandered in Egypt and Palestine after the Legions' demobilization. In the letters, written to his former comrade Yehoshua Davidzon, who served with him in the 39th Fusiliers and then settled in the United States, Zilberman spells out the hardships he encountered once the great experience they were part of ended and he became displaced and disoriented. The letters provide a unique view of the economic and political conditions in Palestine in the early 1920s, with Zilberman's despair over the lack of employment and the prolonged negotiations over the allocation of land to veterans of the Jewish Legions interwoven with despair over deteriorating relations between Arabs and Jews in the country. The letters refer to the San Remo Conference of April 1920, in which Great Britain and France were granted a League of Nations mandate over Palestine, the nomination of Herbert Samuel as high commissioner for Palestine in 1920, the Arab riots in Palestine and the anti-European riots in Cairo and Alexandria in May 1921, and other events. These letters serve as a monument to a sense of comradeship that did not end with demobilization but that was partly overwhelmed by melancholy once the symbolism that accompanied the Legionnaires on their journey to the Promised Land had faded and sites that were associated with biblical images had turned into a hard, disputed soil whose future was uncertain.

We conclude with some thoughts on existential Zionism, the unique form of Jewish consciousness found in the life-writing material of the Legionnaires. The transformation they underwent during their service in the British military, we argue, did not involve dismissal of their former heritage, as national movements often demanded, nor did they resemble the iconic image of the "New Jew" designed by the Zionist movement. To the contrary, they negotiated the soldiering culture they were exposed to and the national mission they were endowed with within the parameters of their personality, upbringing, and religious traditions, thus pursuing a mode of Jewish nationalism marked by authenticity.

2

Leaving Home

LIKE CHILDREN OF A NORMAL AND HEALTHY PEOPLE

We begin with a memoir by Miguel Krel, who was born in Warsaw in 1895 and came to Argentina in 1912. In 1917 he joined the Jewish Legions. In his memoir, published in Yiddish in 1938 while he was living in Montevideo, Uruguay, he reflects on his experiences as a young man who left his home in faraway Argentina to liberate the Promised Land. Krel, who served in the 38th Fusiliers, notes that while many English Jews he met in that battalion joined it reluctantly, he and his Argentinean fellows came voluntarily, which is indeed the case, because Argentina remained neutral in the war and did not have a draft.

> We truly joined the Legion as volunteers, without any outside influences; we were only motivated by our internal force, like children of a normal and healthy people, whose best progeny fight to be the first to give their lives for their people and their land. We have here a small group, too far to be influenced by the official leaders of organized Zionism, who decided to create a movement to join the Jewish Legion and fight together with the British Army to free the land of Israel.

The memoir tells of the excitement caused by the formation of a Jewish military force and the celebrations accompanying the departure of the volunteers.

> In the last days before our departure from Argentina, the Jewish population became more excited every hour. The Jewish Argentinean citizens still

17

remember the farewell-celebration that was held for us in the Coliseum Theater. The theater was overflowing, and the enthusiasm was extraordinary. Among other personalities, [socialist legislator] Dr. Alfredo Palasios gave one of his most brilliant talks. Banquets had also been arranged. One of the most memorable was that of Mr. Max Gluksman [a major figure in Argentina's film and music industries]. This [banquet] had wonderful music, dance, and champagne, which gave us one final taste of the joys of this world. Mothers, sisters, brothers, and just regular people accompanied us to our ship with blessings on their lips and tears in their eyes. There was no limit to the people, who in their co-mingling of sadness and joy, shed tears for our young lives.

Krel makes a clear distinction between the tears shed over the departure of Jewish soldiers to the Promised Land and those shed by Jewish parents in the past.

These were another kind of tears than those our mothers cried, when we, their sons were "new recruits" in Russia or even other countries, and were led to almost certain death. No, these were another kind of tears filled with joy and belief that [now] we would not be giving our lives for strangers but for our own land, for our own people. One entity would be built by us, all together: those who were on the deck of the ship together with those who stood near the ship were united by the same ideal, the ideal of our national rebirth.

The memoir illustrates the excitement stirred in Brazil, which did take part in the war, over the soldiers' departure.

The ship slid silently over the Atlantic. Without banquets and without parades each one of us took stock of our lives. Therefore we were surprised, when upon arriving in Rio de Janeiro, we were met with the music of an orchestra and a crowd of Jews. We were seated in automobiles and were part of a military parade down the lovely avenue. Our appearance in uniforms and the whole parade made a great impression. At that time, Brazil had already declared war on Germany. The hatred of Germany was great. The curious crowd filled the sidewalks and one person told another: These are soldiers in the Jewish Army, who are traveling from all corners of the world to conquer Palestine. The Brazilian populace was very friendly to us. Even common folk found us worthy of being feted with drink and being shown the neighborhoods of this extraordinarily beautiful city. The Jewish residents rejoiced, felt proud, and paraded us around as if we were a precious stone. And at this time, when intellectuals were discussing whether or not we Jews were a nation, we strolled through the streets of Brazil as part of the Jewish Army. Our departure from Argentina and Brazil was triumphant, honored the Jewish population, and was positive and useful to Zionism.

Because of the danger posed by German submarines, the ship's captain was instructed to direct the ship to Sierra Leone in western Africa, which allows us a view of a British colony at the time.

We arrived in Sierra de Leone when the Spanish Flu was at its height; we were therefore not permitted to leave the ship. The surrounding panorama was beautiful, the natural forests between mountains and valleys, looked as if no human foot had ever touched them. I see the black natives, practically naked except for a piece of cloth around their hips. There is coal in three straight rows. One of them fills the baskets, the other one hands it to the third one, who pours it into the ship. They did not look human but more like spirits, with their black, shiny bodies under the African sun. All of them moving at the same time: one, two, three. Bending down with empty hands, straightening up with a full basket of coal, continuously without cessation. And between the rows, on a higher box, stands an overseer with a long whip and also methodically, systematically, he cracks his whip on the naked backs every time one row bends down. The result is that there is not one back the whip has not touched. The crack of the whip on their bare backs bearing black scars, resounds in the air, and after every crack, the song they sing to accompany their work is sung higher. And in this song one hears not only the joy of creating but also a deep moan. That is when I truly comprehended the meaning of English protection.

The volunteers arrived in Britain to no fanfare; no one was waiting there to greet them.

Upon arriving in Liverpool, the Captain ordered us to disembark. No one was waiting for us at the port, so we were left in an uncomfortable position. No one wanted to sell us food. We did not have any ration-cards. We also did not have a place to spend the night; we did not know the language. To tell the truth, one of our number did know English, but the Englishmen could not understand him. We telephoned the Zionist Federation. No one knew about us. They promised to take it up at their next meeting. We turned to the military post and asked about the Jewish Legion. They had never heard of such a thing. By night, someone took pity on us and took us to the British barracks. We stayed there for a week. We were afraid that they were going to send us to the French front, so every day we pleaded that they have compassion on us and send us to the Jewish Legion.

Finally, the volunteers were brought to the Crown Hill camp near Plymouth where the 38th Fusiliers were gathered, and the memoirist was excited to see the Jewish flag fluttering on the barracks. As he remembers it, everyone began to sing the Zionist hymn "Hatikvah" (Hope). Jewish soldiers hearing the singing came out to greet the newcomers, and together they joyously marched into the camp.

The adjustment of the Argentineans to army life in British barracks was difficult as a result of the language barrier.

> The first difficulty that the British officers had with us Argentineans had to do with commands; we did not understand any English, so they were forced to teach us everything a soldier needed to know in Yiddish. However, the Yiddish vocabulary does not possess such elements. For example, rifle down, rifle on the shoulder, close the feet, spread the feet, and so on. Because of this, our first exercises were the cause of constant laughter in the battalion. In principle we did not want to give in and argued that we cannot learn English. So the commands continued in Yiddish for several weeks, until we ourselves saw the impossibility of [continuing to give] commands in Yiddish only to us. Our military course in England lasted 4 months.

Language problems were not unique to the Argentineans—as reported in a May 1918 issue of the *Canadian Jewish Chronicle*, a dictionary of "military Hebrew" had to be composed by the British military. For instance, "Front rank" became *Tor alef*, "Stand easy" became *Amod noach*, and "Mark time" became *El makom*. The difficulty in adjusting to army life stemmed not only from the language barrier but also from the lack of a military tradition. When Krel was promoted to corporal, for example, he felt uncomfortable giving orders to friends who were older than he was: "How would I be able to lead and command older and more honorable comrades, such as Yosl Katz, Yankel Grinberg, and other names familiar in Argentina?" The problem was solved in a meeting in which the Jewish soldiers decided that military discipline would prevail over seniority.

HOLDING WEAPONS

The memoirist then turns to his experiences in Palestine, of which two are worth noting. The first concerns Krel's encounter with an Arab during a walk on the sand dunes of southern Palestine. While the story is probably colored by later events, as memoirs often are, it provides some insight into the perceptions Jews and Arabs had of each other at this early period, as well as into future relations between the two parties once both sides were armed.

> Together with two other friends, Yankel Grinberg and Malenski, [I walked] at dawn with heavy steps on the light sand. We went on our way. After half a day, we were not too far from the sea, and we saw an oasis in the valley, an area of land with green trees. The earth was planted and it was surrounded on all sides with sand dunes, with which the wind was cavorting, driving them from one place to another. Only the oasis was peaceful as if nothing [that was happening around it] bothered it. It was a true wonder of nature.

We descended. A young Arab came towards us. He brought us tomatoes and watermelons. The Arabs were used to soldiers trampling and destroying their cultivated fields underfoot. Their fear of soldiers was extraordinary. A rumor was circulated among the Arabs that there are forty thousand soldiers in Palestine. We calm the Arab down. We do not want to disturb him. Just the opposite, we throw him several coins. This completely astounded him. In the distance we see another Arab. He said that his future father-in-law was coming. He had promised to work for him for 7 years in order to get a wife from him. He complained that wives were, in general, getting to be very expensive. Men pay up to 10 pounds already for one. This is a sum, which he can never attain. "How old is the bride [to be?]" we ask. "He has three daughters. The oldest is 4 years old. He will give me whichever one he wants."

We become somewhat friendly with this Arab. After our bath we go back to this same Arab to rest in the shade of his palm trees. We pay him again for his fruits. He wants to kiss our feet. We do not permit it. We begin to walk. He pleads with us to wait, so that we can protect him, and later he [says that] he will take us out of the sand-dunes in the quickest way possible. It is already evening and we get going. Our heavy shoes sink into the soft sand. The Arab walks near us barefooted. We treat him to a cigarette, but before we finish smoking it, he asks for another one. We did not like the tone in which he asked very much, but we were in his hands. He did not wait very long before asking for several piasters [small coins]. And now his tone was unbearable. His unmitigated gall showed us where we stood in the world. We promise to give them to him later. He walks faster. We call to him. He turns around and with a cynicism that is difficult to describe he shouts to us that shoes are no good, while pointing out how he glides with extraordinary agility over the sand with the soles of his feet. I run with all my strength to catch him. He taunts us by laughing right in my face. I throw my bayonet at him, the only weapon we had with us. But I missed my mark. In the end, the Arab disappeared in the labyrinth of sand. We were alone between the sky and the sand, our bodies targets arrayed for the jackals. In addition, Malenski, the weakest one of us, had fainted from fatigue and fear. We had to carry him or roll him down the sand dunes. It is [now] late at night, and we are dragging ourselves with our last reserves of strength. Suddenly we see light. We go in that direction and only after midnight we barely managed to drag ourselves to the hut of Australian soldiers. All three of us were faint. We rested, received something to eat, and in the morning were sent by train back to our battalion, 20 kilometers away.

The second experience concerns the Legionnaires' reaction to news they got about a pogrom in Poland. The pogrom occurred in the city of Lemberg (Lvov) in November 1918. Following the breakdown of the Austro-Hungarian monarchy, fighting between Polish and Ukrainian troops erupted, and the Poles who won the battle customarily accused the Jews of supporting the Ukrainians. Soldiers and civilians set fire to homes of Jews and killed many of them. The American, British, and French press reported on the pogrom.¹ We have an opportunity to observe the response to a pogrom by a group of Jews who remembered the helplessness of Jewish families when their homes were attacked but who had now left those homes and, holding British weapons in their hands, felt that a new era in Jewish history had come.

At that time, Poland, the very newly-independent country, celebrated its independence with a bloody pogrom on Jews in Lemberg. The news of this pogrom exploded in our circle like a grenade and caused confusion. The soldiers gathered in groups in huts, and each one of us felt that we could not remain silent. To tell the truth, our situation was a strange one. We, who were standing near the trenches of the just recently dismantled front and were serving with the Allies—the same ones who tore chunks of land away from Germany and Austria in order to enrich the new [country of] Poland. This same Poland now dares, in the presence of its allies, before the eyes of the whole world, to organize such a bloody pogrom in which the Jewish corpses numbered in the hundreds.

The storm among us reached the most fervent pitch. The 40th Battalion, in which the Jewish soldiers had organized themselves by selecting officers and sergeants, carried their full packs as well as ammunition and started out to wage war on Poland in order to take vengeance on the martyred Jewish souls.

Today it sounds like a legend. It was, however, a fact. Our despair could find no other outlet.

The Jewish Army consisted of five thousand five hundred well-trained soldiers.

If we had gotten underway, we would have amassed as many provisions and as much ammunition as we would have wanted, and no one would have stood in our way. We would even have been able to commandeer ships. Of course, Poland was far away, and we would have had to traverse many countries in order to get to its borders. [It would have been worth] the effect that such a march route would have had on the world, on the Allied powers and, especially on Poland itself, which would have at least for a moment given some thought to [the fact] that we are not sheep, who can be led to the slaughter whenever anyone decides to do so.

Unfortunately, this march was stopped right at the outset. Colonel Margolin, a nationalistic Jew, who was respected by everyone, was against this [plan] and convinced our soldiers of the impossibility of such an adventure by showing us that the Legion would surely suffer. The world's interpretation would be that the Jewish elements [in the army] could not be disciplined and so on.

That brought to an end our spontaneous outrage against pogroms on Jews. How different this was compared to our usual protest meetings, which had numbered in the hundreds where the same resolutions were always accepted but with different addresses: today about Poland, tomorrow about Rumania, etc. And at every meeting [there would be] a prominent Gentile, who was a candidate in the next election in the country, who gave a fiery speech accompanied by gestures fitting for a future. No! No! Our protest had a completely different character. We lived together with the Jews of Lemberg. Their suffering was [also] ours. That is why our souls hurt and grieved. We would rather have fallen in the battlefield, fighting the enemy—in this case the Polish perpetrators of the pogrom—rather than be caught hiding in cellars looking out at loved ones being flayed and afterwards slaughtered like calves.

One must remember the limitations of a memoir written two decades after the events. In 1920 and 1921, the Jewish Legions were prevented from intervening during Jewish-Arab skirmishes taking place several kilometers from their base. This turns the idea of intervention in Poland into a mere fantasy (although the very fact that such a fantasy came to mind is instructive). In other matters, too, Krel is uttering opinions that are more in line with Jabotinsky's views in the 1930s, when his belief in taking the land of Israel by force placed him in opposition to the Zionist movement, than with the language of 1918. The memoir is influenced by a sense of frustration over the dismissal of Jabotinsky's ideas at the time and by the little appreciation given to the contribution of the Jewish Legions, whose heroism the author compares to that of the ancient Hasmoneans, the kings who ruled an independent Jewish state following the Maccabean revolt in the second century BC. He believes the Legions were not commemorated by Zionist leaders who feared the idea of an independent Jewish military force. From the beginning, he claims, the Legions received no material and moral support from official Zionist organizations: "We were never even in contact with the Zionist leadership in England or even in Palestine itself. This was at a time, when the colonial armies of the brown Indians and the black Africans were treated, as their soldiers, to a cigarette or a piece of chocolate, things which during war time are like a taste of heaven. We had to content ourselves with the meagerest of diets, because as Jews, we were not given any pork products and these were not replaced with any other food."

Krel claims that even Chaim Weizmann, president of the World Zionist Organization, looked down upon the Legionnaires when they attended a meeting with him in 1919 and accuses the Zionist leadership of not backing them up when the British government prevented their members from staying in Palestine after the war. He feels—and it is hard not to concur—that the Legions suffered historical injustice even from national poets, who have not written songs of glory in their praise.

3

In Distant Lands

SAILING TO THE BATTLEFIELDS

The diary presented in this chapter is displayed in a glass case in the Legions House in Aviha'il with no name attached to it. It has been observed over the years by thousands of visitors, but the soldier who wrote it remains anonymous. The diary, written in Yiddish, begins on August 12, 1918.

12) I enlisted today in the Jew. Legion.

13) At 11 o'clock at night, I went off on my trip to Philadelphia. . . . I had barely asked about the address when I was there already. I found out that Luba is in Atlantic City and Tonya somewhere on a farm in New Jersey, but Luba's sister treated me very well and said that she would go to Atlantic City with me, and we would find Luba. She did not know her address.

The diarist searched for relatives in order to say good-bye to them before sailing to the faraway battlefields. Following several family visits on the East Coast he returned to the recruiting station in Chicago, where he did not seem too impressed by his enlistment in His Majesty's military.

26) In the morning I went to the recruiting station. They filled in my papers, and I had to sign [my name] about 10 times. Afterwards I swore to be true to the war, its principles, and to do everything that my superiors tell me to do. At 4 p.m., 30 Christians and I went to the train station and took the train to Canada.

Upon arrival in Windsor, Nova Scotia, where he stayed for ten days, we find the first expression of pride in his new status: "I have no lack of troubles here both from the new recruits and from a soldier's life in general. I am, however, a Legionnaire and bear everything with patience."

The adjustment to army life was facilitated by preparations of a banquet celebrating the holiday of Rosh Hashanah, the Jewish New Year.

[September] 6) For a few days now we have been preparing for the banquet that is to take place tonight in honor of Rosh Hashanah. We work a lot and we also contribute money. I gave 5 dollars.

(Evening) The banquet was actually a success. All the officers were there and the most respected members of the city. There were speeches and good food (not for the soldiers—many soldiers left hungry). When I left at midnight to return to the camp, a terrible storm was raging, and I had a lot of trouble finding the tent, which was full of water.

7) We marched to the synagogue and from there to lunch. We were told that in a day or two we would be leaving for England.

8) All day long we had parades and got ready to leave. At 4 o'clock everyone gathered together, even the sick. The Major gave a speech and told us how to comfort ourselves while in transit. He wished the Jewish soldiers health and good fortune and that we might live to see the Jewish flag flying over Zion. At 7 o'clock, 8 platoons of Jews and 2 platoons of Christians left for the station and at 8 we were already on the train. We traveled a whole night not knowing where we were going.

The soldiers began a long trip through Edmundston, New Brunswick, the Eastern Townships of Quebec, and Gaspe Peninsula to the St. Lawrence River, where the ships were docked that would take them to England. The ship the diarist boarded was the *Durham Castle*, a vessel that was built in 1904, passed to the admiralty in 1939 as an accommodation ship, and was mined and sunk in 1940 off Cromarty, Scotland. Ammunition and other war material were being loaded at the same time as the men. The notebook draws a picture of a ship carrying hundreds of soldiers to the battlefields of the First World War and of the scenery of 1918.

11) I slept very badly last night. We were given hammocks, but there was not enough room for everyone. I spread my hammock out on the deck and lay down in my clothes. Things keep getting worse on the ship. There are more than 400 Legionnaires here. Many are Canadians.

Yesterday 600 Serbians boarded. They are traveling to a mobilization camp somewhere in Africa. Around 10 in the morning, an officer came and asked who wanted to box, and our Legionnaires showed their proficiency in this "art." Out of the 600 Serbians, there was not one who stepped forward [to try], but on the other hand, they sing such beautiful, sad songs, which remind me of Russian folksongs.

12) Last night I slept on a hammock for the first time. It would not have been so bad if the hammocks were not so close together. When we are all in our hammocks, we can't move. We are squeezed in like sardines. The air is also not good. Two hundred and fifty people are pressed together in a space that is barely sufficient for a hundred. We are still in Quebec. The weather is cold and wet. It rains from time to time. But when the weather is nice and the sun comes out, it burns like fire. It is getting boring being on the ship and I would like to be underway already. It is possible that we will depart tonight.

13) Our ship began to leave at 7 in the morning. We are floating on the great St. Lawrence River. We see a beautiful panorama on both sides, beautiful mountains and valleys, villages and farms can be seen everywhere. It appears that this area of Canada is well cultivated and densely populated. There are also many islands. We caught up to an English transport [ship], the "Corsican" carrying American troops. In only half an hour we had passed that ship. (It was 2 o'clock in the afternoon.) During lunch, we were all drilled on how to save ourselves during an accident. Each one has his own place in a lifeboat. Everyone was given a life vest that is two pillows, which are worn. We are not allowed to take it off for a minute. Everything is very well organized. I do not know, however, if order will be maintained when it will be necessary. We are still on the river. There are also a lot of other transport ships.

14) We are now in the Gulf of St. Lawrence. The water is turbulent and the ship is tossed back and forth. Many of us are sick. Today I am quite a fool. Who can even think of food, when one is throwing up gall?

14) Our Legionnaires are showing their human side. Some of them get together in groups and sing songs. Some of them even form a minyan [ten-man quorum required for public prayer] and pray. (Today is the Sabbath.) It is very crowded on the ship. Wherever one turns, weak people are lying on the deck.

15) We spent a very bad night. The ship was thrown about terribly. We lay on our hammocks pressed together like sardines. Many lay on the tables on the deck and any other place they could find, any bit of empty space, because there was not even enough space to hang all the hammocks. Those who were in the hammocks vomited on those who lay on the deck. They were cursing each other and it nearly resulted in blows. That together with the polluted air, because there was no ventilation, created a true hell. In the morning, the ocean became much more peaceful, and the exhausted people slowly recovered.

(In the afternoon) The weather is extraordinarily lovely. We have already left the Gulf and are now going into the Atlantic Ocean. Our Legionnaires have formed little groups and are debating whether or not we should fast tomorrow (Yom Kippur). We have forgotten all about the submarines and mines. They feel that they are now in a New York club, and they do not stop fooling around.

The Jewish soldiers, who came from different backgrounds, engaged in debates over the appropriate way to observe Yom Kippur. Some un-named activists were aware that a celebration of the holiday would be conducive to the formation of a Jewish soldiering culture, and on Yom Kippur an official fast was declared for all Jewish soldiers, including those who were nonobservant.

Some say that Yom Kippur is a national holiday that is why one should fast. Others say just the opposite, that it is a purely religious holiday and one may eat and have a good time.

   (At night) We are not lonely on the ship. Thank God, we have a committee that actually consists of people who like to have a good time, but as politi-cians they sensed that religion goes hand in hand with militarism, and they got the Captain to agree that we could pray Kol Nidre [the prayer beginning Yom Kippur] in the evening. We prayed in our quarters.

16) A very nice morning—but cool. Very early we spied a real piece of land. Today we are having an official fast and not getting any food. The canteen, however, is doing very well. And those who decided last night to fast are eating more than the others. Groups of people can still be seen discussing the fast. During the day we passed a large iceberg, but it was very far away. Af-terwards in the distance there appeared a thick fog like a volcano. We came closer and closer until we entered the fog. It became cold and wet and we could not see each other. Once again a storm came up and the ships began to signal one another.

The next entries describe the fleet's journey at sea during the period of unrestricted submarine warfare. On February 4, 1915, the German gov-ernment declared the area around the British Isles and French coast a war zone, within which all enemy ships would be liable to destruction with-out warning. In the next few months, ninety ships were sunk by German submarines, including the British passenger liner *Lusitania*, sunk off the coast of Ireland with the loss of 1,198 lives, 139 of which were American. America's reaction forced Germany to moderate its policy of unrestricted submarine warfare, but in the course of 1916 it substantially increased its U-boat fleet and in January 1917 resumed unrestricted attacks, which posed a serious threat to the Allies and were a major reason for America's declaration of war on Germany in April 1917.[1] The Allies coped with the U-boat threat by sailing in large convoys in the Atlantic and Mediterra-nean, and the submarine warfare did not determine the outcome of the war, as German admirals claimed it would. But, as can be seen here, it continued to be a nuisance until the end of the war.

17) Another day passed. We see only the sky, water and ships. The whole fleet of ships is sticking close together. It is difficult to be on a transport ship, but I comfort myself with the thought that every day we are coming closer to England.

The YMCA organized a concert and we are passing the time by singing songs and doing other activities. A lot of birds are flying around. It seems that we are not far from land. I think we are heading east and should not encounter any land until England.

The weather is nice, but cold.

In the evening the sky was covered with clouds and the water was turbulent.

18) A cold and wet day. In the evening it started to rain, and we went down to our oppressive cabin earlier than usual. At about eight o'clock, Captain Steed of the YMCA came to show us spectroscopic pictures of a French ball-game as well as some cartoons. He also sang some English songs with us. We would have been more grateful if he had brought us some fresh air.

19) It is an uneasy morning. The sea is agitated. The ship is being tossed about like a stick. The sky is covered with thick clouds. A fog is spread over the water and one can hardly see the other ships. From time to time a thin rain falls, which gets into one's bones. Sleeping at night in that fetid air is making me sick. It has been several days now that I have not eaten any cooked food. Just the smell makes me throw up. I only eat oranges and biscuits that I buy in the canteen.

At around ten o'clock in the morning there was a "bath parade." We all stood in a row naked and took a shower in seawater. The water was as cold as ice. It was difficult to go under that shower. Afterwards I felt newly born.

20) The sky is still cloudy and it rains on and off. The sea is still turbulent and the ship is [still] being tossed about; however, we are already used to these problems. During the day we had a medical check-up. We were [also] told that if we heard whistling or shooting, we should not be afraid, because it is nothing more than maneuvers. I am certain, though, that we are getting ready to encounter a submarine. We are coming closer and closer to England and the sea-demons are getting worse.

In the evening we had a talk from Capt. Steed. He spoke about London, England and our being there, and also about the ten days vacation that we will have there and how we could spend the time. He warned us about the women in London, [and hoped] that they would not mislead us, because the licentiousness in England is terrible. He also wanted to show pictures, but something was wrong with the electricity, so he left it for another evening. We asked him all sorts of questions, which he answered.

We went to sleep on our hammocks. The ship was being tossed every which way. We heard the water roaring and pounding the walls of our ship. The air was so thick that we could not catch our breaths. I wonder how people can live in such air. If I ever get tuberculosis, I will know that I caught it on this ship: [Durham] Castle.

21) I got up quite early and ran out of our cabin with its polluted air. I took deep breaths, like someone who swims a long distance underwater and surfaces to breathe. Rumors are going around that the ship had been attacked during the night by a submarine but that the torpedo missed its mark. I do not know how true this is. The fact is, however, that at dawn I did hear the whistling and shooting of a cannon. We got an order not to wear our uniforms and not to tie our shoelaces, and if something happens we were to throw off our shoes and jump into the water. We were also not allowed to take off our life jackets for a moment.

The sea is still choppy. The boat is being tossed about like a toy. The ship is constantly being filled with water and we are always getting wet, but we laugh and make jokes. It seems almost as if we are going on a picnic not into war.

(Later) A heavy rain is falling. I hope that the sea does not get overly full.

(Later) The water roars and boils and tosses the ship about as if it were a stick. Now we are on the top of a huge mountain of water, and now we are sliding down into a pit. The ship bends to all sides. The water is constantly covering the deck. The forces of nature cannot do us any harm. It is the torpedoes and mines that frighten us. They are the only things that can kill us.

(Evening) We are once again in our cabin and are breathing the polluted air. Ugh, that air! If we only had some more air, we would be happy. But we are already used to it. We sing and we exchange jokes, clean ones and dirty ones. And for lack of anything to do, we even gamble a little.

After eight it gets dark and we are already lying in our hammocks, but it still takes a lot of effort on the Sergeant's part until he quiets everyone down. From time to time, someone still speaks up and tells a joke. Then everyone goes to sleep. A piper, who sleeps on a table under my hammock says to me: "We are going to sleep now, and in the morning we will wake up in a shark's belly like Jonah the Levite [the Prophet]."

22) The weather is the same as always; a cloudy sky, a turbulent sea, and it rains on and off. Today, for the first time, we were permitted on the upper deck near first class, because the water was beating the lower deck and we could not stay there.

At around three in the afternoon, we encountered eight small "greeting boats," which had surrounded our ship. They will accompany us and protect us until [we reach] England. We are now entering the most dangerous place, where the submarines are most often found. I know full well that I am in great danger, and yet it does not bother me at all. One becomes accustomed to every bad thing, and I am, after all, a soldier.

(Evening) Capt. Steed showed us spectroscopic pictures of London and other parts of England. However, he did it quickly, because it seems that he could not breathe well in the air in our cabin.

23) The sea is still stormy, but the sun is shining and warms us. A wave crashed over the deck and soaked me from head to toe. When I took off my shoes they were full of water. It was not destined for us to enjoy the nice morning. At around ten o'clock we were all told to go down; our things were [going to be] inspected. This occupied us until three in the afternoon. The result was that thirty soldiers were inspected and then they stopped. It would have taken a few days to look through everyone's things. I will never forgive our sergeant for the crime committed against 250 people—that of keeping us cooped up in the suffocating air [of our cabin]. It is enough that we have to suffer through it each night.

During the day we passed several islands, and now, in the evening, we are close to the English shore. We passed by a city, and an airplane flew over our ship. We are now over that dangerous place where there are hundreds of submarines and mines. I comfort myself with the thought that soon I will be out of this pig-sty of a ship and our troubles. It is already getting dark, and soon we will be driven down to our grave. We will spend one more night in the putrid air.

We all had a very bad night full of fear and anxiety, but we took it in stride, as much as possible. As soon as we got to our cabin, the Sergeant-Major came and told us that we were going to be in great danger this night. We have to be ready for an accident at any moment. He told us how to act in the event that a tragedy occurred. Everyone should sit in his place at the table, and each of the N.C.O.s [noncommissioned officers] have to stand at their posts. Good guards have also been stationed at the exit with orders to shoot anyone who tries to escape. If we get the signal that the ship is sinking, everyone should leave his place quickly and quietly one after the other. When one table has left, the other one should start [to exit]. I sat down at my place and sat there from 7 in the evening until 5 in the morning. I did not sleep at all. I dozed deeply and had bad dreams. The water kept pounding the sides of the ship. The wind outside blew loudly, and the ships sent signals to one another by whistling 2, 3 or 4 times. There were also a few shots. Many bed down on the floor and slept quite soundly, and the whole thing did not bother them at all. That is how I spent a night full of fear, waiting to be torpedoed at any moment.

24) When I went out onto the deck at 6 a.m., I found a lovely morning. The sea was very still, and far in the distance on the right side, land was visible. Since I had seen England on the left side yesterday, I decided that this [land] was French islands and we were entering the English Channel.

A few ships of our fleet were missing. It seems that they went to other ports, or perhaps they had been sunk. Everything is possible.

The little war boats are still running around us searching for submarines. The latter are smarter and are not showing themselves, but one can feel it in the air that they are there. Everyone is looking at the surface of the sea to try to see a ship with a periscope.

(In the afternoon) We are in the English Channel. The water is still. It has a pretty green color instead of being blue as the ocean. Many airplanes are flying around looking for submarines. We have also met a lot of English ships, war ships it seems, which are patrolling the waters.

Now it is a pleasure to be sailing, but we still have to be prepared lest we be attacked at any moment by a submarine.

(In the evening) We passed through Hasting on the English side and half an hour later we saw the lighthouses on the French shore.

25) Last night we entered the Thames and stayed there until five in the morning. Then the ship went as far as Tilbury. That means that to spite the Kaiser we arrived in England in peace, and we will finally be rid of our cabin with the polluted air. I do not know when we leave Tilbury. In the meantime, they are once again driving people down to the cabin. I wish that this were the last time.

At ten o'clock, a small boat took us to the other side of the river, and with great joy I placed my feet on the ground.

A MILITARY ON THE MOVE

The troops boarded a train and rode to Hounslow Barracks in London. The next day, they began to experience the confusion associated with military troops on the move.

26) Today we were supposed to be sent to Plymouth, but [instead] we paraded several times. A sergeant with a big mustache (and even greater anti-Semitism) counted us a number of times and called out our names. Afterwards we were divided into groups. I was in the first one. At two o'clock in the afternoon, my group was lined up, and everyone was given two pieces of bread and butter. We took three municipal trains and got to the station. We were tired and soaked in sweat from [carrying] our heavy packs, when we arrived at the station. Then we found out that they had been on strike for several weeks already, and we could not depart. We returned to Hounslow Barracks. When we arrived there in the evening, we were told to go eat and to bring with us the bread, which we had been given to eat on the way. But since I had already eaten my bread long ago, [I was dismayed] to learn that we were only going to be given one bowl of tea for every two people. So I got out of line and went to the canteen. I bought tea without sugar and a few pieces of cake.

27) It is a beautiful morning. After breakfast, 120 of us—the same ones who had gone to the station yesterday—were arrayed in two rows. Six men were added. They were coming into the Jewish Legion from the English Army.

It is now eleven o'clock and we are still standing here with our packs awaiting orders. It seems that they want to get rid of us as soon as possible, but we cannot be sent away due to the strike. Now we are waiting, because someone has been sent to find out if the strike has ended or not.

We left Hounslow for half a day, and when we got to Paddington Station our train had already left. We went into a free lunchroom, where we were given cocoa and crackers. We are now sitting and waiting for the next train.

At 4 in the afternoon our train left for London. I have been riding now for an hour. The neighborhood is very nice. Every plot of ground is built up or worked [planted]. We see several towns and villages. Some are pretty and some have long streets and one house just like the other. Practically all the houses are red and squeezed right up against the other.

After six o'clock at night, we rode through the city of Bath. It is a very pretty and original city, and I found out that it has been named "The Clean City of the West." When it began to get dark, we arrived in Bristol—a large city and completely different from Bath. There are a lot of factories here and the city was enveloped in smoke as if it were in a cloud. Many passengers got off here, among them many soldiers, who it seemed were on leave.

At half past ten at night, we pulled into a station. . . . Our packs were taken from us and loaded onto train cars. There we were given tea, bread and pie. Then each one of us was given a blanket and [we were shown] into a large room, which contained two billiard tables, and there we went to sleep—some on the floor and some on the tables. By now it was already one o'clock at night.

28) Eggbuckland [Devonshire]. We ate breakfast, found our packs and went to a new camp. As I heard it, those whom we had met in Eggbuckland were also transferred to the camp we are going to. Camp Eggbuckland, as I understand it, is an old castle in which more than one historic battle was fought.

So far, the diary includes only occasional references to the journey being part of a Jewish experience. The reference to Colonel Patterson in the following entry is therefore instructive, as it shows the difference between Patterson, who, from the beginning, saw every episode concerning the Legions as related to the redemption of the Jewish people in their homeland, and the diarist, whose awareness over the meaning of the journey to the Promised Land is still nascent.

There are only Jewish soldiers here, with a Jewish flag. Most of the officers are Jewish, but there are also some Christians. The officer who's in charge was an Irishman, that however did not prevent him from wearing a Star of David on his hat—something he was very proud of, more so than many Jews.

We ate a good breakfast, much better than the one in Hounslow, and for the first time since I have been in England, I ate until I was full. There is a library in the camp. [There are] also a synagogue and canteens.

I wanted to go to the barber, but I saw a sign that [indicated that] he was
closed on the Sabbath.

The diarist had great interest in the sights around him. His descriptions
of the geography of England, and later of Egypt and Palestine, are quite
detailed and show the impact the encounter with foreign lands had on a
soldier coming from abroad.

We do not go far from Plymouth. The area is pretty and the houses and
streets are very varied—like in America. With every step one takes [how-
ever] one can tell that one is in Europe.

It is a beautiful morning. If it weren't for the packs that we have to carry
ourselves now, our march would be a pleasant walk in the fresh air.

We arrived in Devonport and went downhill to the ferry, which brought
us to the other side of the river in five minutes. We came to the town of
Saltash [Cornwall] and walked uphill with our packs. We were drenched
in sweat by the time we came to Camp Verdi, which is on the other side of
town.

It is a lovely high place. Many wooden and tin houses are situated on long
streets. From our camp we can see the town and Fort Plymouth as well as
Devonport. Many ships are [docked] in the port and a new whistle is always
heard from ships that are either coming or going.

We were given a meal and we went off on foot to see our new quarters.

With a change for the worse in the English weather came a despondency, which officers helped overcome by reminding the soldiers of the
larger cause that made the suffering worthwhile. The major mentioned
in the following entry was probably the old recruitment officer William
Shonfield, an English Zionist, who became deputy commander of the
42nd Holding Battalion in Plymouth.

29) A dreary, rainy Sunday. It is bleak outside and one's soul is melancholy.
The older soldiers tell us of hard work and strict discipline. The food is bad
and meager. If it weren't for the ideal [that we have] and the thought that
this difficult road leads to Zion, things would be bad indeed. I am certain
that I will get used to the life of a soldier, just as I have many times [in the
past] adapted to various conditions. But there are some brighter moments as
well. In the evening there was a concert. Major Shonfield gave a talk in which
he recounted the history of the Jewish Legion: how the idea developed and
spread. With Hebrew passages he showed that it was close to the time of
Jewish revival, and [he said] that the Jewish Legion would play a large role
in this revival. Then there was a program of songs, recitations, and skits. At
the end, everyone sang "Hatikvah," the English hymn, and the oath. Both the
soldiers and the officers raised their hands while singing the oath. It was a
beautiful moment and like balm to our despondent spirits.

[October] 2) Our training continues. We get better every day. In the evening, we had a big parade. A general came and greeted us. He gave a short talk in which he said that we were welcome and that he was very happy to see that people from Canada and the United States came to help Great Britain. He hoped that we would be good soldiers and would excel on the battlefield and that we would uphold the reputation of our race and of the regiment to which we belong.

3) The same thing all over again: training, training, and training. It is not difficult but one has to really pay attention, because the whole sense of militarism is to make a person an automaton, a screw in a machine.

One thing is good about the English Army; from time to time an officer explains the reason behind every movement. That makes it more interesting.

From time to time we also have a few lectures. Some are even interesting, but most of them are foolish.

A JEWISH SOLDIER'S CONSCIOUSNESS

The diarist, while ambivalent about military life, gradually developed a soldier's consciousness.[2] On October 4, he wrote, "It is a very nice day. We march, drill and make progress in our new country," and complained about those who "make fools of themselves and do not want to drill the way one must." He also began to call his officers by nicknames, as soldiers have always done. The combination of army life and rituals stressing the uniqueness of the Jewish Legions becomes more apparent in the notebook. Captain Redcliffe Salaman, mentioned in the following entry, was the battalion's medical officer.

5) Today is Saturday and we are free. I say free, but in reality we have to wash, clean and then we have an inspection by the "Crazy One," Captain Salaman. Then there is a parade inspection and we walk to the synagogue accompanied by music. We pray as the English do, half in Hebrew and half in English. At the end will sing "Hatikvah" and the English hymn. The cantor is Major Shonfield himself and he sang the prayers with a nice melody. He also read Balfour's Declaration concerning creating a home for the Jews in the land of Israel. Then another officer gave a short talk in Hebrew. In general, we do experience some good moments, but we feel bad being under the heel of militarism.

There was a baseball game in the afternoon, which I did not attend, because I am not very interested in that.

6) Today we only drilled for half a day. The second half of the day we played football.

7) We did gymnastics for the first time today. Exercise is very good and it will [help us] develop physically. Today, for the first time since I left Chicago, I received three letters that had been forwarded from Windsor, Canada. I am very happy.

10) It has been raining for a few days now, and we are drilling in the huts for the most part. We went on a long march today. We went out of the city through several towns and farms.

It is a pleasure to walk for a few hours through open fields.

12) Saturday. We had a minyan, under the open sky, on the parade ground. A table was set up with the [Torah] ark. We were arrayed in square and a civilian cantor led the service. In the afternoon I went off to Plymouth.

13) Today I got a rifle. But it works on an old system and is only for drills. Later we will exchange it for a more modern one with which we will learn to shoot. Rumors are circulating that Germany agreed to President Wilson's 14 points, and there will be peace.

26) In the evening, three other soldiers, a sergeant and I were "town pickets." We walked around the streets of Saltash from 6 until 11. We were armed with bayonets, which we did not have to use, because the residents were peaceful and order was maintained.

29) Very soon we will go to London on leave. In the morning we had a hike. In the afternoon, we had a lecture and did an exercise with gas masks. In the evening, each one of us got four pounds and we started to get ready for our leave in London.

We took our rifle and some other equipment into the store[room] and left some other things behind as well.

Each one of us received a red Star of David, which we have to sew onto our left sleeve.

30) At eight in the morning, the Colonel inspected us to see that we were properly dressed, and at about ten we took the train to London. The trip was very interesting and [we were] happy. We got to London at 5 in the evening. A committee was waiting for us. We were taken to a large hall, where a good supper had been prepared for us. There we also heard several speeches. One was from that Irish officer who had brought us to London. Later we went to sleep: some in the YMCA and others at private homes. Two other Legionnaires and I went to the YMCA.

31) Two other soldiers and I found a room. We left our things and went to see the city. I saw the Victoria Monument, Buckingham Palace and other sites. [Later] in the evening, we walked the dark streets of the city. We made the acquaintance of three Christian girls and went to a vaudeville theater to have a good time.

The diarist visited the British Museum, the Tower of London, the Parliament buildings, and Westminster Abbey, where he saw the "very old and large local temple full of historical monuments and graves of the greatest men of England" and fell into "a mystical mood" while listening to the sound of the organ. He also saw several ballet performances. On November 3 he went to a conference at Queen's Hall, where he listened to a report given by Dr. Chaim Weizmann, president of the World Zionist Organization, who headed the Zionist Commission that went to Palestine in 1918 to study the conditions there and made recommendations to the British government, which was planning to establish its rule in the Middle East after the war.

[November] 3) In the evening, I went to a conference of English Zionists in Queen's Hall, and I heard the report of the Palestine Commission given by Dr. Weizmann. He told about the great difficulties that the Commission had encountered with the new life that was forming in the land of Israel, and there is great hope that our ideal will become a reality. [Journalist and Zionist leader Nahum] Sokolov also spoke and representatives of [the religious party] Mizra'hi spoke in Hebrew. Mayers, a representative of the [socialist party] Po'alei Zion spoke in Yiddish and some others in English. It was a very nice evening, but what was missing was the lively, creative spirit of the delegates.

4) In the morning, a hundred and fifty legionnaires marched to the station, where we took the underground to Queen's Hall to attend the second meeting of the Zionist Conference. We entered the hall singing "Hatikvah" [and] the oath and were nicely received by the delegates. Dr. Weizmann greeted us and asked that we maintain quiet and not disturb the work of the conference, which had now become practical and very important. We sat down and the conference continued with its work.

As the Legions prepared to leave London for the front, the diarist wrote of a soldier who died of influenza in the hospital and expressed his hope that "before we go to war an armistice will be signed, because the newspapers are full of this." On November 11, Germany agreed to the Allies' armistice terms.

11) At about ten in the morning, the ships that were docked by the fence began to whistle and blow. Rockets were also shot off and [the men] shouted Hurray! This was to let us know that Germany accepted the conditions of the allies and an armistice had been signed. The whole camp was lively and happy.
    There was a parade during the day and Colonel Miller [a South African Jew who headed the 42nd Battalion] gave a talk. He told us that we will be leaving for Palestine soon to take "garrison duty." Many were happy and

many were not, because they would like to get back to America as soon as possible—and the Englishmen to Whitechapel. The British Jews are very angry at us, the Americans. They are foolish enough to think that if we had not come from America, they would have been let go.

Although the war in the Middle East was not yet over, the German sur-render brought a decline in motivation to serve in the army. The soldiers were therefore subjected to "full-pack" marches and gymnastics activities intended to keep them busy until a decision concerning their fate was made. A rumor spread among the Legionnaires that only those who were truly devoted to the mission would be sent to Palestine brought in a new sense of mission. As the following entries indicate, the symbolism of the journey to Palestine became very much a part of the diarist's consciousness.

26) We continued our preparations to leave, until this evening we suddenly received the news that the draft for Palestine was cancelled, and only young men would be sent who want to volunteer again. There was a great commo-tion, and as usual, lots of discussion. Several sergeants came and wrote down the names of the young men who wanted to go to Palestine. Now we will find out who the real Legionnaires are. In the meantime, everyone is happy. There is singing and dancing. The joy cannot even be described. It is only now that we can see the devotion of the Jews in the Legion.

It turns out that this whole thing is an intrigue [initiated] by the Jewish as-similationists who were using Colonel Miller as their tool. They are working as hard as they can against Palestine and the Jewish Legion. With this volun-teering business they were trying to confuse the soldiers, to make them want to go home and then show the world that no one wanted to go to Palestine. They were not successful. The majority [of us] wanted to go to Palestine, and it is better without those who fell by the wayside, because we wanted to get rid of them for a long time already.

27) After another rainy night, it is a lovely morning. The sun shone brightly and dried up the wet ground. We hiked the whole morning. In the afternoon, signatures were collected from those who volunteered to go to Palestine. The others were jeered as they were sent back to Saltash. The majority [of us] had volunteered to go to Palestine and finish our tour of duty there.

No one knows yet what will happen to those of us who go. I hope that we do not have to wait much longer.

Everyone's morale is high. Everyone is waiting for the time that they will ship out.

Major Lipski came from London this afternoon. He is a Reverend. Our two companies were combined and joined by the British soldiers. First he led the afternoon prayers. Then he gave a talk in which he told us to be good, disciplined soldiers and good Jews. (A good Jew to him means someone who prays and obeys his superiors!) Then we sang "Hatikvah," "God Save the King," and the oath. But when are we going? No one knows that.

28) Today is the first day of Hanukkah, and our company had a party. We had a good time after blessing the Hanukkah candles. There was singing and dancing and no lack of speeches.

29) In the morning a platoon from C company and my platoon from E went to meet the two companies that are supposed to come from Saltash. These are the guys who came from America when we were in Tregental and fifty guys from Argentina. We went to higher ground than the camp and waited for them. They arrived a short time later. They marched with Jewish and British flags, while singing songs. We greeted them by shouting hurrahs. The platoon of C company went first, then the newcomers and my platoon brought up the rear. It made a pretty picture to see the Jewish troops stretching far, far down the road. If there had only been nice weather, it would have been much more lively, but it just kept drizzling. This weather is really getting us down, and it just will not improve.

[December] 2) There was a nice concert this evening given by our company, and we had a good time. This is the only thing we can do in such gloomy weather, when it rains continuously and the wind is blowing. Everyone is waiting for that happy hour when we will be rid of all of this and be on our way to Palestine.

4) I am on guard duty for 24 hours today. I will have two on and four off, and during the time that I am not on guard duty, I still have to be in the guard room in the fort. If I were guarding something important, it would be worthwhile, but I have to stand outside with a rifle in the storm when it is raining buckets to guard the bathroom and the toilets while everyone else is sleeping; it is just plain silly. But go teach them common sense if the "King's Rules and Regulations" say that it must be that way.

7) Today, Saturday, I was in Devonport, where I bought some necessary items to take with me when we travel. I also bought a silver Star of David with the word "Shalom" [salutation meaning "peace"] on it, which I sent to Miss Shapiro. On the way back, I got caught in the rain and I got soaked to the skin.

9) It is raining once again. It hasn't stopped for the last two weeks. It stopped for an hour and now it is pouring again. There is mud everywhere. We are looking forward to the time when we can leave Tregental, but we still do not know when we will ship out. It seems that it will be this week.

12) Various rumors are circulating. They say that we will not go to Palestine at all. There is dissatisfaction among the Legionnaires, and some of them are speaking quite openly about a strike. Some have already refused to parade, because the food was bad. If they will not send us out of here soon, I do not know how this dissatisfaction will further manifest itself, because remaining in this camp, with this rain and this fog, is very bad. And our goal is, after

all, not to stay in England and wait until we are sent back to America. But who cares what soldiers think?

13) In the morning, our company had a parade. The weather was bad. It was cloudy and the thin rain did not let up but crept right into your bones. A truly English rainy day. Our Captain Salaman showed up with a thick book and read to us about how insubordination and rebellion is punished in the army, and so forth. As someone said: "Children, you should know what to expect if you will not be good and pious." Then we had a good drill. This was done so that we would understand that a Captain's dissatisfaction and heavy drilling go hand in hand.

In the afternoon, a notice was put up stating that the draft will be abolished, but we don't yet know when.

Today, Saturday, we did not attend synagogue. Instead we were all gathered under one roof, and Colonel Miller told us the news that this coming Friday we would depart. I have, however, become so pessimistic that I will only believe it when I will be on the ship.

16) We are preparing to leave and wait impatiently for these next few days to pass. But time is going very slowly. The weather is still the same. It rains and the sun shines. In the course of five minutes, the weather can change several times. If there were this much rain in Palestine, it would be a Paradise.

In the evening we had a fine concert. A small orchestra was put together: three violinists, a flute, a cornet and a piano. They did not play at all badly. There were also several solos, recitations and so on. We had a good time.

17) In the morning we drilled. Afterwards, those who had signed up to learn Hebrew were marched off to the institute, where they were divided into four groups. Lessons, however, will only start once they are on the ship. The second half of the day was spent in cleaning and polishing our equipment, because tomorrow there will be a general inspection, and everything has to be in order.

18) In the morning we had a general inspection. The Colonel and the Major as well as a whole raft of officers inspected us, and it seems that we were found to be satisfactory. Then we drilled and marched.

Later we were all marched into the fort, and the Colonel and the officer, who will lead us, gave short talks. They told us that we would be leaving tomorrow and told us how to behave on the trip. My back was killing me after carrying the full pack for the last four hours, but it is all worth it as long as we leave!

IN THE MIDDLE EAST

In mid-December, the diarist's unit departed for the Middle East on a ship named *City of Calcutta.*

19) We were busy a whole day getting ready for our journey. We were constantly returning things and taking things. We left at seven in the evening. We passed through Antony, Torpoint, Devonport and Plymouth. When we got to North Road Station, we saw the Colonel and other officers, who had come to say good-bye to us. A band played music, some popular tunes, and a quarter of an hour later we were on our way.

The four hours of marching had exhausted me, but the thought that I was on my way gave me strength and made me happy.

If one waits, it happens. We had been fooled so many times, but we are finally on our way.

23) All of us had a very difficult time of it today. The sea was very stormy and we all suffered from sea-sickness. I did not eat a thing the whole day.

24) The sea is still stormy. It is still very turbulent, but we are already used to it, and with a few exceptions, we are feeling better. The weather is still cool, the sky [still] cloudy, but when the sun appears for a while, it warms [us] well. We can already feel that we are getting closer to warmer lands. In the meantime, all that can be seen is sky and water. I think that we will soon see the shores of Spain and Portugal.

25) The sea is calm and the warm sun is a pleasure. It is getting warmer and warmer. The sky is still cloudy. We still see only sky and water, but I think that we must already be near Spain. It is possible that we are traveling far from the shore.

Now everyone feels fine. One seldom sees anyone being sick anymore. I feel very well, and my appetite is returning to me with a vengeance.

In the morning we did a cleaning of our cabin. We got rid of some of the dirt, but quite a bit of it remained, since it is difficult to keep such crowded quarters clean.

26) Last night was very cold, but one hour after the sun came up it was warm. However, a cool wind is still blowing. We see a large mountain in the distance. [Also] an island or part of Portugal's shore.

(In the afternoon) The mountain turned into a long stretch of land, which keeps getting larger and clearer. The sun is wonderfully warm. I remember last year at this time in Chicago—there were many snowstorms and it was freezing, and I see that it is much better to live in warm country.

Onboard ship, Hebrew lessons were given, and the diarist seems more conscious than before of the ideological meaning of the experience. When the ship passed through the Strait of Gibraltar, he compared the present experience to his travel through Gibraltar on his way to London (probably as an immigrant from Russia) fourteen years earlier: "27) What a difference. I was young then and full of life and hope. And now I am older, and who knows if my present hopes will not dissipate like those of

14 years ago. Then I was just traveling for no real reason, and now I am going to Palestine."

While he did not specify what hopes had dissipated in the intervening years, he did distinguish his position then from his present journey to the Promised Land. The difference between the two experiences was related to his being in the company of others sharing the same goal and singing the Jewish hymn of hope. "28) The sea is calm and the sun warms pleasurably. A mild breeze is blowing and it cools the air. We can no longer see the shores of Spain. We are now following the coast of Africa: it appears [to be] Algiers. Long rows of tall mountains stretch along the edge of the sea. Today is Saturday, and we have gathered on the top deck, where we prayed and ended with 'Hatikvah.'"

These high spirits did not curtail the routine grumblings of this soldier, who commented that "if it weren't for the parades and mess tins, things would not be bad at all. But we are bothered too much and we are not allowed to forget that we are soldiers."

The nature of the trip to the Promised Land was not clearly defined. While it is unknown whether the major mentioned in this entry was Jewish or not, the discussion described in it provides an example of the discourse taking place at the end of the war about the future of Palestine.

30) In the afternoon our class stayed in the cabin and studied Hebrew. Then the Major showed up and asked that we read him something and say [something]. He briefly described the situation of Palestine in older times—how the country once served as a bridge between the two great centers of the old civilization: Babylonia and Assyria in the north and Egypt to the south. That was why the country played such an important role. Now its situation is different. There are no more important centers near the land of Israel. Mesopotamia will develop quickly, when the old canals will be rebuilt and the country will export a lot of merchandise. The transports, however, will no longer go through Palestine as they used to . . . but much further north through Aleppo. That is why he advised us not to settle only in Palestine but also in Mesopotamia and Syria. "If I were a young man," he said, "I would settle in Aleppo and would quickly work my way up."

Several Legionnaires responded that we were going to Palestine not to become rich but to live a natural life as farmers and workers, because we had already been intermediaries in the Diaspora. He answered that he was surprised to hear that our ambition was to be farmers. He believed, however, that the second and third generations would not be satisfied with that, and then they would have good opportunities in Palestine's neighboring lands.

For some—especially the socialists among the Legionnaires—the goal was well defined. The diary mentions lectures by socialists as well as gatherings of the Labor Zionists, who were well organized on the ship, and on the morning of October 31, they "had a lesson from Comrade

Kretzmer from Palestine on the topic: 'Economic Conditions of Jewish Workers in the Land of Israel.'"

The ship arrived in Port Said and the diarist, who had been seasick for a few days, described the Egyptian port city at the beginning of 1919.

[January] 3) Finally land appeared: first, the tops of chimneys and minarets in the port. Then [we could see] everything clearly—the port and the city. The ship gets closer and closer. We are now passing the monument to Lesseps, the builder of the Suez Canal. The statue greets our ship with a stretched out arm, as if to say, "Come in and see what I have accomplished." We are standing in the harbor of Port Said. I look over the city from a distance. [I see] a lot of very pretty buildings, a mixture of Oriental and European architecture. Many Arab boats surrounded our ship on all sides. They were selling oranges, dates, and other fruits. And with every swallow of the juice of the orange, I actually feel my strength returning, and I become a totally new person.

There is a lot of noise and it is like a fair. We stand on the deck, each one of us with his pack and rifle, and wait for our orders. When we have eaten our fill of oranges and other fruits and really strained our backs with our packs, we docked; and the picture that I saw made a very deep impression on me. Men and children in long, tattered shirts or completely in rags were sitting idly on the sandy streets. I did not see any women at all. This picture was completely different from that which I had seen in my life to date. But the most important thing only came later, when we went into the train cars and put down our packs. That's when the real "business" started. Hundreds of Arabs ran over [to us], and with wild cries pleaded with us to buy oranges and dates.

We stood there for half an hour before the train started to go. That is when I saw a picture that I will not forget my whole life. Young and old men together with small children ran after us screaming in wild cries, bakshish, bakshish [Arabic for "tip" or "charity payment"], at the same time that some Arabs, dressed as shabbily as the ones [mentioned] above but with a patch on their chests (It seems that they were some kind of police) with long whips and sticks in their hands were beating [people] left and right. The whips and sticks hit heads and split backs, but it seems that they were already used to this, and as soon as the "keeper of order" let one person go and went after another one, the first one [once again] chased the train shouting, bakshish and manga (food).

This scene made a deep impression on me. These were, after all, the grandchildren of the ancient Egyptians mixed with the proud Greeks and brave Arabs, who had [at one time] conquered half the world and continued civilization during the time when all of Europe was pressed down under the bitter yoke of Catholicism.

The unit rode for several hours toward Quantara, where we get another description of life during the war—here, in one of those desolate desert spots that during war turned into major military centers. Quantara was a small Egyptian village containing a mosque and a few mud houses that happened to be located close to the Suez Canal and served as a gateway to the Sinai Desert. It was, therefore, transformed during the First World War into a huge British military base looking "more like a modern metropolis, with macadamized roads, electric lights, miles of railway sidelines, workshops, cinemas, theatres, churches, clubs (including a YMCA establishment), and even a golf course."[3]

Night fell. There was no light in the [train] cars, and we rode in the dark. When we left the train in Quantara, it was already late in the evening. Then the business of parades began. We were counted once and then again and some kind of order was imposed. We were exhausted. Our backs ached from our packs, and we still had to drag ourselves over the sandy and stony roads until we came to the camp and were allotted tents. Then we were given a little something to eat, and we fell asleep on the sands of Sinai.

4) The place where I am located is Base #1. It is the beginning of the desolate Sinai near the Suez Canal. For as far as the eye can see, there are only sandy plains covered with tens of thousands of tents. There are masses of soldiers here. It is a piece of civilization forcibly shoved into the wasteland. Wide roads were made; hospitals were built as well as churches, a Y.M.C.A., canteens and clubs. [There are] large stores, where one can get anything: sardines from Norway, canned fruits from California and Australia, meats from Australia, Argentina, Africa and the Chicago stock yards. Even chewing gum. One can get souvenirs from Egypt, Palestine, Damascus and even Japan, that is flooding the east with inexpensive merchandise. One can get everything in the host country, where our ancestors wandered for forty years. Eating and sleeping here is very bad, but I do not want to think about that. I am standing on the threshold of the land of Israel and my only thought is of when I will cross that threshold.

I visited the cemetery today. Here are buried Turks, Germans, British and others. There are about a dozen Stars of David here, a symbol of the sacrifices we brought. The cemetery affected me deeply. So many sacrificed and for what?

In Quantara, the soldiers went back to drills and parades during the day and sleepless nights due to the crowded conditions and the cold desert nights. Dust and fleas were everywhere. The Legionnaires were told that some of them would be stationed in Rafa, a desolate spot on the border of Palestine, which led to unrest within the group. But on January 9, the diarist expressed a great deal of excitement over the entrance to the Promised Land.

Finally the dream that I have had my whole life is being fulfilled. Today is the day that I will enter the land of Israel. I did not sleep the whole night. At around three o'clock in the morning, we began to prepare to go, and at seven we were already seated on the train. Our trip took us through . . . a wasteland where there is only sand and more sand for as far as the eye can see. Every once in a while we come upon a bit of an oasis of palm trees, as in El Arish. The work that England has put into this wasteland is marvelous. It built a train which unites Egypt with Palestine.

It is 1 o'clock in the afternoon. The train stopped in El Arish, but I do not see anything of the old city. Everything is new. Actually, it is not even a city but a camp.

It is a desolate area but pretty. The Mediterranean makes a nice contrast to the desert. There are scattered groups of houses and tents, and wherever one casts a glance one can see heaps of war materials. When we passed through the station, I noticed a palm grove, and there were Arab houses among the trees. I saw the old city at a distance. It was not very large. More like a village than a city.

In the afternoon we arrived in Rafa, where we stayed for a few hours. This is already the border of the land of Israel.

In the evening we rode through the town of Gaza. Great battles with the Turks took place here, and the city is quite shot up. There is also a very large cemetery here. We passed through several other villages and Jewish settlements, but it was totally dark, and I could not see anything. We arrived in Ludd [a town in central Palestine] at ten o'clock at night. [This is] where our camp will be.

A LAND OF MILK AND HONEY

However cherished the Promised Land in religion and folklore, when it was covered by military tents and railroad tracks moving tired soldiers from place to place it hardly resembled a land of "milk and honey," and yet it was seen as such by the diarist.

I did not see anything important there: only trains. Wherever one turns, there are railroad lines and a handful of houses. Wherever one goes, one sees soldiers' camps. We started to march out of Ludd, and marched quite a lot until we finally, finally came to our camp. We did not find any tents. We were given a little tea without bread and we fell, like the dead, on the ground of Judea and slept. It was already one o'clock at night.

10) I woke up very early and began to look around at where in the world I was. [I saw] an endlessly large field covered with tents. In the distance one could see the lovely Judean hills. An awesome beauty suffused it all.

I walked over to the water to wash. It was quite a long distance. On the way back, I bought oranges and refreshed myself eating them. It is not at all a bad food. Well, as usual we had a parade, and we were divided into new companies. We also heard a short speech from our Colonel Margolin.

I am writing these notes, and I myself cannot believe that it is really true, that after striving for so many years, I am finally in the land of Israel. Well, I am going to stay here. How will I settle in here and how much longer will I remain in the army? These are questions that trouble me, but I will not dwell on them. Beautiful nature makes me forget about everything. I look at the long mountain range, at the lovely valley and at the clear blue sky covered with small, white clouds. A cool, mild breeze is blowing. It is delightfully refreshing.

The discrepancy between the love of the land and the conditions encountered by the soldiers is striking.

11–12) These two days were bad. It rained cats and dogs. We did not have any tents, just bivouacs [lightweight and temporary tents]. The bivouacs washed away and we lay in rivers of water. Our rifles and things got soaked. And many things were lost. Then they gave us tents near the "English," who were unhappy and unfriendly. It turned out that there would be twenty of us in a tent. The conditions were so crowded, that we could not move. It was pouring outside and whole rivers were created. And people say that there is little rain in the land of Israel. The rain stops every once in a while and it is nice out for a time, but in the distance one can already see new black clouds, which will soon drop more rain.

We had a talk here from an Agronomist. His words really discouraged us. I wish that he had kept his talk to himself.

I visited the [Jewish] colony of Beer Yaakov. I went to the workers' club and saw the impoverished lives of the workers. I also visited the 40th battalion and visited Glazer and a few other friends from Chicago. [I did] all of this during the torrential rains. Not far from my camp there are several Jewish colonies. For now we have not been drilling and we do not know what our prospects are. There are rumors circulating that we will be freed very soon. Others say that we will be kept for six months. No one knows the truth.

16) (The 15th of the month of Shvat ["new year for trees" in the Hebrew calendar]). Today the whole battalion marched to Ben Shemen, a farm [supported by] the Jewish National Fund, where the Herzl Forest is located. This farm is situated three hours away from our camp. We passed through several Arab villages and a lot of "camps." When we arrived at Ben Shemen, someone greeted us with a short talk in Hebrew. Then the school children sang some songs. In honor of the holiday we were given carob tree seedlings to plant on both sides of the road. With great love and energy planted the little trees which had been prepared for us on both sides of the road. I planted about 6 trees. We spent some more time there and looked over the farm and then we headed back. It was already dark when we returned to camp.

18–19) This was my first time serving a 24-hour shift as Quarter Guard. A cold rain fell at night; it went right through my bones.

21) Today I met the Turkish prisoners. I led them to work. They do not work too hard, but considering the wages they receive, they are doing too much work.

30–31) I was on guard duty in Ramla. I stood near the [mosque], and from time to time, the imam sang out his melancholy songs from the minaret calling the faithful to their prayers. Ramla is an Arab village. A very dirty one. There are also some Jews there as well.

The entries in February and March are marked by exhilaration over the first Jewish settlements in Palestine, like Peta'h Tikva, founded by religious Jews from Jerusalem in 1878; Rishon Lezion, founded in 1882 and supported by French philanthropist Edmond de Rothschild, who built a winery there; Re'hovot, a farming community founded in 1890, where Colonel Margolin lived as a young man before he moved to Australia; and Tel Aviv, the "first Hebrew city," founded at the outskirts of Arab Jaffa in 1909.

[February] 5) Today the whole battalion took a route march to Re'hovot. The route was very difficult. We became tired walking. It was, however, worth it. When we arrived at the colony, we were taken up to a little hill from which we could see the whole settlement as well as a really beautiful panorama of the whole surrounding area. We were given wine, fruits and other good things. We spent quite a bit of time there. Re'hovot is the third [largest] colony after Peta'h Tikva and Rishon Lezion. There is a lot of building going on, and they have a lot of vineyards. There is a large wine cellar, where the wine of the colony is prepared. When we got back to the camp, it was already late in the evening.

[March] 1) This is the first time I was in Jaffa and Tel Aviv. I was very happy to see the old city of Jaffa and the new [city of] Tel Aviv. Tel Aviv is not yet entirely finished, but it nevertheless gives the impression of a modern European city with its broad streets and nice houses. The gymnasium building makes a very nice impression.

And yet the inconsistency between the joy of being in the Promised Land and the realities of living conditions there was still apparent.

4) We spent a terrible night. In the middle of the night, when everyone was already asleep there was a big rain storm. It flattened all the huts, and we were left under the open sky.

My hut remained intact, but it shook on all sides as if it would collapse at any moment. Many half-naked soldiers came into our hut shivering from the cold. Our hut was so crowded that the hut simply could not fall down. I got dressed as quickly as I could in such crowded conditions, but I was soaked through to the skin and freezing cold. Yes, it was a terrible night. One I will long remember.

Many half-naked [soldiers] went off to Tel Aviv, where they knocked on doors. The storm quieted down in the morning. It became warm. The camp looked as if it had gone through a war; the huts had collapsed, rifles were scattered everywhere, clothing and blankets were half covered with heaps of sand. In the morning I went to Tel Aviv, where I ate a good breakfast.

In the morning we cleaned out an empty building that had once been a cinder-block factory, but during war time it had been a barn for horses. We worked hard until we cleaned out the manure, which was several feet high. We moved into this building.

19) We have been in Tel Aviv the whole time since after the storm. We worked continuously to finish the range. I enjoyed this time. I go into town every evening. I have already attended several concerts. I had a good time on [the Jewish holiday of] Purim. In the land of Israel, Purim is quite a holiday. There were several masquerade balls, and on [the last day of] Purim there was a carnival on the streets of Tel Aviv. There were several very interesting groups. The streets were so crowded that one was lucky to be able to get though.

Training on a shooting range, the diarist noted he could only hit the sea or the sand. "I guess I will never be an ace marksman," he concludes. He finally gave up on a career as a sharpshooter but continued to seek out cultural entertainments.

20) I have not improved my marksmanship at all. I still shoot into the sea. It is very rare that my bullet hits its mark, and that is certainly through no fault of my own. It happens.

In the evening I attended a concert of a flautist and pianist. They played very well. They played a classical program and several popular pieces.

The military leadership of the Legions was aware of the disconnect between the expectations that accompanied the formation of the Legions and the tasks they were commissioned by General Allenby's headquarters to perform at this stage of the war: guarding Turkish prisoners and forming labor legions. When the unit was moved to the camp of Serafend in central Israel, Colonel Margolin explained the situation.

25) In the morning we had a battalion parade and the Colonel gave a short speech in which he told us that we would have to do things which we would not find very pleasant, and it was not very pleasant for him either, but we were, after all, soldiers and we would conduct ourselves well and follow orders. We did not really understand what he was referring to, but from his vague words we inferred that many British soldiers were being released and

many Indians were being sent to Egypt, where there is now some unrest. This meant that we would have to work harder, because we would have to fill in all the gaps. We also understood that we would not be demobilized so soon.

The next day, however, when fifty soldiers were ordered to perform infrastructure works in the city of Ludd, a strike was organized.

27) In the morning, we were called out to work, but no one went. The officers' threats were to no avail. No one moved a muscle.

At about 9 o'clock we got the order to march to the place where the Colonel would hear our complaints. The Colonel was very upset and angry. He asked that one person step forward and state our demands. It appeared, however, that of all the speakers at yesterday's meeting there was not one who had the courage to step forward and speak. In the end, someone did step forward and said that we did not want to be a "labor battalion" and that the G.I.s laugh at us when we go to work and that no one has any respect for us. The Colonel said that it was his duty to ensure that our battalion was respected and that he would see to it. [He said] that our working was not disrespectful to us. He asked us not to do anything foolish and to return to work. He would see to it that this job would soon be taken away from us but through legal means not by strikes, which are not the army's way.

We returned to our companies, but when the "fall in" order came . . . no one stepped forward. The officers tried all their tricks but it was no use. The Colonel himself was very upset and ran from one company to the other shouting that he [would force us to go] with the help of Indian soldiers and machine guns. But nothing worked. No one wanted to go. They asked for volunteers, and they barely, barely got together a work detail consisting of subordinate officers and some British soldiers. Seeing that force was of no avail, our Captain gathered us around him and speaking nicely he tried to convince us that no one wanted to turn us into a "labor battalion." It was only that there was a temporary emergency. He spoke about some other side issues also. They asked him questions, which he answered. In this way, with kind words, he convinced us and we agreed to go back to work after lunch. The same thing happened in other companies. And that is how the strike ended. It was actually not a strike, since there is no term for such a thing in military parlance. There is [the word] "mutiny," but thanks to Colonel Margolin's tact and love for his people and this land bloodshed was avoided, something that surely would have occurred had we had another Colonel.

From April on, the notebook records the demoralization caused by the unfulfilled promise. The diarist worked, drilled, guarded a hospital for Turkish prisoners, engaged in another failed attempt to hit the target on the shooting range (which led his superiors to send him to Quantara for eyeglasses), and recorded the confusion over the Legions' demobilization.

[May] 8) I walked through the camp today to hear a speech by Colonel Margolin. All kinds of rumors are circulating. Some of them say that we will be demobilized, and others say the opposite, that we still have a long time to wait. In the meantime, we are expecting trouble on the 11th of May, because that will mark six months since the armistice was signed, and according to our interpretation, the end of our contract with England. But as the Colonel indicated in his speech, an armistice is not a peace [treaty], and we have to have patience and wait. In general, his talk was so vague that it confused us even more and we knew nothing at all about what world we were in. We all want very much to leave the army. Our life as soldiers disgusts us more every day that passes.

A curious traveler, the soldier spent the weeks before demobilization getting acquainted with the country. Upon his departure, he looked back at its landscapes with love and nostalgia.

2) I miss Haifa and the Carmel. The two months that I spent there imbued me with a love for that place. I [often] see a picture of it before my eyes—the majestic Carmel, the city and the river shore and the city on the other side of the water.
    Then [I remember] the snow-covered mountaintop of Mount Hermon, which is visible from afar after a rain when the air is as clear as crystal. I saw Mount Hermon twice from [Mount] Carmel, and both times it was after a rain.

The diarist celebrated his last Hanukkah service in the military camp of Quantara and boarded the *Teutonic* in Alexandria, which sailed back through the Strait of Gibraltar ("It is really a wonderful piece of work made by nature and finished by the British") to Devonport, where a musical band played for the returning soldiers. In Winchester he returned his rifle and equipment, and in London, before departing for Chicago, he managed to see the motion picture *With Allenby in Palestine and Arabia*. The film, he writes, left no impression on him.

4

To the Front

CHAIM BARUCH BEREZIN BECOMES A SOLDIER

The notebook discussed in this chapter was written in Yiddish by Chaim Baruch Berezin, who was born in September 1886 in Mohileff-Podolsk in the Ukraine and studied in various technical schools in Europe. The outbreak of the war found him in Belgium, which he left for the United States with the help of Reverend Bernard Steinberg. He traveled as a tenor with a traveling band and in 1917 joined the 39th Fusiliers. He took part in Allenby's battle in the Jordan Valley and was a member of the battalion's band, called the Schnorrers (Yiddish for "beggars").

The notebook has no dated entries, but it was composed by Berezin while he was hospitalized in Quantara at the end of March 1919. He mentions at the outset that it contains a short overview of his experiences from March 17 to October 13, 1918, and it was likely based on notes taken during that period, for it is too detailed to have been written later strictly from memory. It begins with a reflective statement in which the diarist tells of his melancholy at the time of recruitment, probably as a result of the death of his parents, and his urge to do "something meaningful."

March 17 1918 while in New York:

It was Sunday. I went out confused and returned alone. What can I do? I had devoted my whole youth to our land and was always a devotee of those who talked about accomplishing something in one's life—something meaningful.

At that time, my situation was also not very good. My cousin, Raboy, went to the hospital at that time and there was a great wound in my heart that no

51

one could find a cure. At such moments, a person feels like accomplishing something great.

And that is what I decided—that the greatest thing that I could do is to devote my whole existence to the rebirth of my people, who spent many years striving to become [something]. Well, what we Jews have experienced during the time of our exile . . . I certainly do not have to write about this, because I am sure that you are more knowledgeable about our history than I am.

On March 18, 1918, Berezin went to the British recruiting office on Forty-second Street in New York and enlisted. "It was the greatest feeling that I ever had in my life," he wrote. "I felt that I was fulfilling my heart's desire." He was, however, ambivalent about joining the British army. The oath the new recruits took included the following wording: "I, [name], swear by Almighty God, that I will be faithful and bear true Allegiance to His Majesty King George the Fifth, His Heirs, and Successors, and that I will, as in duty bound, honestly and faithfully defend His Majesty, His Heirs, and Successors, in Person, Crown, and Dignity against all enemies, according to the conditions of my service." This pledge did not make the new recruit too happy: "I was given a green card with the number 5339. On the 19th I took the oath, although the contents of the oath did not impress me. But I closed one eye, remained silent and swore. I changed [the words to] 'fire and water.'"

Having sworn to defend His Majesty "in fire and water" rather than "in Person, Crown and Dignity," Berezin and his comrades were now ready to march in a parade through the Bronx before they left the country.

> I cannot describe my feelings of pride and how great was my happiness, when I heard the speeches at "Borland Casino," that [said] "The Jewish People are with us!" There were many speakers there, but I will never in my whole life forget the talk given by a young Jewish Serbian officer. He fought for Serbia from 1914 on. "Tens of thousands of our Jewish brothers spilled their blood on foreign battle fields for foreign nations, and we are now about to fight on our own soil, for our own flag. Kiss the ground of the land of Israel for me!" These were his last words.
>
> On the 21st we left for Boston on the ship "Providence." I kept a little back from everyone, because most of the young people who were leaving had relatives to see them off.
>
> I was all by myself.
>
> In my imagination, I pressed my parents to my heart and asked them not to forget me. But it was only a fantasy.

On March 22, he left Boston for Yarmouth, Nova Scotia, on board the training ship *Governor Cobb*: "I felt fine, but I could not sleep. My thoughts soared to the seventh heaven. I was filled with great optimism, and this gave me great courage. But [there was] one thing: If only I could see my parents! Unfortunately, I had to be content with my fantasies."

The recruits arrived in cold, snowy Windsor, Nova Scotia, on March 24.

I kept on studying the types of Jewish young men who were about to give their lives for our rebirth. There were many interesting, fervent idealists, like in the Russian Revolution, but there were also some "bums"; American guys, who go for the adventure of it without any of the idealism and without any reason. Many of them answered me in very halting Yiddish: "Well, I am going to fight there where our forefathers once fought." Isn't that an enlightening response?

Passover has arrived. Three guys were selected and sent to Halifax to buy something for a soldier's Passover. Unfortunately, they were not successful. As it appears, the Zionists forgot about us as soon as we left New York, and we had to spend our own money to celebrate Passover.

This is what it was like! On the first day, we had a festive meal with three officers. They gave nice military talks and kept on giving us hints that things would not be very easy.

But who was listening to them?

On April 3, the recruits departed Windsor for Halifax, and the writer was impressed by York Redoubt: "a fort, cannons, barracks, training, etc." When given a day off, he spent it raising money for the Palestine Workers' Fund. A day later, the soldiers boarded a ship headed for England.

On Monday we boarded the ship Vilaya for England. The ship is now on the open sea. A German submarine tickled her. It is a small boat that was previously used for transporting animals. We were packed in like herrings in a barrel.

One of the guys named Mitchell wrote a song and it goes something like this:

I
We lie in our hammocks and sweat as if in pot,
We are packed in like herrings in a barrel.*
Chorus: Throwing up is not good,
Good soldiers do not lose courage.**

II
Our food is fit for cattle,
But we are sated with our dreams.
Chorus: Throwing up . . .

---

* Translator's Note: In Yiddish, *kesl* (pot) and *fesl* (barrel) rhyme.
** Translator's Note: In Yiddish, *gut* (good) and *mut* (courage) rhyme, and this pattern repeats.

III
The ship is tossed hither and yon,
To arrive in the land of Israel is our desire.
Chorus: Throwing up . . .

We left on the 9th of April at 5 in the afternoon after about 10 other ships also packed with soldiers in a convoy with the American dreadnaught, Pittsburgh, in the front. The ride was not very pleasant. Day and night we had to wear life preservers. In addition, there were big storms and it was cold. Most of the soldiers were seasick. I had made up my mind to be a hero and not get sick and indeed I wasn't.

There are parades every day [and we are told] how to prepare ourselves in the event a submarine decides to play a joke [on us]. In the space of 2 minutes, everyone had to be at his lifeboat. In this way the days flew by until we arrived in Liverpool at 6 in the morning on Friday the 19th.

Our happiness cannot be described. We fooled the Germans and stuck out a long nose.

We sang, danced, jumped, and did not know what else to do to express our joy. We survived a serious trip.

The recruits departed Liverpool for London and marched about six miles to the YMCA with their packs on their backs, holding a flag out in front. When allowed to go to the city, Berezin chose to go to a meeting of the Labor Zionists in Whitechapel.

They were having a gathering. The mood was very pessimistic, but there were a lot of people there. The English people could not get over our singing. They were all despondent, and whoever I spoke to wanted to give everything away, if only the war would end.

The city affected me greatly. At night everyone was sad and afraid of poison [gas] attacks. On Monday we left for Hounslow near London. In a barracks there, I saw a lot of American soldiers getting ready to go to France. They once again asked me all the same questions as in the beginning, but the most important thing was whom should they call in the event. . . . It seemed to me that I was going to die. The Angel of Death, however, laughed at them all. It seems that in the other world, they were able to manage without me. They didn't need me for a minyan.

On the 23rd we left for Plymouth. We got there at 3:30 in the afternoon and marched away at 9:30 to the Crown Hill Barracks, 4–5 miles from town. The moon shone. It was a clear, bright night. I can now say that wherever we went good fortune followed us. Our friends from the group were waiting for us and greeted us warmly. We were drilled right away, like the Rabbi [drills] his students in Chumash [Pentateuch]. They worked us hard, but we had Saturday off. It seems that the English government respects this: six days of work and the seventh day is a day of rest.

The Jewish humor found in the above paragraph (the Angel of Death assembling a *minyan*; the military drills compared to a drill in *Chumash*) shows how rooted Berezin was in Jewish tradition. He therefore got a lot of satisfaction when the military routine incorporated that tradition.

On Saturday morning, we got all dressed up and accompanied by music from the battalion we rode to the synagogue. It was the most beautiful moment that I had ever experienced in my life: to see Jewish soldiers from our 1,200 men, marching all dressed up as Jewish soldiers and going to synagogue. Everyone prayed in the soldiers' way: short and sweet. They took out a very small Torah* and read. Then they sang "Hatikvah" and "God Save the King" and that was that.

CHAIM BARUCH BEREZIN BECOMES AN ARMY SINGER

On the Jewish holiday of Lag Ba'omer, when the barley and wheat harvest in ancient Israel is celebrated, Berezin's talent as a singer was revealed, enhancing his sense of belonging and commitment to both Jewish traditions and the wartime mission.

There was a Jewish concert, but there was very little in the way of talent. Until this day, I held back the fact that I could sing. I was interested in other things. But seeing the voices of the guys, the already-mentioned officers, and Colonel Samuel,[1] I began to sing, but then they did not want to let me go. Unfortunately, I had left my music in New York, and I had to show my talent as best I could. I was the hero of the day. From that day on, the guys and also the officers began to look at me with different eyes.

On Friday the 3rd of May, we were invited to sing at Devonport Hospital for officers wounded on the battlefields of France. I will not forget that day. That was the first day in uniform that I saw crippled people lying in agony due to the damned weapons of the Germans. One [soldier] moaned terribly. He had lost his eyes. Another one lost a foot and so on. And I was supposed to sing for them. Perhaps my nice songs could ease their pain.

I can also say that my heart was crying and that my voice resounded with sympathy for them.

I was happy when, after my singing, I saw smiles on their faces. It was one of my happiest days, since I felt that with the gift God gave me, I was able to comfort, for a while, several broken, unhappy souls.

Berezin went on a ten-day visit to London, and the notebook provides a firsthand view of that wartime city and his activities there.

---

* Translator's Note: In the Yiddish, this phrase is a colorful idiomatic simile that doesn't translate to English very well—the Torah was *azoy groys vi a genets* (as big as a yawn).

The 15th of May: The English Parliament—something wonderful, sat in the place where Lord George sits. Also saw Westminster Abbey.

The 16th of May: Saw the palace, but one could not go in, because the royal family was there. Saw the changing of the guards at 12 noon. It was a nice ceremony but only for the royals. Who knows if we Jews will have a guard for our president. I do not think that we will need this.

The 17th of May: Because it was [the holiday of] Shavuot, [I] was invited to the West End Synagogue, to the rich, genuinely British Jews. [There were] speeches and words of Torah.

The 18th of May: Invited to a Zionist friend's house and spent the time as Zionists do.

The 19th of May: Spent [the day] seeing the city. Rode around on buses and saw British trains.

This day will also be noted among those days that I will not forget. This was one of those days when the English people used to tremble and not sleep through the night. A visit from the German air force at about 11 o'clock at night. I was taking a walk with a Jewish girl, when suddenly a whistle was heard: "Take Cover." This is a signal of danger, which gets on even iron nerves. Right after this whistle, bombs started falling. Screams for help and shouts of pain [were heard] from all sides. Men, women and children in nightclothes were running around looking for a place to sleep . . . in houses and in underground tubes. I was actually standing near the post office at that time and looked with shock at the misfortune, which the Germans brought to the British people. A horrific picture. Everything stood still and all that is heard is screaming and sobbing. Pieces of windowpanes fall everywhere, and the hospitals and doctors get busy. A piece of a shell fell about 5 steps from me. I picked it up. [It] was still hot, but unfortunately, I lost it. If that piece of shell had hit me, perhaps I would not be writing about it so cavalierly. But thank God! . . .

The 20th of May: Went to see the damage that the bombs made. 12 machines did the bombing, but 8 of them were brought down.

The 21st of May: A departing dinner in Shakespeare's House and "good-bye" London.

Unfortunately, I cannot describe the city here. That would be a book in itself. The moral side [of things] did not impress me at all. The answer to this was: "[It is] war time." Thousands of unfortunate war brides are wandering around and thinking of their beloveds, who are shedding blood for England. There are also others wandering around with broken hearts—for the most part soldiers on leave. That is how things go . . . needless to say for me too.

London also has a beautiful park—Hyde Park. Thousands of unions are made there and ruined there, both seriously and not seriously. The park is beautiful. It is divided into 2 parts. On one side, young couples pour out their bitter hearts [to each other], and on the other side, toward Piccadilly, music plays every evening, mostly military music. The finest classes of English society can be seen there. I hear that the Germans had also fallen in love with this park and did not forget to honor it with several bombs. I was also told that many romances were started in this unnatural way. Young people, however, are not [so easily] frightened, and by 2 or 3 in the afternoon the next day the park was already filled [with people]. Many soapbox orators take advantage of this opportunity, until the sun goes down, and there are talks about everything—both good and bad. Sometimes I like to listen to them. One can discern the humor of a nation sometimes. Englishmen possess very little of this gift of God. They should come learn humor from us Jews.

Back from London, the soldiers trained in Eggbuckland, where a platoon was formed and Berezin was made section commander ("A very interesting job. Here I could learn everything about how more quickly to kill the enemy"). His singing career was also taking off.

On Monday there was a concert for the soldiers on the roof of the fort. (Near our camp, there was a fort.) I sang and was very successful. Lt. Roth, a rabbi's son, was the officer who used to arrange these concerts. He became very fond of me. (He could speak Hebrew and English but disliked Yiddish very much.) After the concert he took me over to Colonel Samuel. He thanked me and praised my singing and asked me if I would accept a gift, "Music Notes." On Thursday, I received leave and permission to go to Plymouth, where he bought me music for over 10 dollars. This was very nice of him!

The New York Jewish singer, soon to become a fighter on Britain's eastern front, began to feel the personal effects of military training, which were interlinked with growing national pride.

On Wednesday we had a field day. The whole battalion went out on a march in full gear (this amounts to between 100–110 pounds). We marched for 10–12 miles and stopped in a large field, dried our shirts that were soaked with sweat, and cooked a meal for ourselves. (We had been given a piece of raw meat, a potato and a chunk of onion.) We gathered together several twigs from trees and did our own cooking. I do not need to describe how good that dinner tasted after such a long march. I licked my fingers! In the afternoon we did field attacks and then [went] back to camp. This time the guys wanted to show off and marched the whole way back without stopping. Unfortunately, many of the guys fell by the wayside, but I did not. You cannot even imagine what willpower a person has. It was only as a soldier that I discovered this. (I wish that I had known this before. Perhaps I would be in better condition now.) When we entered our camp, sweaty and dusty, we saw our Jewish flag with the Star of David flying over the camp. No matter how tired we were, there was a smile and a "Hurrah" [on everyone's lips]. We began to sing "Hatikvah" and the Labor Zionists' "Oath." The spirit that we had among us cannot be described. Every day we felt more heroic, and nothing could have stopped us from achieving our goal.

His singing gave Berezin an opportunity to observe other aspects of wartime Britain.

On the 7th of June, I was invited by the General to a concert in Government House, Devonport. Here I had the opportunity to see various types of English Generals and Admirals. It was a palace; no worries were felt there. That was the life! They were dressed up and decorated with their medals. Their young wives were dressed in silk and diamonds adorned their décolletage. They all sat in their seats to listen to the Jewish tenor sing. I had to sing and sing. Generals and their impressive ladies came to congratulate me and to ask me questions. I felt like a king.

My feelings and my whole heart were with my fellow soldiers. Several days later I received a letter of thanks from the General. Unfortunately, they did not want to give me the letter. They kept it from me in the battalion as a souvenir. If I were to have such success in America, I would be a rich man today.

The unsuccessful American singer by his own account had now found pride both as a singer and as a soldier and noted that "[e]very day I became more interested in the life of a soldier, and I began to feel like a true Jewish hero."
On June 16, 1918, the unit prepared for its departure to Egypt.

A concert was arranged at that time. I felt that this was one of my happiest days. I was wild with joy. My joyous temperament could not be contained and I sang for all I was worth: I sang in Russian, French, English, Italian, Hebrew and Yiddish. At that time, I showed off everything that I knew in the field of singing. In Yiddish I sang a song which very much impressed the guys, and they helped out. It goes something like this:

> I
> Question: Tell me brother,
> I will ask you a few words:
> What will you do in Palestine?
> Answer: There I will lift my flag*
> And will fight for my beliefs,
> But only in Palestine!

---

* Translator's Note: In the original Yiddish, the last words of the first two lines of the answer rhyme.

II
Question: Tell me brother,
I will ask you a few words.
What will you eat in Palestine?
Answer: I will eat rye bread there,
And completely forget the exile.
But only in Palestine!

III
Question: Tell me brother,
I will ask you a few words.
What will you strive for in Palestine?
Answer: I will weave the future of my people,
And give my life for that,
But only in Palestine!

IV
Question: Tell me sister,
I will ask you a few words.
What will you do in Palestine?
Answer: I will cut rye,
And not suffer at all.
But only in Palestine!

After the concert, I and a friend of mine went to an English farm, bought a large pitcher of milk and sold [the milk] to our friends and officers: the profits went to the Palestine Workers' Fund. This earned [the fund] 45 dollars (9 pounds). Afterwards we paraded around the streets with our flags: Jewish, British and American—and sang. We were so happy that we did not know what to do with ourselves.

TO THE FRONT

On June 18, the unit moved off to Southampton, and the diarist describes his march among chanting Jewish soldiers with bayonets secured on their guns and the Jewish flag in front. He boarded the *Queen Victoria* and crossed the channel to Cherbourg, France, avoiding German submarines ("This time too we stuck out a long tongue"). Traveling from Normandy through the Italian Alps toward the Adriatic coast, he notes that bystanders were staring at the Jewish soldiers in surprise. He seems saddened by the view of Allied soldiers waiting "for their Judgment day" and is amazed by the beauty of Italy ("I would have to be a kind of Turgenev to be able to describe all this natural beauty"). He caught a fever and was taken to a hospital, where he was kept until July 4. He then boarded the *Rose-Glasgow*, which took him to Alexandria, and from there he proceeded to Cairo.

> Unfortunately saw very little of the city. Saw some Oriental types, Arabs and gypsies. They are very dirty: dressed in dirty caftans. (The caftans were once white.) They beg continuously: give bakshish (that means, give some money or bread). The trip was very interesting. For the most part, nice, tall date trees and here and there Arab villages with very original clay huts, in which they live together with their animals. Because of the filth (the word hygiene is as far from them as a good Jew is from pork) they suffer from many eye problems, and a large percentage of them are blind.
>
> On the same day, we arrived in our camp, Helmiah, near Cairo and also not far from Alexandria. It is located not far from the beginning of the Sahara Desert. Our friends from Palestine were waiting for us there. Among them was also my friend from home, Aaron Zelner. We lived in the same house as his parents for quite a while. He did not know that I was in America and was very surprised to see me. [He is] an interesting young man. [He] graduated from the Jaffa School, is a devoted member of the Labor Zionists, understands farming very well.

The soldiers were working hard ("Every day there was something new in the field of soldiering; in other words, learning how to kill the enemy more quickly") but also saw some tourist sites in Egypt: "On the 18th of July our Major Hopkins, a Welshman, took a group of us to the pyramids near Cairo. It took an hour to get there on the electric train and then we were at the historical pyramids and the sphinx, which were created thousands of years ago. It is amazing that human hands were able to create these. It is unfortunate, that our forefathers also had a hand in [forming] these creations. This time, however, we stood near these works as protectors of our long-suffering people."

A similar sense of pride can be detected in Berezin's description of his meeting with Egyptian Jews, who still lived in the ghetto while he had advanced to new frontiers.

> On the 27th of July, I returned to Cairo and devoted myself to examining the ghetto of Egypt. [It had] extremely narrow streets, very dirty, and thousands of families live squeezed together like in a tenement house in the east side of New York. Horrible and terrifying! Especially the streets where the Sephardi Jews [Jews of Spanish origin] live. On the Sabbath, they get dressed up and sit with their neighbors. They are very religious, [they] speak, for the most part, Arabic or Spanish and a little Hebrew.
>
> I took advantage of this opportunity to see the Rambam's [Maimonides's] synagogue. The three rooms in which he lived are very small and dark. There is a sanctity there. There are still a lot of his things there: a menorah, a curtain from before an ark and so on. The Sephardi Jews are so superstitious that when someone becomes sick, he is sent to sleep in that place. In that way,

they think, he will get well. It is also interesting to hear the melody of their psalms on the Sabbath after the meal. It sounds very close to Arabic. They also listen to someone giving a sermon in half Arabic and half Hebrew.

The rest of the days flew by very quickly with very little to upset me. Every day the work became harder [due to] the terrible heat [and] the dry air, and one could see that every day we were getting closer to the battlefield.

On the 17th of August, Jabotinsky came to talk to us. For the Palestinians, he spoke in Hebrew and for us in English. [His talk was] very short and made an impression; few words, but good and sharp:

"You are about to go to the land of Israel," he said. "This whole time, this land has been under a government that was against civilization. You, however, must look at the land of Israel as a sculptor looks at clay before he makes and creates his work. You should look at the land of Israel with the same eyes as a sculptor. The future creation depends on you."

He spoke in Spanish to the Sephardi Jews. The majority of them are, however, Moroccan. A kind of Jew that doesn't look like a Jew at all. They are black like Negroes, dirty, live like Arabs, have several wives (they buy their wives for 5 pounds), [and] treat their wives like slaves. They work for their husbands like cattle. Their husbands are very lazy and religious; [they are] constantly reciting the psalms. This is the kind of Jew that we will have to civilize in the future. Years will pass until something will become of them! Morally, they are on a very low level. They will, perhaps, see our generations rising in respectability.

The words of one of my friends made a deep impression:
"In blood Judah fell;
In blood Judah will rise!"

The next day we went shooting. [It was] a very interesting experience as a sport but not if it meant shooting people. I got a very good score, especially in shooting fast. I got to be very fond of my rifle (AG 3924). [I] kept it very clean and shiny. I kept her looking like a Parisian coquette. I knew that in the trenches, my rifle would be my best friend.

The unit moved to Quantara and from there by train to Palestine. What it was like for Berezin to enter Palestine was described with no particular excitement. The main event mentioned is the warm reception given the soldiers by the local Jews.

On Saturday, I went to see Rishon Lezion. Even from a distance, one can recognize that it is a Jewish colony. [It has] nice, white European houses and lovely gardens. Since I did not know anyone there, I just walked around by myself having a look at the colony. When I entered, Jewish children came up to me. [They were] clean, dressed in white, and delighted that they saw Jewish soldiers. They were able to recognize us by the Stars of David on our sleeves. Unfortunately, they speak very little Yiddish. Most of them [speak] Sephardi Hebrew [i.e., modern Hebrew]. I am not yet proficient in this language. I have been in the Diaspora for too long!

A friend of mine, who left before I did, was already seated on the balcony of a family. When he saw me, he called me over and introduced me to the Broytman family.[2] I became very attached to them, and it is now like my second home.

On Sunday, many of the people from Jaffa came to see us before we left for the front.

Among those who came to see us, I recognized a colleague, Mr. Doynin, with whom I had studied in Mittweide, Germany and with whom I had founded the Jewish Party: Verein Jüdisher Techniker. It was a friendly meeting and [he] invited me to his house in Jaffa. I did take advantage of this opportunity to go back to Jaffa with him. The city made quite a grotesque impression on me with its nice section "Tel Aviv," very European, spreading out from the shore of the ocean. Quite nice. Unfortunately, I did not have a lot of time then to see the city, because on Monday we were supposed to march further.

WAR

The diary describes the hard walk to the front and the solidarity that developed among the Jewish soldiers on the way, inspired by biblical locations like the Judean Hills, Jerusalem, Jericho, and the Jordan River. As the diary was written by a simple soldier rather than a general, it does not provide a comprehensive and accurate account of Allenby's Jordan Valley campaign of summer 1918, but a few elements of that campaign can be discerned from the following entries. First and foremost, the weather conditions were unbearable. The retention of a bridgehead over the Jordan was deemed necessary by Allenby in order to secure the Palestine forces and threaten the Hejaz Railway, but, as official British documents noted, this was hardly possible because of the shade temperature, which reached at times 131 degrees Fahrenheit, and because of the dust: "A single column of half a dozen wagons would toss up a vast dun cloud, which would then hang for a long period like fog in the overcharged air. The insect life of the place seemed to accord with its pestiferous character."[3]

In August 1918, at the hardest time of the summer, the 38th Fusiliers were stationed in Nablus, on the hills of Samaria, where they were attached to the Tenth Irish Division. They eventually went down through Ramallah and Jerusalem to the Jericho area at the Dead Sea, where they were put under the command of Major General Edward Chaytor of the Anzac Mounted Division, and a month later the 39th Fusiliers, under the command of Colonel Margolin, joined them. The salty land in the Jordan Valley near Jericho, known as the Mellah, has been known since Roman times as one of the hardest spots for human survival.[4] As Legionnaire Elias Gilner notes in his memoir, "The worst spot in the entire Jordan

Valley was the Mellah . . . a ten mile long canyon about 80 yards wide at its narrower points and almost a mile in width in its broadest part. . . . In the event of a massive attack, the Jews there would have been exceedingly vulnerable not only because of their exposed position but because they had no support that could have come to their aid with reasonable speed. A West Indian regiment was stationed miles away at the foot of the Judean Hills, and the Twentieth Indian Infantry Brigade held the Jordan three miles south of the Jewish Battalion, leaving a gap that a determined superior enemy force would have found easy to penetrate."[5] Berezin reported on the difficulty of moving through this region.

This was the first long march—from 3 in the afternoon until 10. We walked 18 miles. The road was very bad, full of stones. One could feel every pebble like a nail in the foot. There was a lot of dust and the air was dry. I could not use the water that I had without permission. Many areas along the way had been destroyed by the Turks. However, I managed to stay on my feet and keep up. The rubbing of my shoes gave me blisters on my feet, and the next day I opened them up with a knife and continued marching. Our food was biscuits, bully beef and tea. This day we walked only 8 miles. We rested and then on Wednesday, we were supposed to reach the Judean Hills, a distance of 20 miles. This march was very difficult for me. I felt like I was going to die! Some of the guys fell like stones along the way from fatigue. I was determined that I must make it. . . .

And God helped me.

We arrived very late at night. [It was] a night that I will never forget. Small tents were spread out on the stony hills of Judea. In them were our former buddies of the two Jewish companies, A & B. In honor of our arrival, a light burned in every tent. It looked like a Venetian night with Bengali lanterns. I dropped to the ground like a dead person, and fell asleep near a rock.

In the morning, I felt very good and admired the beautiful Judean Hills, of which our history contains many stories. We rested for a day, and on Friday, the 6th of September, we went on a practice attack. The whole battalion was dressed in "Battle Order," that is, [we were not carrying] our large packs on our backs. We marched over hill and dale, over big boulders and [through] thorns. . . .

No man had ever set foot there. Ultimately we came to a place where other battalions were waiting for us. Among them were also a lot of Indian soldiers. Airplanes began to fly over our heads, and after resting for an hour the "advance" started. The soldiers were divided into groups. One vanguard (a group of people who go first to find out where the enemy is strongest) went out, and shortly after them the procedure started.

I jumped over the stones like a wild goat, even though the thorns bloodied my knees. On this front, we wore short pants in the summer, leaving our knees exposed. But we did not stop. "Onward!" Who knows if I would have felt this way if the Turks were flying around me. Many of my comrades were very brave and many were very weak.

One comrade in my group, Levitan, a former Bundist [member of the non-Zionist Jewish Russian workers movement] (A younger brother of his [who] was an ardent Zionist and a sculptor by profession was beheaded by an Arab near the colony of Re'hovot)[6] . . . kept on begging God to break one of his legs, because he could not take it anymore. That is how weak many were during this procedure.

I, however, was very courageous and watched every step that our officer was taking. Suddenly we were told to take out our bayonets. From this I understood that we were getting ready for hand-to-hand combat. With lots of shouting and a "Hurrah," we conquered the imaginary enemy. The groups gathered together and with songs we returned to our tents. The sun was burning like hell, and one could pass out for a drink of water. Nothing! We were swallowing the dusty air and pressing on. Many Arabs stood close to us and wanted to sell us grapes, but we were not allowed to buy anything from them. Captain Barnett comes over to one of the guys, who cannot speak English and asks him: "What would you do if you were attacked by several Turks when you were alone?" He answered, "May God help me, I would pass out!" So I ask you: is there another nation in this world with a sense of humor like the Jews?

On Saturday we marched to the synagogue. [It was] the eve of Rosh Hashanah. Colonel Margolin wished us all a good year and read two telegrams out loud. One was from our Jewish American soldiers in France, who were wishing us luck and saying that their hearts and their thoughts were with us. The second was from the 38th battalion, which was at that time near Nablus and had already been successful on the battlefields and had won several medals for their bravery.

After the services, several of us were dropped off in Jerusalem [for the remainder of] the holiday.

Unfortunately, I had to stay behind.

I, however, took advantage of my free time and went with several comrades to look for a well. After walking for an hour, we saw water flowing from a small hole in the hill. [It was] cold as ice. No matter how thirsty we were, we did not drink it. [Later] we drank our fill, washed up a bit and went into an Arab's garden, picked figs, oranges and grapes and ate until we were stuffed, then went back to camp. Here and there we came upon Turkish and German shells. One could see that there had been some fighting there.

On the 2nd of September, right when the sun burns brightest, we were marched out of hills of Judea towards Jerusalem, towards our historical city. At 6 o'clock we arrived at the walls of the city, where we stopped. Jews came to welcome us. The next day we marched through the city singing and stayed on the other side of the Mount of Olives until the morning. We left for Jericho in the morning. The night was very cold in Palestine. As hot as it is during the day, that is how cold it is at night, especially in Jerusalem, which is situated very high above sea level (1,200 feet above the sea). It was [not] pleasant to walk.

The night was very dark and it felt as if we were walking into an abyss. The dust was unusually deep. Here and there we came upon traces of where the enemy had been. After marching for 12 miles, we stopped and we could see the graves of the fallen soldiers with their names written on them or simply "unknown."

At midnight on Friday, we continued on to Jericho, where we arrived at 7 in the morning. The road was awful: stones, deep dust reaching over our knees as we walked down into a chasm.

Some of the men fell by the side of the road for lack of strength. One friend of mine fell and pleaded, as if with God, to help him get up. But who would do this, when our own struggles were so great? Towards the end, going downhill, I [also] fell, but with my last ounce of strength I got up and continued on.

Day started to break. We could see the Dead Sea in the distance and the hills across the Jordan. They looked like large waves on the sea during a big storm. [We had] a short respite and pressed onward. The only star in the sky remained the North Star, which shone on our faces with its full power. As we were descending the last hill and had stepped onto the ground of Jericho, which lies 1,800 feet below sea level (that is the deepest point in the world), an Australian officer and [some] soldiers came to greet us and showed us where we could camp, because the Turks were on the hill across the Jordan and were constantly "treating us" to shell fire. We scattered among the trees, because if a shell should hit, it would not be able to do as much damage.

Not far from my tent a small stream flowed unusually swiftly. I immediately took advantage of this opportunity to wash myself, because one could not drink this water. Then I felt like a newborn person. Even though I was tired and weak, I washed my laundry. The sun was very strong there, so strong that the wet clothes dried right on one's body in a matter of minutes. In addition to the powerful heat, millions of mosquitoes and flies were eating us alive.

Many of my fellow soldiers fell like the dead and I could not close my eyes, so I went to Jericho to buy something at the canteen. After a walk of about 3/4 of an hour, I arrived at Jericho, where only Arabs live—in great filth. . . . In the middle was a marketplace and there were several government buildings; that was Jericho. I bought [something] and on the way back I began to feel sick with a bad headache and shivering all over my body. I lay down, and later when I got up, I noticed for the first time a building. I did not know what it was.

I headed back to camp, and later an Australian on horseback came riding in my direction. I stopped him and asked him what that building (palace) was. "The Temple of Temptation" was his answer. "The place where [Jesus] rested. A very holy place." This was on Saturday the 14th of September.

Sunday was my birthday. I went to sleep and dreamt thousands of dreams. I got up, washed and felt very happy that I was in Jericho on my 32nd birthday fighting the Turks for my people.

The military operation described in the following entries was part of Allenby's Megiddo campaign of September 19, 1918. Having had to send many of his elite forces to the Western Front, Allenby regrouped a large multinational force with which he defeated the two Turkish armies stationed west of the Jordan River and attacked the Turkish 4th Army in the Jordan Valley and Hills of Moab. On September 23, the Jewish Legions fought side by side with the Anzac Mounted Division and the Twentieth Indian Infantry under the command of Major General Chaytor in the conquest of Es Salt, a strategically located village in the Jordan Valley, which the British had failed to hold in two earlier battles. It so happened that the assault began on September 15, the eve of the Day of Atonement, an event in which Berezin took center stage, according to Elias Gilner's memoir.

> At sundown on September 15, 1918, the eve of the Day of Atonement, when Jews throughout the world gather to pray and to seek forgiveness for their transgressions, the 39th Royal Fusiliers was ordered to put on full pack and equipment and to march to the front. The men stepped out northward toward Wadi Aouja and were told to march in silence. But soon Turkish shells fell and exploded in the thick, soft dust.
>
> Since the enemy was clearly aware of their presence there, Private Berezin, who had been a cantor in New Jersey, decided to ignore the order of silence and began to chant the Kol Nidrei, soon groups of Legionnaires joined in and the strangest Kol Nidrei service ever heard resounded through the valley of death. The mournful tune which the martyred Marranos had surreptitiously intoned in subterranean synagogues was now chanted in the face of an oppressor; it mingled with the howls of jackals and was accompanied by the rhythmic tramp of marching feet. Some of the men wept quietly, smearing the desert dust over their faces as they tried to wipe their tears away.[7]

Berezin reported on the occasion in more detail.

> On Monday, the eve of Yom Kippur, we were told to be ready to move on, that is, to the trenches in the hills. That evening, precisely when the rest of the world was saying [the prayers] Al Khet and Kol Nidrei, we marched bravely out. It was unusually dusty—over our knees. In a very short time, we were white as lime. Even when I had no strength I kept on singing our Kol Nidrei, as a cry for help to our Master of the Universe, to wake Him up from his ancient slumber and to let Him know that here were the first Jewish volunteers to spill their blood for the revival of the Jewish people.
>
> It seems that He heard my cry for help! Immediately there came an order to be silent, not to speak, and not to light any matches. The moon shone. The air was cool. There was not even a breeze. One could suffocate from the dust! All of a sudden, we were told to divide ourselves into groups. There were about 1,000 men, because many had become sick in Jericho and they were sent to the hospital. It seems that the Turks had spied us. I kept my composure.

Our Captain Smiley gave the order to walk single file. We entered something that looked like a narrow street and jumped from one rock to another until we came out into a free area and gathered together. We walked a bit further and then stopped. Our advance guard showed us the way. At about 10 at night, we saw lights in a valley, which was between 400–500 feet deep. We had to go down there with a partner. When we got down there, the whole battalion broke up [into companies]. Every company went to a different corner somewhere in the hills. My company . . . went further away than all the others. (A battalion has 4 companies or 16 platoons, that is, every company has 4 platoons. I was in the 14th platoon under Lt. Harrison. . . .)

We kept on walking. Suddenly we were in a stream. The water was above our knees. When we had gotten across and we had come to our appointed place, we dropped down right where we were standing. The Turks kept right on shelling us. They were flying right over our heads. This was a Turkish welcome in honor of Yom Kippur! Many of the guys were a bit frightened. I, however, kept calm. Why, I do not know. An order was given that no one could leave. [We were] to keep quiet and not move. I was fortunate enough to have taken a box of pineapples with me from Jericho. That gave me a bit of energy, because that night no one got anything to eat or drink. [The pineapples] revived me. I still have the taste of it on my tongue. Despite the whistling of the shells and the dust, after that tasty morsel, I fell asleep [and slept] like the dead. [I had] a sweet sleep and a sweet dream. I saw my parents in my dream.

At about 4 o'clock, we were awakened and every platoon took a place between two hills. We could not go up the hill. That was where the Jordan flowed. The Turks were on guard there and treated everyone, who dared take a peek, to a bullet. The next order was from that day on, no one could leave without letting the Sergeant know. And when one does leave, he has to have his rifle with him as well as 2 bandoliers full of bullets (100 in 2 bandoliers) and his iron helmet. If someone had to go to the bathroom (you should excuse me), he had to get all dressed up, [wearing everything] as mentioned above.

At this point our privations of food and water reached a critical point. The food was bad and there was no water! We had only one batch of water every 24 hours. That was supposed to suffice for washing, shaving, and sometimes even washing out a pair of socks or a handkerchief. I pity the poor fellow who did not wash or shave. That was tantamount to risking one's life, because if anything was noticed, what one heard was, "You're on active service. . . ."

At about 2 o'clock in the afternoon, I saw an air-raid, a battle in the air. Five airplanes were fighting in the air. Unfortunately, this took place very high up, and I do not know the end result. At such a time, one has to be cold-blooded, lying stretched out on one's belly, wearing one's steel helmet on one's head and waiting until someone blew the "all over" [whistle].

On Wednesday, someone came to announce the good news that it was finished, that the Turks had erected a wooden bridge over the Jordan, and we were waiting for them to attack us. I was very upset; why shouldn't we attack them? But I bit my lips and remained silent. Every night from 8 in the evening until 4 in the morning was a "stand to": that means, one had to be ready to fight at any minute. One could not lie down, nor sit down—only stand and wait. There has to be dead silence, so that in the stillness of the night the enemy should not hear any noise that we were making. The Turks were 150–200 yards from us.

There was a lot of commotion.* We had no lack of problems. We could not sleep during the day due to the great heat and the biting of the mosquitoes and flies and also because of the hard work we were doing, such as repairing the roads, and at night we were not allowed to sleep! The order was to go and take Es Salt. If they said [to go], then we had to [do it]! This was the time that General Allenby gave the Turks the final death blow. We crossed the Jordan and continued on.

There were dead people—Turks, German, British—wherever we stepped, dead horses, camels, donkeys were everywhere. We walked without stopping. Every once in a while we came across the body of a person. The smell was unbearable. Friends began to become ill, to fall, to faint. We had no food, and there was also no water. The Turks left handfuls of ammunition. We came across two cannons, which had shot at us. We captured them. The Turks and Germans lay dead. A Turk begged for mercy but Sergeant [unclear name] killed him with a rifle. The attack was so very surprising and [carried out] with such great military strategy, that they had left everything in their great hurry to escape. The further we went, the more ammunition [we found]. We also took a large Austrian cannon from a battleship. Then Turks began to appear. They immediately surrendered and begged for ekmek, that is Turkish for "bread."

Fifty men and a sergeant had to go back through Jericho to the city of Es Salt, which is situated on a high hill (the hill looks like a straight wall), to stand guard. I was among those 50 men. We boarded trucks and went down to the place from which we had come. From there we went by foot back to Jericho.

The heat was unbearable. I was exhausted, totally wiped out. I felt that it must be better in the other world. I did not, however, lose my courage and kept on going. We covered the distance in 8 hours. We were all scattered like sheep. The sergeant lost control over us.

ON JEWISH FATE

Berezin's recollections also include an amazing story on the fate of Jews in the First World War.

---

* Translator's Note: In Yiddish, the original reads "all the joy and gaiety," which is, of course, meant sarcastically.

They started to bring prisoners there by the thousands, in tatters and rags, starving, sick. We felt pity looking at them. It is impossible to forget how they looked. All of them were happy that they had been captured, because their situation had become unbearable.

When I ended my guard duty, a friend of mine [named] Asinovski, arrived and told me that he had brought the German and Turkish officers that we had captured to the Government House in Jericho. I went to see them. They were lying on the grass very down-hearted. [We had captured] Germans: no small matter! They were waiting for their fate. As I was standing and speaking to a German officer from Hamburg, I see a guy in a Turkish officer's uniform wandering around. I stand there and look at him and thousands of thoughts fly around in my head.

Suddenly, he comes over and asks me [in Hebrew] "Are you a Jew?" As soon as I heard his voice, I screamed out at the top of my lungs, "Meylikhzon! Oh, my friend, Meylikhzon! A Turkish officer! Just a day ago, my enemy. I shot at him and perhaps he at me. And now we are friends again. Oh, great God! The Jewish people, [what] a cursed people!" We kissed each other, and I did not know what to do, I was so happy. The German, Turkish, and British officers stared at us with wide eyes, open mouths and ears, and could not understand what had just happened here. I immediately ran and bought him food at the canteen and secretly gave it to him, but then I, unfortunately, had to leave him. He told me that during his past 4 years as a soldier, he had been awarded the highest decorations for heroism from both the Germans and the Turks. He also told me that he, himself, captured three Jewish soldiers from the 38th battalion. When he asked them from which battalion they were, they responded the 38th, and he had understood that it was the Jewish battalion. Not a pretty tale. It could be that they were really frightened and that is why they began shouting Ekmek!

Something about my friend Meylikhzon:

We were raised together. Our house was next to his house. We were neighbors. He was younger than I was. He had two brothers: Avram and Meyer. We were together day and night. His parents were very wealthy. I think that his father was the richest one in our town. He was raised on milk and honey. They were spoiled like only rich children can be spoiled. He got it into his head that he wanted to go study in the gymnasium in Jaffa. This was not the best place from an idealistic or educational point of view.

The following was told of him: Once while he was in Jaffa, he received a lot of money from home, so he decided to make a dinner for his fellow students, male and female. Well, the crowd was happy and probably everyone made a toast. When it was his turn, he said the following, "I wish that a year from now all Jews would be in the land of Israel and all those from Popelukhe also." From that time on, he was no longer called Melikhzon but Popelukhe. This is also a propos. I had to leave my friend, my former enemy, and I never saw him again. When I left him, he gave me the impression of being a German sympathizer, but I cannot say that for certain.

I was on the side of the Jewish people, before their liberation, and he was on the side of the Turks. For now, I do not want to think about that at all.

On the 9th of October, we took the prisoners and marched into Jerusalem. When we got to the Mount of Olives, Jews wearing prayer shawls came to greet us. (It seems that they were in the middle of their prayers.) They brought us some whiskey. Everyone was joyous. The same Turks, who not too long ago were bathing in Jewish blood, we Jews were now bringing back as prisoners of war. Despite the fact that I was tired and sick, I, nevertheless, felt proud. We rested in a field below Jerusalem, and the next day we were supposed to bring the prisoners to Ludd by train.

Another friend and I were responsible for one [train] car [holding] 40 prisoners. As we traveled, I could see what dirty, low people these were. Unfortunately, this filth cannot be described by the pen. We brought them to their compound and we returned to the Ludd station and went to sleep.

On Friday, we went off to make our camp near Serafend, where we are still. I worked quite hard and thanked God that I returned to the same place.

On Saturday, I went to Rishon Lezion, and the first thing I did was go see the Broytmans. You cannot imagine how happy we all were. The wife and the children cried from joy. No one had expected such a quick victory over the Turks and that we would see each other so soon.

Well, if God wills it, even a broom can shoot.

We had a really good time, and on Sunday, I went to Jaffa. I could have kissed the houses and everyone there from happiness that I had remained alive and could see this city again.

Berezin was demobilized in 1920 and returned to Belgium. A year later he moved to London, where he settled permanently. In the short autobiographical note he left in the Legions House he did not mention whether he ever continued his singing career.

5

On Bravery

WE CAME TO FIGHT FOR OUR COUNTRY

In his memoirs, Ze'ev (Vladimir) Jabotinsky, founder of the Jewish Legions, makes a distinction between the English soldiers who manned the 38th Fusiliers and the North American volunteers. He felt that the former lacked the idealism characterizing the latter. Spelling out the difficulties of recruiting in London's East End, Jabotinsky complained about young men who were born in Russia, Poland, and Galicia and grew up in London, Manchester, and Leeds. Having not become British citizens yet, they enjoyed the good life while their peers died in the trenches. The restaurants, coffeehouses, and cinemas in London's Jewish quarter of Whitechapel, he wrote, were filled every evening with young, healthy, well-dressed fellows who were indifferent to their surroundings, as if they lived on a separate island. They lacked national or class consciousness; any idea introduced into Whitechapel would sour like spoiled milk. They defined themselves neither as Jews nor Englishmen but as *schneiders* (Yiddish for "tailors"). Jabotinsky admits that the English Legionnaires turned out to be brave soldiers demonstrating responsibility, endurance, and fortitude, but felt they lacked the spirit that tied the individual with higher national or human ideals.[1]

The association of "spirit" with adherence to the ideals of Zionism led to dismissal of the *schneiders*, especially by the 40th Fusiliers recruited in Palestine. These Labor Zionists were puzzled when they encountered Jews who did not share their Zionist worldview and consequently portrayed them as devoid of any worldview at all. One such portrayal can be

71

found in Baruch Gurevitz's notebook. On his way to a training camp in Egypt as one of the Palestine recruits, Gurevitz stayed for a few days in a tent with three soldiers of the 38th Battalion. He describes them as having "typical Jewish faces, of the type we would call 'Whitechapel folks'" and tells of their lack of interest in the Zionist project. As one of them told him, "We helped conquer the land for you, and we don't hold it against you, to the contrary, let you be successful and let the land flourish, which will give us satisfaction that we did not fight in vain. But we do not need your country. We have a beautiful country of our own, a gigantic kingdom with developed cities and kind, generous, goodhearted people. Our living, with God's help, is also good. We are simple folks, artisans with no great aspirations. For what does a person need?"

The soldier added he was proud of his occupation as a shoemaker and of his two friends' occupation as tailors who used to make clothes for high officials in the British government and for members of Parliament. He complained about Jabotinsky, who founded the Jewish Legions, which was not his business, or—as the Yiddish expression goes—his grandmother's business. He told Gurevitz that he and his friends had warned Jabotinsky several times that if he did not stop recruiting English Jews to the military, they would beat him up, but the stubborn guy did not stop, which forced them to fight with the British army in Palestine. While they did not share the Zionist values, said the soldier, "We have not inflicted shame on the King, the battalion and the Jewish people [but] now we want to return home."

Martin Watts, who reviewed ninety-eight short biographical notes by veterans of the 38th Battalion, writes that "apart from the testimony of three or four of Jabotinsky's keenest supporters . . . none of the ninety-eight records mentions any Zionist activity, which contrasts sharply with the testimonials of the American volunteers."[2] The lack of concern for Zionism, however, did not make these soldiers devoid of "spirit." Having been less impressed than the North Americans and Argentineans by the symbolism attributed to the fighting in Palestine, having often enlisted as a result of the fear they would otherwise be deported back to Russia, and having included few persons of letters in their ranks, English recruits to the 38th Battalion have written fewer diaries and memoirs. But those who did depicted a strong consciousness of being soldiers and Jews.

In this chapter, we explore a memoir written by an English-born Legionnaire named Abraham Jacob Robinson who fought with the 38th Fusiliers and received a Military Medal for bravery. Although Robinson may not have been versed in the Zionist literature of the time, his self-consciousness as a Jewish soldier fighting for the British Empire contains a large degree of idealism. This memoir displays what we shall later call existential Zionism—namely, a Jewish national consciousness that stems from religious roots rather than from an imagined model formulated by political leaders and intellectuals.

Robinson was born in Boston, England, in 1899, and, as he puts it, "My adventures started at a very young age." His father fought in the Boer War and in 1902 the family joined him in South Africa. In 1914, during a trip to England and the Continent, the war broke out and Robinson, being big for his age and of an adventurous disposition, joined the army at the tender age of fifteen. After seeing active service, he was discharged for being underage and obtained work in the Royal Arsenal in Woolwich, where thousands of employees engaged in improvements of weapon design and manufacturing techniques. According to the memoir, he came into contact with anti-Semitism there in the form of a foreman and relinquished the job. Though still underage, he joined the army again and was put into the training reserves. One day, during synagogue service, he heard about the formation of the Jewish Legions and enlisted.

When Robinson and others arrived at the training camp in Plymouth, they were joined by veterans of the Zion Mule Corps who fought in the fierce battles of Gallipoli. These were tough soldiers, recruited in 1915 among the Palestinian Jews who were exiled by the Turks to Alexandria. Jabotinsky, who joined the 38th Battalion as a lieutenant, was vocal about their audacity, curiosity, and adventurism in contrast to the *schneiders*, but the Robinson memoir does not depict less of these qualities.

Robinson participated in the march of the Legions with fixed bayonets through the city of London. He does not elaborate on the meaning of the event but writes that this was an honor granted to few regiments. His description of the embarkation at Southampton for Cherbourg and of the train trip to Taranto is not colored by grand ideas. At the same time, the symbolism connecting the soldier's journey to higher values such as the redemption of the Promised Land requires little mental adjustment, as this symbolism was very much part of Robinson's consciousness. In describing, for example, his travel on open trucks in the Egyptian desert, the biblical verse "And the Lord went before them by day in a pillar of a cloud, to lead them the way; and by night in a pillar of fire, to give them light; to go by day and night"[3] is so much part of his upbringing that it becomes a natural metaphor in his writing.

> On the 1st of March [1918] we marched through Alexandria, and had a service at the beautiful temple in the street of the prophet Daniel, and were very well entertained by the ladies of Alexandria. After saying farewell to these good ladies, we entrained for Helmiah, just outside Cairo. Our camp was situated in a sandy desert, where we finished our training. Pesach [Passover] celebrated in Helmiah, as in days of old before leaving the land of Egypt on our way through the Sinai Desert to the land of our Fathers. Towards the end of April, two months after our arrival, the Thirty-ninth Battalion joined

us, and there was a gathering of many old friends whom we were forced to leave behind at Plymouth. Our unit consisted of many celebrities, and our concert party was in very much demand, and requests were made for some members to stay behind and be incorporated in Lady Allenby's Concert Party. This they refused to do, as Anthony Tchaikov, the world-famous violinist put it, "we came to fight for our country, not to play for it." Travelling in open trucks with a cloud of smoke leading us by day and a column of fire from the engine by night, we eventually arrived at Ludd. After a short stay at Ludd, during which we visited Rishon Lezion nearby, we finally left on June 9th and marched across to Umm Suffah on the main road from Jerusalem to Nablus, where we arrived late at night on the 12th. Here we were attached to the Tenth Division.

The division referred to above was the Tenth Irish Division, which fought under Allenby in the battle of Jerusalem in December 1917 and in the battle of Nablus in September 1918. Robinson describes his experiences during the preparations for the Nablus battle: coming under heavy shellfire during Saturday service, experiencing an air raid, building gun emplacements, and going out on night patrols over the crest of a mountain with the Turks encamped just over the crest. In August, before being given an opportunity to participate in the battle, the Jewish Legions were redeployed by Allenby's headquarters to the burning hot Jordan Valley.

We were the only European troops in the valley at this time. Our march was a terrible ordeal. The moment we got down to the Jordan Valley our real trials began. The heat was intense and the dust lay a foot deep. It was exceedingly fine and looked like cement. As we marched, clouds of it rose to choke us, while our feet were actually sucked down at each step, and it required an effort to draw each foot from this dust. We were considerably spread out to try and minimize the choking and blinding effect of this sulphurous dust. As I was Company runner on this march, my job was to take the O.C.'s watch and move down the column, instructing each section and platoon Commander to synchronize his watch with the O.C.'s, and to stop for a rest at a certain time so as to retain the spacing. While the others were resting, I had to make my way back to the head of the column. Fortunately youth was on my side, and I was very fit from my training in the Training Reserves.

The 38th and 39th Battalions were attached to the Australian and New Zealand Mountain Division and took up positions in the Wadi Mellah (the wadi mentioned in the previous chapter), where they were vulnerable to a Turkish attack. They managed to hold off any such attack through raiding parties intended mainly to conceal their vulnerability.

It fell to our lot to harass the Turks as much as possible by means of raiding parties, in order to prevent them from discovering how weak we really were. Also patrol parties would go out nightly to reconnoiter the strength of Umm esh Shert Ford over the Jordan. These duties fell mainly to my company, and as it was discovered on our arrival in the Mellah that my eyesight and hearing was particularly keen in the dark, I was placed on permanent patrolling. This suited me fine, as it enabled me to have a good sleep from about 1 a.m. until dawn, whereas on post duty, lying down, staring into the darkness, with two hours on duty and four hours off, it was almost impossible to prevent oneself from dozing. . . . During these patrols we were able to gain much information regarding the strength at the Ford and the best way in which this strongpost could be attacked and taken.

ADVENTURE AND INJURY

Calculations of which night shift allows one the maximum hours of sleep possible are a major preoccupation of soldiers everywhere. It is the mention of such matters without referring to the ideals behind one's presence in the Wadi Mellah that gives meaning to this memoir. Robinson, a runner in a battalion composed of English Jews thought to be without ideals, may be seen as fulfilling the cause pursued by Jabotinsky to the utmost in spite of—or because of—the lack of explicit references to that cause. This is particularly apparent when Robinson describes in a matter-of-fact manner the adventures that led to his injury and earned him the Military Medal.

> Often Private Angel would come along and suggest to me that we go out after some snipers that were giving us a certain amount of trouble. We would creep through our barbed wire and lie among the dead and decayed bodies of a number of Turks that had been killed many months previously, and never buried. Owing to the dry heat there was no stench, but on turning the bodies over, scorpions and tarantulas etc. would be seen in large numbers. Why these bodies have never been buried I have no idea, but there must have been about twenty of them. During these excursions we took many foolish risks, but fortunately came to no harm. Private Angel was afterwards awarded the Military Medal.

As water was scarce, Robinson repeatedly climbed down the cliff his unit was holding to the Jordan River below and brought up water in canvas buckets, ignoring all risks in doing so.

> Things ran smoothly for a few times, and then an occasion arose when I met two Turkish soldiers below. These I captured, and disarmed, and on our way back made them carry the water. But all did not go well. We had no sooner reached the foot of our steep climb when snipers opened up from three sides. Instead of running for cover as the two Turkish prisoners did, all I could think of was to return their fire. Bullets were hitting the ground all round

me, knocking the sand into my face. Eventually one found its mark, and from that moment fire ceased. The day incidentally was the first day of Rosh Hashanah. At first, on seeing the manner in which the blood poured from me, I thought it was the end. Eventually I decided to get up and see if I could walk. I managed to stumble along for about twenty paces, when my legs just collapsed under me. This, however, brought me in view of my two prisoners. I made them come to me and had one pick me up and carry me, while the other went ahead, climbing the steep slope in soft sand. As you took a step forward, you slid back half the distance. When I felt the one was too tired to continue, I let him put me down, go to where the other one was, and made the other one come and take his turn. Fortunately I never lost consciousness during the whole of this procedure, and had in my possession a revolver, my rifle having been left below at the place where I was wounded.

The ordeal went on until soldiers in the observation post noticed what had happened and sent stretcher bearers to come down and fetch the wounded soldier. He was bandaged by a doctor who estimated that he had no chance to live and was sent on an "ambulance," a camel with a stretcher placed on one side, to the first field dressing station. He reached Jericho and was then sent to a hospital in Cairo.

It was when I was lying in the Twenty-Seventh General Hospital in Cairo that Sister Oppenheimer, who was in charge of Jewish volunteer nurses, came in one day and pinned a ribbon to my chest and informed me that I had been awarded a Military Medal for bravery in the field.

Stereotypes survive long after they are proven to be wrong. Just as the image of the English Legionnaires as lacking in spirit found itself in the history books, Robinson fought bravely in the First World War and later during the Second World War while he was living in the South African town of Uitenhage. There he joined the local police reserves and saw action in Ethiopia and Egypt. But he still had to do battle with stereotypical remarks about the unwillingness of Jews to fight, as shown in the conclusion to his memoir.

While at Sonderwater in a lecture hall I heard the following conversation immediately behind me.
"In the town where I come from none of the Jews have joined."
"What town is that?"
"Uitenhage."
On hearing this I immediately swung round and was able to refute the statement, mentioning the names of some Jews who had joined, together with names of others that were vaguely connected with Uitenhage, a little white lie that I hoped would sow seed.

6

Hope and Disenchantment

DISPLACEMENT AND IDENTITY

Ira Jacob Liss was born in Russia and at the age of fourteen immigrated with his family to Detroit. His exact date of birth is unknown, as is the case for many Russian Jews, whose ages were concealed to avoid being drafted to the czar's army. During the First World War, he tried to join the American army, but being too young he was rejected and found his way at the age of seventeen to the Jewish Legions. This diary, written in Yiddish in thirteen notebooks, provides a picture of military life in the First World War from the perspective of a young man who was aware of his religious origins (his father was a *melamed*, or teacher of religion), the uniqueness of the experience, and the historical significance of Jewish soldiers landing in the territory of Pharaoh and the land of their forefathers. At the same time, the writing is earthly and mundane; the diary reads like so many First World War diaries by English, American, French, and German soldiers, who reflect on army life, war and killing, fear of death, cruelty toward prisoners, and peace, for example. The lengthy entries display no fear of anti-Semitism and make no attempt to construct an intellectual model of a Jewish combatant. The following are simply the daily thoughts and insights of a Jewish American soldier on the way to the Promised Land.

The diary begins on May 1, 1918, when Liss, along with a group of American volunteers to the Jewish Legions, sailed from New York harbor to the British recruit depot in Windsor, Nova Scotia. On this day of departure, he felt uncertain about the life awaiting him; the need to swear allegiance to King George in the company of people he had never before met gave him palpitations. Despite his anxiety, or perhaps because of it, he was not pleased to see his parents, who had come to say good-bye. "I am sick and tired of their tears and moans," he wrote, as if the old world they represented, where Jewish parents mourned children who were forced into the czar's army, was now gone. In the evening, the recruits boarded a ship and in the morning were surprised to see a big crowd of Jews on the shore, waving American and Zionist flags.

Everywhere the recruits came into port there were crowds to greet them, prominent persons made speeches in their honor, and Jewish girls were keen to kiss them farewell. The diary shows how these experiences become the basis for bonding among the Legionnaires—especially when they realized the bewilderment they caused. Liss wrote that Gentiles, who had never seen Jewish recruits on the way to war, gazed in amazement and took their hats off in reverence.

The entries written in Windsor record the soldiering experience with a sense of parody, as when Liss describes how his comrades fainted when they were vaccinated. With no military tradition for two thousand years, the Jewish recruits found it difficult to adjust to military customs, such as saluting, and envied the Gentile soldiers, who seemed more disciplined and adaptable to army life.

On May 28, when a new group of recruits arrived at the camp, Liss and his company welcomed them with songs. It is hard to exaggerate the role singing played in the development of a national consciousness within the Jewish Legions. A popular song, considered more sacred than the official Zionist hymn "Hatikvah," was the "Marching Song of the Judeans," written by Nina Davis Salaman, a well-known English poet who was married to the Legions' medical officer, Captain Redcliffe Salaman.

> Zion, our Mother, calling to thy sons,
> We are coming, we are coming to thine aid.
> Spread among the nations, we thy loving ones,
> We are ready, we are coming, unafraid.

Other songs popular with the Legionnaires were "Ya ha li li," a Hebrew labor song, and "Se'u Ziona Nes Vadegel" (Carry your pennants and flags to Zion).

May 31, 1918. Today we had a wonderful experience. We marched about five miles carrying our folded blankets. When we got out of town clamorous singing began. We sang our old songs "Ya ha li li," "S'eu Ziona," etc. The "Marching Song" we no longer sing. We are fed up. We sang it so much that it is getting on our nerves.

The unit sailed for England in early June. Only one month had passed since they had been recruited, but the soldiers marching from the military base to the railway station already felt like a national army: "Today there was no need to wake us up because from four in the morning we stood in line to return two of our four blankets. Until five o'clock we managed to finish breakfast and were standing in line with the kit bags. After a speech by the Sergeant Major our Jewish army went marching toward the railway station, lifting our three beloved flags: the Jewish, the American and the British. We marched proudly, singing national songs. On the way we received blessings from the local inhabitants, including women who wiped their tears."

The unit then embarked on a British warship sailing for Plymouth. Liss describes a boxing match won by Jewish Sergeant Rosenberg and a meeting with a Jewish English payroll clerk on the ship, who expressed his hope that one day a Jewish navy would be established so he could serve his own people. In what seems like another step away from his past, on June 15, 1918, Liss noted that he had tears in his eyes while listening to this rootless man, whom he calls "a victim of our national fate."

Liss describes the past, when Jews could not fight for their own people, as tragic and rejoices at the change that was occurring. On his arrival in England he visited the Jewish enclave of Whitechapel, where he got into debates with local Jewish residents who voiced their objections to a Jewish army, describing it as adventurous and treasonous. As if he belonged to a different breed, he tells of a visit to a Jewish family in London who ate the traditional Jewish dish of gefilte fish behind closed curtains so the neighbors would not notice. He also felt alienated from the Russian Jews he met, who had been detained as conscientious objectors.

At the end of June, only two months after enlisting, Liss no longer belonged to the ranks of the dispossessed and had found himself a new "home," as the following entry indicates.

> June 24, 1918. In the afternoon we were sent to the Plymouth camp. We arrived there after a six-hour drive. A sergeant with two Stars of David on his sleeves welcomed us in friendly manner and took us into the camp cheering us up, while we marched and sang national songs in Yiddish. When we arrived at the camp . . . we saw the white and blue flag blowing in the wind and we knew we had arrived home.

This feeling of being at home in a British military barracks was expressed by Liss both as a Jew and as an American. As he became increasingly secure in his Jewish identity, his American consciousness strengthened. He describes a June 26, 1918, visit to the local YMCA when he felt like an "American in every respect," and said in reply to an Australian who asked him on July 13, 1918, who he and his comrades were, "We are

American Jews going to fight in Palestine." On Independence Day, he was full of pride at belonging to America.

> July 4, 1918. Although we were signed up with the British Army, we feel first and foremost as Americans. And when American Independence Day has arrived, we immediately announced that today is a holy day and we refuse to go out for training. Our officers were considerate and brought us to an American Army base that is not far from here, about half an hour drive. Apparently this is where the Americans keep the German POWs because I saw them working in the base, preparing it for a softball match against the American soldiers. The game didn't take place because there were not enough American soldiers there, but the few Americans were very happy to meet us. Right away, conversations had begun, typical of chats taking place between citizens of the same state, and since our friends are from all over the United States, everybody found someone from his own hometown. I also found a soldier from the Bronx.

The entry goes on to describe how the Americans expressed their objection to American soldiers serving in the British army because the two nations did not trust one another and because British troops had shown poor performance in the war: "We explained to them of course who we are and what made us come here. We departed in great friendship." Liss concludes the entry by expressing his and his comrades' satisfaction at being "in an American atmosphere on our first Fourth of July of our service in the British Army."

A JEWISH SOLDIER

In August, Liss explained his motivation for recording his military experiences.

> Aug. 3, 1918. Now that I have put my life in danger, my life is becoming so interesting that I feel it must all be written down, so that I can [remember it], if I will survive or so that my friends [can read it] if they survive this day. Today, Sabbath, is my day of rest as a Jewish soldier in a Jewish camp. Oh, how interesting! I felt like a bridegroom marching to the synagogue in cadence to the music that was playing. Yes, I forgot that I was in the army.

> Aug. 4. It is [like] the night before Passover here in camp. Everyone is getting ready for a 10-mile hike. Our company is going to . . . learn to shoot. There is a bit of tumult, a bit of excitement in our lives. We left the camp at 2:30 [carrying our] full packs. We pass the city of Devonport. The residents, probably thinking that we are going to the front, come out to greet us. Some are happy and some cry deep inside themselves. They were most likely

reminded of their own children, whose fate is the same as ours. The road is difficult, [but we have] young blood. We sing; we encourage each other and we forget that we have already been walking for 4 hours, hungry and tired. At 3 p.m. we arrived at our target, and it was wonderful [to see] the boys forget that they were tired. They went right to the canteen; they're singing, dancing and are extremely happy. May God grant that our whole journey be in the same spirit.

The whole journey was not, unfortunately, conducted in the same spirit. As time went on, Liss's mood shifted from exhilaration, inspired by the sense of mission conveyed by his superiors (especially Colonel Patterson), to a soldier's depression resulting from drills, barracks routine, military discipline, insufficient food, boredom, longing for one's home, and—not least—bad weather.

Aug. 5, 1918. I do not know what makes me feel so bad. Is it the heavy rain that has been coming down now in buckets for the last month or because I will soon have to go shooting. For some reason I feel so sad, lonely . . . I walk around sad and disappointed, and after teatime, I look around the place where I am located. On a high hill very close to the shore of the ocean there are rows of huts, where soldiers, people, children with various thoughts and aspirations [go]. Here and there one can see a soldier looking through the semi-dirty windows. I walked around deep in thought until I came right to the shore of the sea, the sea that seems so vast to me, that separates me from my parents. Yes, my soul certainly remembers the conversations with my parents. A letter from my parents eased my heart a bit.

The diarist was often preoccupied with the disruption to civilian life caused by the war and the state of a world that would allow thousands of young men to lie in trenches. He also reflected on the need to kill other human beings in war.

Aug. 6, 1918. Yes, the words of Isaiah the Prophet have already come true, but just in reverse. Our scribblers and writers have tossed away their ideals for other tools; they have taken up their rifles. It is hard to believe that our boys, raised with books, are now speculating about their shooting: Would they have hit their target if they were aiming at a person? Right now, things are not going well for me at all. I simply cannot hit the target. It's a real shame. I am worried about this. . . .

Aug. 7, 1918. Another day spent shooting. At least, [I now have] some idea of what it means to be in the trenches. As a marksman it was my duty to see if the shooter hit the target or not. Every time a bullet flew over my head and sank into the ground, it made a sound as if the crying bullet was not yet ready to be buried. . . . My luck in shooting improved. Oh, how happy I was. At night I attended the concert in the canteen: by the soldiers for the soldiers, except for the few women who had been invited by the officers. I had a good time. I especially enjoyed seeing the spirit of our Jewish boys: of those who performed and of those who kept praising our boys, the Jewish boys.

Aug. 9, 1918. Spent another homey Passover Eve. Before leaving our huts in Tregental, we washed the floors [and] the tables, so that everything shone. At a quarter to one, we were already in full marching order. By 2 o'clock, we were already marching. Under the burning sun, we marched with a 70-pound weight [on our backs]. Everyone was hot and sweaty, barely able to drag his feet. Nevertheless they sang with spirit: "I am a soldier, and I will build the Galilee," and other songs. A Corporal or a Sergeant cuts into the air with a tired voice, keeping the tempo, "Left, right, left, right. Keep in step." And in four hours we covered the distance from Tregental to the edge of Buckland—10 miles. Just like locusts, we fell upon the dining room to have tea. Thank God, we did not lack an appetite, after such a walk. Then we got paid. Oh, when I received those 10 shillings, for which I had waited all week. . . . Because for the first time since I was in the army, I was broke: didn't even have a penny in my pocket.

The unit prepared to leave for Egypt. The commotion involved reminds the diarist not only of Passover Eve, when Jewish families are traditionally involved in housecleaning, but also of the commotion preceding his family's trip to America. He also cannot escape the biblical symbolism of an exodus in reverse. The preparations for the trip to Egypt reminded him of those made by the children of Israel preparing (although in greater haste than the British army) for the original exodus.

Aug. 10, 1918. Today was a big day for me. Because we are getting ready to go to Egypt, we did not have our Saturday parade to the synagogue. Instead we had a pack inspection, and then we received khaki drill suits, which were very reminiscent of my Palm Beach suit, which I had left at home. I very much regretted that my parents were not there to say: "Wear it in good health," which they always said when I put on new clothes. Then I got 2 letters from my sister and brother, which I opened right away. Also a returned letter to my cousin, Iza Liss, stamped Wrong Address.
  I still suffer from my old curse; I cannot find a good friend,* even though I know so many boys. I nevertheless do not have a true friend, so I went off to town by myself, a distance of 3 miles from camp, and bought necessities like soap to shave with and soap and a brush for washing my things, needles for sewing etc. [I am] a regular homemaker. I turned back early, because I was afraid that I would spend my whole pay, which is so small; there were only 2 shillings left of my ten.

---

* Translator's Note: The original Yiddish, *a fraynd tsum hartsn*, is a beautiful phrase that means "a friend to my heart."

Aug. 11, 1918. I found last night very interesting, because for the first time since I have been in the army, I slept outside, my head leaning on the tent, because of a comrade who did not get a blanket. In order to help him out, I shared his bed outside, because it was very crowded inside. It was a beautiful, starry night, a little cool. I lay with my face to the sky, where the stars—and many times, falling stars—entertained me well. In the morning, I got up shivering a bit from the cold, but pulled myself together for the day and a kit inspection, an arms drill and the inspection of our rifles. I must mention the joke that was played on us when our rifles were taken away: "Hey boys, we have peace. The war is all over." And other such comments. Then once again, for perhaps the tenth time, we were asked for our "particulars": where and when we were born, our address, our profession. I finished my day's work with doing my laundry. Due to our departure, we received an order telling us not to leave the camp. I got a letter from my sister Ida.

Aug. 12, 1918. Today reminds me of a trip to America; things are really jumping. So much is going on. We are getting ready for the long trip to Egypt and then to the front. Something about getting up this morning was different than other days. The N.C.[O].s pound on the tent at 6 o'clock in the morning harder than usual, and the boys themselves get up more quickly than they usually do. They get busy. It is the same with the officers and the whole company. There are inspections all day long. We march to get the guns, which we left in the company's orderly store to be checked; we march to get buttons for the khaki drill suits; we march to sign the pay book, and for everything there is a separate parade. Every hour we hear only: "Fall in! Look sharp!" and there is an inspection. Why? Tomorrow there will be another inspection. One general is particularly happy, [so happy] that he gave us half a day off to polish our things. Anyway, [it reminded me of our] trip to America.

Aug. 13, 1918. If I called yesterday "a trip to America," I have the right to call today "leaving Egypt," with the only difference being that at that time our ancestors were leaving Egypt and today, we are going to Egypt. Today's preparations were impossible to describe. The whole camp was buzzing and frothing with waves of soldiers. The day began with a general inspection, and right from the start one could see that today was a day different from all others. To begin with, we got up an hour earlier than usual today, and there was no early morning roll call at 6:30. We had breakfast at 6 o'clock instead of 7:30, and at exactly eight o'clock, we were already lined up in rows according to company, platoon, and section. (I am in D-Company, 15th Platoon, and 3rd Section.) [We stood still] as statues. We did not dare move a muscle.* I still remember a crow flying by and we could hear its cawing so clearly that I was certain it was conveying some heavenly message to us, which I, unfortunately, could not understand. The march started at five minutes after eight. Colonel Samuel (a truly typical, sympathetic Jew) and his

---

* Translator's Note: The original Yiddish is more colorful—"We did not dare buzz a wing."

adjutant rode in front. Two blue stars of David decorated his shoulders. They immediately put me in mind of King David riding into his victorious battles, and his captains reminded me of the Jewish "commanders of thousands and commanders of hundreds,"[1] because everyone, with a few exceptions, were Jews. For several minutes I thought that our redemption had already come, and that the Colonel was the Messiah. But the pack on my back and the rifle in my hand reminded me that I still had a long, long way full of dangers to go before being redeemed. Then came the cops led by the Captain riding in front and the officers of every platoon and the Sergeants of every section. Of course, the band went first. The rest of the companies kept the same order. In this order we walked 3 miles, where a General inspected us. It seems that we made a good impression on him, because on the way back, the General gave us a few compliments and added that we had a long, unpleasant journey ahead of us. After dinner, we had foot inspection, got paid 30 shillings, that is [we got paid] for the whole trip. [I] also got a pay book with my identification and a will to fill out: tags with my name and address to wear around my neck, so the corpse can be identified if something, God forbid, should happen. [We got] an order to have our kits packed [and ready] for the morning. My personal happiness of the day was [that I received] 2 letters, [one] from my parents and [one from my] brother. Oh, how happy I was to hear of my mother's health and to see her own handwriting. Because of a shortage of paper and stamps, I did not answer.

Aug. 14, 1918. I've heard of enthusiasm, patriotism, mob rule, but I had never felt it like I did last night. Our boys were extraordinarily happy that they were going to Palestine. They got together in a mob, and beating on tin pans, they danced and sang, "It is good to fight for our country." This filled everyone's heart, and we all hugged one another from joy. Even the officers, whom a private cannot even approach, were drunk on patriotism and danced together with us. Every once in a while, there came a thundering shout of "Long live our future republic in Palestine," which I think frightened the twinkling stars. I actually did notice many falling stars. It was a lovely night. In the morning all the excitement started ([like] Khantshe going to America).[2] We turned in our blankets, kit bags, old things and shoes. At about 12 o'clock, the General addressed us as the Jewish Regiment of the future Jewish nation. After dinner, we were decorated with oriental hats, which had on them blue stars of David. They made us look like true Maccabees. Helmets of steel and to protect us from bullets, some household items . . . bandages, a blanket, and a sheet. In any case, it was lively and everyone had a good time. We had an inspection that night. I would wish any Jew, who has Jewish blood coursing through his veins, to see this scene: Jewish children standing there like heroes. This was something our enemies always threw up to us.

The "new Maccabees" were now mingling with soldiers of many other nations as they left the Plymouth port.

Aug. 16, 1918. I found a whole world there on the dock: like flocks of sheep, there were groups of soldiers from Australia, England and America. Everyone was waiting happily to ship out. Our boys met the Yankee soldiers. At half past six we were already aboard the ship Londonderry, packed in just like sardines. Like in a real Lithuanian tavern, the boys lay down on the tables and chairs. Due to a lack of space to lie down, I had no more than [a few] hours of sleep.

Aug. 17, 1918. At half past 7 we landed in Cherbourg, France, where [we] stopped at a military camp. We stayed there until half past one. Our rations consisted of a quarter of a loaf of bread and a piece of bully-beef until morning. The Colonel had given us a talk before boarding the train in which he had said there would be scarcity [of things] and hunger. And that we were now in active service, where for any triviality we would be punished. At half past three, we were packed like sardines [into the train] because it was a freight train and there was only enough room for eight horses and we were packed 25 to a car. . . . It seems that we were to travel this way across all of France. At night, when we lay down to sleep, we really began to understand the meaning of "packed." Feet were by heads and heads by feet. We could only sleep on one side and even then 3 had to stand. After having slept for 3 hours, I gave my place to one of the guys standing. This is the 3rd night that I have seen the morning star come up. Now I also feel that I am in a strange country, because in England I could still hold a conversation and I felt at home. Here, however, things are different; I have to use my hands as language.

Aug. 18, 1918. We are still riding on that packed train. Oh, how I ache all over. I have had enough. Hungry a whole day. Our rations: a dog biscuit for breakfast, a slice of bread for lunch and a slice for supper. But the scenery is so beautiful that it makes one forget all one's troubles. Like now; it is the time when the fields are ripe. All one sees now are large, broad fields that are being worked by women. Beautiful trees. Lovely green woods, and I just rode by a neighborhood, whose name was unfamiliar to me. For miles and miles, I see high hills, which have been dug into, and on top of which there are ruins of previous inhabitants or homes of current residents. Some of these people have made their homes inside these stone hills. As I rode by, I thought of Emile Zola's "The Human Beast," many of whose heroes also lived in this way. A little further on, one can see how Uncle Sam has made himself as comfortable as if he were in his father's vineyard. For miles and miles one could see Uncle Sam's camps packed with thousands of his nephews, who probably feel quite at home here, because on the road I saw a lot of them strolling with French girls, kissing them quite openly. And if we met any of our own comrades, it was a miracle. Today [we] have our own rough roads, cars, tracks, cannons, and airplanes operated by our own people. One could think that we were in America instead of France. I was also amused by the Chinese camp. Then I saw the Algerian Arabs. There was a whole world here. They [the Arabs] were prisoners, who were working on [laying] tracks and in factories. I saw the whole picture in one day: British, French, Americans, Chinese, Germans and Austrians.

Aug. 20, 1918. Well, I had another sleepless night. I stood guard. My first turn was from 10:30 to 12:30. Oh, what a pretty picture that was. [I] was born in Russia, lived in America and am now guarding a train in France, so far away from my home. Everything is strange, but the moon, at which, for some reason, I looked last night more than ever before, was familiar to me. It is exactly the same. I had a little fun last night, because while on guard I saw two Frenchmen, who were working on the train, and for a joke I aimed my bayonet at them, like a regular hero. It seems that I shouted: "Halt." And the two stood there like little lambs and tried to tell me in sign language that they were employed to work on the train. Oh, how I laughed at that prank.

The train traveled through Italy and arrived in the port of Taranto, where the troops boarded another ship that took them across the Mediterranean to Egypt.

Aug. 25, 1918. At about 6 o'clock, our ship began to move. We were called to breakfast, but my God, the crowding. . . . [It was so bad] that one did not even feel like eating. One doesn't feel like doing anything. Standing on one's feet, sweating terribly one grabs a bite and we go for inspection at about 9 o'clock. Once all the companies are arrayed, we hear the command to be quiet, and everyone becomes mute. Only the hum of the ship's engine can be heard and the airplanes in the sky. In this stance, we left Italy. As the ship passed through the large gate, a lot of Italians were gathered on the shore and were saying "Good-bye." We, however, stayed in position and could not respond to their farewells. It almost gave me the impression of being in a funeral, like when one accompanies a corpse. Several hours later, we were already on the open sea, where land was already a thing of the past. We could only see our escorts, the destroyers near us and the planes above and the Mediterranean Sea, with its blue* color, on which the sun beat down very intensely. It was a very amusing scene, when lying there on the deck trying to rest, I heard an English officer having a conversation with an Italian officer, who could hardly speak any English. He told him who we were: "These are Jews, who lived in America. They can barely speak English, but enough to understand the commands. They are going to fight for Palestine. You can tell this by the Star of David on their hand." Several more such questions and answers ensued.

Aug. 26, 1918. May we not have to get used to everything we can get used to. The overcrowding, it seems to me, has become my way of life and things are not so difficult for me now. Yesterday after tea time, I took my blanket and

---

* Translator's Note: In the original Yiddish, the word is *tekheylis*, a particular kind of blue dye that in biblical times was obtained from a mollusk and predominantly used to dye *tsitsis* (the fringe tassels of the prayer shawl).

ran to grab a spot on the deck of the ship, and when I got it and lay down to sleep, I got more pleasure out of my sleeping place than I ever did from my soft bed as a civilian. The next morning I got up a little earlier than everyone else, a quarter of an hour before the morning call. What a pretty scene it was to look at the sleeping masses lying every which way: this one at right angles to the next one. It was also interesting to see them move in their sleep changing their positions. No matter how sleepy I was, I had to smile at this scene. Then I looked at the sea which always looks the same to me. After 2 days of traveling, I do not know if I am further or nearer [than the day before]. When I cast my eye at the horizon, I saw the sun rising. Here it looked just like a bridegroom coming out from under the bridal canopy. First one sees a fiery red edge at which it is easy to gaze, but every minute it gets bigger and stronger, until one can feel it during the day no matter where one hides. The order of the day, I mean our rules, are the same; we fall in in the morning and we fall out. I do not understand why we do this. I had a nice afternoon today. I lay on the deck with a friend, who had spent some time in Palestine and still thinks of it, and together we fantasized about our future lives in our land. Yes, such moments give me the strength to survive the troubles of the last several weeks. I pray to God that my fantasy should soon become reality.

Aug. 27, 1918. I suffered from insomnia, and the result was that I spent the greater part of the night sitting on the railing of the synagogue and looking at the sea seeing how beautiful the night was falling, and I thought how light it still was. One could still see our 3 companions, the destroyers. Slowly it got dark and everything disappeared from view, and the ship which, being afraid of submarines, was completely enveloped in darkness continued to work. It pushes ever forward, but one can sense a kind of danger. And looking at it going, one's heart becomes sad, and without wanting to, I began to think of the barbarity of war. As morning approached, I fell asleep, and when I got up, I found that the friend who was sleeping next to me had been robbed of 650 pounds. It seems that many of our group think that since there is a lot of transgressing [of the commandment] "thou shalt not kill," therefore "thou shalt not steal" also does not apply. The epidemic of stealing has gotten worse among us but especially among those on the ship. Today we had a rifle inspection. It looks like child's play to me, because this whole place is very crowded. The whole inspection seemed more like an imitation [of an inspection] than a drill. It seems to me that if we had to be here for very long, we would want to get away from here. It is better to be at sea. When one is at sea, however, one longs to be on land. After only 3 days on the water, one can hear the guys talking about land. It seems that we will shortly land, because they are already making all the necessary preparations to land.

Aug. 28, 1918. Well, thank God, we have finished our 3rd trip on the sea, and we haven't even seen any submarines. We received an order [saying] that if the ship were to sink, we should either dive or roll into the sea but not jump. Since we wear our lifebelts day and night, it is understandable that we would be happy to be on land. At 10 o'clock in the morning, we saw land, and at 2 we disembarked from our gigantic ship, Armanda [*sic*], and we were right in Egypt.

When Liss arrived in Egypt, he had a sense of familiarity with the place, as if the Old Testament had provided him with a frame of reference with which to absorb it.

As soon as we entered, I could see the British culture. Right on the shore, there were advertised all kinds of houses built in the European style. We got off the ship and immediately boarded a train. We squeezed into open air cars, that is, the same cattle cars but half open. There near the train, I saw our friends—the Arabs. It seems that Egypt is eternally blessed with slaves. And when it is not the Jews, then it is the Arabs, who are at the port by the hundreds, working and guarding England's granaries, of which, may no evil eye befall them, there are plenty. Just looking at that warehouse made me certain of the Allies' eventual victory. Wearing old, torn rags, which for the most part consist of a long robe and a few scarves wound around their heads, so that it is difficult to recognize whether this is a man or a woman, they stand around and work in such a haphazard manner that many of them are beaten by the older ones; exactly like in ancient times. Today many beg. It disgusted me to look at them. At about 6, the signal was given. (When our ancestors went down to Egypt, they were 70 souls.) Our train took us into Egypt. We remembered that we were going to Cairo, but we were very disappointed when, at about midnight, we got off the train in a place that we could not identify in the dark. But I do know one thing—I was deep in sand. I comforted myself with the fact that sand would be soft to sleep on as I made myself a place to lie down. And after several hours of scratching, because sand is very itchy, I fell asleep.

Aug. 29, 1918. When I got up in the morning, the sun, which was shining hotly on my face, made me understand what kind of country I was in. And although I was sleepy, I began to think about what I had learned from the Chumash about Egypt. First I saw the great swamp, which looked as if it could have been a sea, without the slightest, tiniest indication of life, except for the places where there was a bit of water, which were besieged by birds. This immediately made me think of the clay that our ancestors had to knead, and the birds reminded me of the quail that they received in the desert. I had thought of this while still traveling, but now in this place where I was, I was reminded of the desert in which our ancestors walked, because this is a place of dry land covered with deep sand, on which the sun beats down mercilessly. In order to house soldiers, they had erected huts, which looked like Succoth [the huts the children of Israel stayed in during the exodus], which they had to build in the desert with some stones held together with the kind of grass that grows here. Here was the house. We had our meager meal, and we fell in [line] to wage war with Pharaoh's third plague [lice]. First they took our things that were not made of rubber or leather and threw them into a pot, which was boiling with some stuff and boiled them for half an hour, and we ourselves were given a milk bath, that is, the water was white, and when we got out, all the delicate places on our bodies burned like salt poured on wounds. Yes, even if Pharaoh had been subject to [this] plague in the 20th century, he would not have managed. Afterwards we once again ate our meal, more scanty than ever. And at about 7 o'clock, when the sun went down, we erected our linen tents, and in a few hours a lavender city had been created. The epidemic of thievery now even affected me; my helmet, which I had washed and hung up to dry, has been stolen.

Aug. 30, 1918. At 4 o'clock we were awakened, and we fixed the tents that had not been put up right in the dark, and after breakfast we moved into our new homes—the tents, and got busy right away decorating them so that they would look pretty. We gathered the white stones, which are more plentiful here than anything else. I became a stone specialist, splitting the stones so that we could use them. Another person [became] a paver, and a third formed the name of the place where we were: Tel El-Kabir. In a few minutes, the 7 people who were in our tent, had a small palace, with a ring around the tent and a white path leading to the entrance. When I had finished my job, I went to see what was going on in the tents of my friends, who had also done a lot with the white stones. My friend, Lartsnu, [wrote out Jabotinsky's motto] "Our land was destroyed. Judah fell in blood and fire, and with blood and fire Judah will rise" and other such decorations. Well, we tried to make things as homey as we could. We didn't have many inspections, except a kit inspection, which consists of laying out everything a soldier owns, like an auctioneer selling his wares. In the evening, I went to see what I could buy in the canteen in which the Arabs were selling things. As it turned out, it cost me a lot of money. I still had 10 shillings with me and I was able to buy very little with that. I had practically nothing left. All I know is that the Arab mentioned piasters and figured things out so that I was thoroughly confused. But now I know that there are 5 piasters to a shilling. I hope that I will not be fooled anymore.

The biblical frame of reference was applied not only to the environment but also to the Legionnaires themselves, who are compared by the diarist to ancient Hebrew warriors.

Aug. 31, 1918. They had told us last night that tomorrow, Saturday at 5 o'clock, there will be a parade to the synagogue, and we got ready, put everything to rights: our belt and the bayonet on top. Exactly at 5 o'clock in the morning the bugle blew and in a half hour's time, our heroes of Israel, who numbered 1,500 men—excluding the staff—stood at attention in perfect order, ready to go pray to their God. It was a beautiful sight to behold our boys dressed in khaki drill suits, [wearing] their helmets with blue Stars of David and their belts with their bayonets. It made us look like real warriors, and with great energy we marched a quarter of a mile away from our tents, where we sat in U shape, the opening was occupied by our officers. And the cantor immediately shouted the prayer that had been especially written for active service. Even though I was very hungry then, I was soon satiated with happiness at seeing how Jews once again went to pray to their God in the desert and [hearing] the cantor, one of our boys, chanting the Shema[3] with such fervor. Our land is mentioned there so many times, the land which we are so close to now and Egypt, where we are now. Then we took out our battalion's small Torah scroll and an officer read [from it]. I was sorry that I did not hear what he read, but I did hear one thing—that he was reading from Bamidbar [the Old Testament Book of Numbers]. This was also touching. It was where it mentioned the desert. Then he prayed Hagomel* because we had come successfully through such dangers. The Colonel wished us success, and when he spoke the words, "For his day and in our days," my heart melted with joy. I saw clearly what was coming. We ended the service with "Hatikvah" and "God Save." Then the Colonel gave a good speech in which he praised us and thanked us for our [good] behavior and work. He said that even when we were on the ship, the Captain of the ship had said good things about us. Then he gave us regards from our brothers, the two Jewish battalions: the 38th and the 39th and said that one of them would soon join us and also that we would very soon receive our Jewish badges: the menorah.[4] [In addition], he said that our name was to be Kadima [Forward], and he was sure that we would earn that title as soon as we distinguished ourselves on the battlefield. Of that he was certain! ("The person whose eyes witnessed all of this should rejoice.") And then we left in order and went to eat breakfast. I forgot to write something interesting about the Colonel. [He said] that for the first time in five thousand years, we will once again sit in Succoth in the desert, just like our ancestors did. And I want to add that just as our forefathers succeeded after much suffering, we too will succeed in the end and be happy. To my surprise, I was so happy that even my rations, which used to seem so meager now appeared bigger. My joy grew even greater during the day, when we were asked for the addresses of our relatives in Palestine. As I understand it, we will be given a leave for the holidays. When it got cooler, I became a tailor. I sewed a pocket on my shirt, and it came out not at all bad. If my mother had seen this she would no longer be able to say: "My son, you cannot even tie a cat's tail. If not for your mother you would be walking around barefoot and naked." But now I even make a pair of cuffs. May no evil eye befall me. Yes, life is a good teacher.

Sept. 1, 1918. It is said that if one laughs a lot, one must then cry. This was the case with me. [I was] happy all day yesterday because of the early-morning spiritual pleasure that I had, but at 7 o'clock, when it was already quite dark here, pitch black in Egypt,** I began thinking very sad thoughts. In order to drive away my sorrow, I took off between the empty rows [of tents], since practically all the boys had gone to hear a concert at the Y.M.C.A. While

---

* Translator's Note: The Hagomel is a prayer said after one survives a life-threatening danger.
** Translator's Note: This is perhaps an allusion to the darkness that overtook the Egyptians when the Jews were about to leave.

walking, I met a sergeant who had just returned from one of the Colonel's lectures given [specifically] for sergeants. He told me that we would very soon go to the firing lines, where it was very dangerous, and that was why we had to learn to be very good soldiers so that we could protect ourselves from danger. A half hour later, when I was lying on my bed unable to sleep because hunger was keeping me awake, I began to ponder my situation. I felt that I was in the same position as Moses, who, after having suffered so much, was told by God that he would die and would not be able to see the land [of Israel]. It was the same with me: I was now suffering so that I could see a future Jewish republic, but who knows if I will achieve that after being in the line of fire. But I nevertheless comforted myself by [convincing myself that] I would live, continue and see the fulfillment of my dreams, which would shortly become realities. At half past 4 in the morning, the bugle woke us up, and at 5 o'clock it was: "Renew our days as of old."*

THE LONG ROAD TO PALESTINE

While he may have felt like Moses on the road to the Promised Land, the diarist still had to go through several weeks of routine life in the British army before reaching it. In the weeks that followed, the diary was filled with descriptions of drills and inspections, thefts, fistfights, a lost battle against flies and insects (compared again to Pharaoh's plagues), and thoughts on war and peace.

Sept. 13, 1918. It is difficult for Jewish boys to devote themselves entirely to the sword and the rifle, and that is actually why we have started classes in Hebrew for those who are beginners and those who already know how to speak Hebrew. In the evening, while I was at bayonet practice, I thought of something strange. What? I will really have to kill a person? I had absolutely no worries about my own life—[I just thought] about how I would do this. No! It cannot ever get that far. I just became a student in Hebrew school, how could it possibly even be imagined that I would kill someone? That made me sad a whole day. A vaudeville show that was put on for the benefit of the rifle brigade, which was staying in our camp until they could get to England, lightened my mood a bit. . . .

Sept. 17, 1918. Peace! Millions of people are waiting for this. Thousands of fathers and mothers are praying to God for the time that peace will come, but I doubt that anyone wants it as badly as I do.

Some of the reflections in Liss's notebooks concern the Turkish and German prisoners of war. The difficulty in coping with the large number of POWs taken by the advancing British army in the Middle East has been

---

* Translator's Note: This is a quote from the Sabbath prayers.

described in various sources as a "nightmarish situation."[5] Elias Gilner described trainloads of prisoners in Palestine whose condition was appalling.

> There was nothing soldierly about them; in fact they hardly looked human. They were shadows of men, with emaciated, grimy faces, from which sunken eyes glared with the sick, ravenous hunger of jackals, or stared with dull resignation. They had all been victims of starvation, fever and vermin. Some of them would take a few steps, then totter and fall flat on their faces. The odor they gave off was so nauseating that no soldier could stand close to them for any length of time.[6]

In another study, Eran Dolev described the terrible condition of Turkish prisoners in Damascus, with thousands of the sick and wounded among them having been abandoned by their retreating units. As one eyewitness reported, "Deserted by all save a handful of Turkish Medical personnel, starved for three days, and suffocated by the stench of their own offal and unburied dead, the plight of these wretches was more than miserable."[7] With the number of German and Turkish prisoners estimated in September 1918 to have reached forty thousand,[8] POW camps were erected, and the Jewish Legions were charged with the unpleasant task of guarding them.

> Oct. 6, 1918. I went to see the prisoners of war in a small camp illuminated by gasoline. I could only hear their voices but not see them . . . except for about a hundred, who had arrived not long ago. [They were] dressed in all kinds of uniforms. Their faces were troubled and they looked so beaten down, like someone looking at the person who could spare their lives. Oh, how my thought processes were working. I saw the world in beautiful colors, like crowds of people standing and reveling, rejoicing in God's world, when suddenly one attacks another and kills him or drags him behind himself like a dog or a slave. The slave was once also a respectable person. And I myself am here. I came to take part in these horrible events. Then I immediately thought: I am a Hebrew, and who knows if tomorrow I will not be a prisoner in worse condition even than these. [Smoking] one cigarette after another stopped me a bit from thinking [too much], and I felt my way to the canteen, which I could barely make out in the darkness. I left that place quickly, so that I would perhaps forget what I had just seen—factually and emotionally. When I had not even gone 100 yards, I heard a guard shout, "Halt! Who goes there?" and I was stopped by a Corporal. I responded, "Friend," was recognized as a friend and continued on my way thinking: How much longer will the world go on this way?
>
> To tell the truth, it warmed my heart to see one of our Jewish soldiers leading some 50 German prisoners to work. These were people, who more than once shouted out "Damned Jews," and now they are forced [to do what] Jews [tell them to do]. A little further on, I saw thousands of Turks sitting

in rows, probably for a roll call, and although I was saddened to see people imprisoned for no more than what the other side would call bravery, I also thought that if they weren't sitting here guarded by soldiers with swords, they would surely have shot me or one of my friends, or they would have run me through with a bayonet. Then a happy smile spread across my face.

There were exciting moments, too, like when the battalion's blue-and-white flag with a golden Star of David was erected ("My heart filled with pride looking at this flag. Yes, I do not think that there is anything else that differentiates us from the old Christian battalions") and when the Jewish Legions celebrated Rosh Hashanah, the Jewish New Year, in the Egyptian desert.

Sept. 7, 1918. In honor of the holiday, we slept a little later today, because our parade to synagogue was at 6 o'clock. We marched to the place where we were to pray, in the same order as yesterday, and held our prayer service. As soon as we had finished, the Colonel gave a speech, which did not make everyone happy. To begin with, he did what the old [traditional] rabbis did on The Sabbath of Return,* knowing that on Rosh Hashanah many hearts are softened, he first asked us to love our fellow [soldiers] as ourselves, to live with each other as brothers, and he especially asked that the thieving stop. Then he commanded that they stop, and he ended to our dissatisfaction that we should not look for [extra] privileges because we were Jews and we, therefore, could not observe the holiday for 2 days. We were in active service and tomorrow we would have to work. Then he wished us a good year for the second time and we were dismissed. All day long, the camp was filled with a regular holiday atmosphere. Having been paid, the guys went off to the canteen to spend their money. In general, serenity ruled the camp.

In September, the Jewish Palestinian recruits arrived in Tel El-Kabir. As we shall see in some of the next chapters, relations between the Palestinian recruits and the other Legionnaires were not always smooth; many of the former held strong ideological convictions according to which they, as inhabitants of the land of Israel who had farmed the land and established collective settlements there, were the vanguard destined to transform the Jewish people into a strong, secular, productive nation. The volunteers from abroad were seen by some of them as immersed in an outdated religion and waiting to be transformed. Liss's diary, however, presents a very different picture, as he saw the recruits from Palestine as true brothers in arms and in faith.

Sept. 19, 1918. Ah, another day without drilling. We are getting ready for the Palestine boys to arrive, and of course tents have to be erected for them.

---

* Translator's Note: Shabat Tshuva, the Sabbath that falls between Rosh Hashanah and Yom Kippur.

It is true that I worked very hard, but I was, nevertheless, very happy, first of all, I did not have to drill, and second, because I have been waiting impatiently for these boys to arrive for the last two weeks. So I was happy to erect those tents and finally see them arrive. At about half past 9, we [all] gathered near the train to welcome them. After we had waited for an hour, they arrived. Impatient to see them, I had gone ahead quite a distance, and while the train was still moving, I jumped on and I shook hands with a lot of them, and some greeted me with shalom a'hi [Hello, my brother] and some asked me questions in Hebrew. Then they immediately began singing "Se'u Ziona." Then I spent until noon talking Hebrew to the Palestinians and sign language with the Egyptians.[9] Well, I was as delighted as someone who sees his brother after not having seen him for a long time. For me this was a very festive emotional "holiday."

Due to the arrival of the Palestinians, we were allowed to sleep an hour later and we did not have to go to the first parade, which we have every day from 5:30 to 6:00. For the second parade, we had a road march in the desert until we came to a place . . . where a battle occurred in 1882, and it was built in that year.[10] It was built halfway up a hill* that is one semi-circle and then another semi-circle. That is where we viewed the spot, and our officer then explained how a battle is fought. Then we actually practiced. The more I learn, the more I see that war is not a simple matter. At night, I spent time with the Palestinian boys, who make me feel good with their Jewish patriotism.

Sept. 22, 1918. Last night we gave a name to the historic night and it was accurate. It is true that we suffer every night from itching that we think comes from mosquitoes, but last night surpassed them all. We went to sleep, and after a few hours of scratching ourselves we saw that it was useless to try to sleep, so practically everyone left their beds, and thanks to the moon, which shone with all of its might, we sat down to play [games]. Some played chess and some cards. We sang and danced to forget our woes. It was a beautiful sight to see the future fighters defeated by the tiny mosquitoes and sitting powerless in the middle of the night because of them. Finally it was morning, and we had a full-pack battalion march; that meant that all the co[mpanies] marched together in full marching order as if they were going to battle. In previous times, I would have done such a march easily, but today, suffering [as I did] from a lack of sleep and food . . . I did not even have any money to help me [buy food], because we did not get paid this week, so I became very weak and felt faint as I walked, but thank God we did not march more than 3 hours. Yes, it is very difficult to serve one's country. I thank God for the comfort He gave us by sending the Palestinian battalion. In the evening I was in their camp and speaking in Hebrew I found out what patriots they were and that these were people one could respect. There I met someone who was 58 years old, but so strong in his beliefs that he could surely best the strongest youth. When we got to talking about our [respective] countries

---

* Translator's Note: In the original Yiddish, this is poetically called the "lap" of a hill.

and our ideals, we found ourselves so close that we practically kissed one another. At night we had a concert at which we welcomed our brothers. The Colonel opened the concert with the happy news that the wireless had just now reported that 20 some-odd thousand Turks had been captured as well as 20 car loads of machine guns and 30 some-odd thousand pounds of gold. It is difficult to describe our enthusiasm. After the concert, the Palestinians went to the flag[pole], where our flag was flying and repeated that which we did when we left England.

Sept. 23. As much as I felt that I was not a good soldier, no complaints had been made about me, but I fell down on the job today. Because of a stomach ache, I had not cleaned my rifle and during inspection they took my name and reported me. All day, I suffered terribly due to my stomach. At night I felt better and went to see my Palestinian friends. There are some with whom I have become more or less good friends, and the old Jewish soldier is someone I consider a grandfather. [I am also close to] one of his friends, who spread out a rubber sheet in front of his tent and made a party with whatever he had. I will remember this supper for a long time. It is worthwhile for me to describe it: the bread was soldiers' bread, [there were] several olives, a kind of cheese that I had never before eaten in the army, and some good brandy, which was simply delicious. Dessert was some nuts. This is what the three of us ate; we ate and talked about American life as well as life in Palestine. It was already late at night when I blessed them with peace and went to sleep. On the way back, I ran into 2 Palestinians, whom I had never met before, but after a few words of greeting we walked together like brothers and once again I spoke of our country and our future.

Sept. 28, 1918. Well, we are no longer celebrating the Sabbaths as we had been doing: praying first and then having the rest of the day off. Today we [expected to] follow an order received yesterday—that there would be a route march on the Sabbath, but it was cancelled and we did have the afternoon free after lunch. Instead of seeing a vaudeville show, I watched a gambling show. I watched guys losing yesterday's wages. It was very dark at night, and I heard a familiar melody coming from a hall. When I went inside, I found out that tonight was Simchat Torah [the holiday marking the completion of the annual cycle of weekly Torah readings] and the Orthodox minyan was celebrating the holiday. A soldier stood at the podium. I cannot call him a soldier, because his prayer shawl was covering his uniform. He had a Jewish appearance, a big, gray beard, and was praying so sincerely us-ing the [typical] Jewish melody. After the prayers, they, the Palestinians and our boys, walked around the ark with our 2 little Torah scrolls, and each time they completed a passage, they sang "Who Gave Us the True Torah" or "The Jewish People Lives." At first I was afraid for the Torah scroll. I wanted to go kiss it, like most of them were doing, but I could not justify it, since I was not observant. But after seeing the older man and a young Palestinian soldier carrying the Torah scrolls around so joyously and singing "Am Yirael Hai" [The Jewish people lives], I developed such love for the little Torah scroll, which was making it possible for young and old to be so enveloped by the same emotions, that I did kiss it lovingly.

Sept. 29. A full pack march: that is how we started our day. At about 7 we started out with the whole kit and caboodle, and after our walk we did maneuvers on the field in which the main activity was running, and although most of us are good runners, it is still very difficult to get through all the drills. In the evening, we had a real Simchat Torah; in addition to our regular supper we had wine, which the Palestinian Jews sent to our battalion. The very fact that the Palestinian Jews sent that was enough of a reason to be happy. In addition, everyone also got a bottle of seltzer and cake, which means the whole world to half-starved soldiers, so we were joyous indeed. Some [soldiers] did get a bit tipsy and some pretended to be. Our camp showed some life.

Sept. 30, 1918. For the first time today I saw a Lewis gun, because this morning, I was part of a . . . party where we carried over Lewis guns and ammunition from one place to another. In the evening we were in high spirits over the news that Bulgaria had asked for peace, and our boys immediately began talking diplomacy, [discussing] where the war would end and when. But for the most part they discussed how soon we could go home, and because of this news, the guys began to dance and sing between the lines. I had something else to be happy about; one of the Palestinian guys treated me to almonds from the land of Israel, and I was overjoyed at being able to enjoy fruit from my land.

Oct. 19. If someone had come into the dining hall last night he would certainly have asked himself in surprise if he had come into a soldiers' camp or into an inner ministry in which the most important people in the country were seeking ways to make the lives of the populace easier. In a hut illuminated by 3 lights, soldiers sat listening to someone who was also wearing a uniform but seemed more like a friend than a soldier. [This was] Ben-Zvi, who was talking about the near future of Israel. . . . He explained the industries that are possible there. He spoke of social reforms, and our soldiers, who love nothing more than to talk and debate, sat so quietly. It seemed that they did not want to miss a word. But when the lecturer permitted it, they asked pertinent questions. It would be impossible to believe that these were the same soldiers of whom it is said that their only job was getting drunk and fooling around when they were not murdering [people]. It was a shame that we were on the fire brigade this evening and did not have more time to spend [talking] at the lecture.

Liss's enthusiasm over his encounter with Ben-Zvi and other Palestinian Jews made him want to settle in Palestine.

Nov. 20, 1918. As soon as we finished our P. T. [physical training] today, they immediately called out that those going to Palestine should fall out and put on their tunics in order to parade in front of the Colonel. Immediately there was a big tumult among us, among the 90 percent who will remain in our land and among the rest, the 10 percent, who saw the possibility of quickly returning home. As a company, we marched to the Battalion Orderly Room. No co[mpany] needed to be ashamed of these 2 [camps], because everyone was a patriot . . . a full 90 percent [wanted to remain]. Afterwards, our company was arrayed in the form of a U-shape with 2 companies being at the head. It would not be an exaggeration [to say] that I, along with everyone else, felt this parade to be the happiest since we entered the army, because for the first time we saw our Freedom for Palestine Army in all its glory, and second, it gave us the possibility to hope that we would soon be sent there, [to the place] to which we have wanted to devote our whole lives. When we were already standing at attention, the Colonel and the Major marched past every rank and asked various questions. Then we were dismissed. I am certain that everything that has been said and written about Palestine has not mentioned it as many times as [it was mentioned] today in front of us. Right after the parade, we began to ask each other, "Are you staying in Palestine?" And if not, why not? Then we began to argue about it or to conjecture about when we would be sent there. In general, it was as if we were dizzy with joy. Later, after lunch, 50 men of our co[mpany] were told to get ready to leave early the next day. Among these 50 were those who were going to remain in Palestine and those who were going home. This completely puzzled us, and there was no end of discussion about what would happen.

IDEALS AND REALITY

The vision of the Promised Land, evoked by national movements, is hard to maintain once the actual land is reached and reality does not match the ideals. In the case of the Jewish Legions, the decisive moment came when the soldiers were stationed in places like the desert city of Rafa, on the southwestern edge of Palestine, where the main source of excitement was boxing matches with other British military units. While the recruits from Palestine overcame setbacks to their socialist and nationalist ideals with endless political activity, many North American soldiers like Liss found themselves in a spiritual void. His diary entries written after arrival in Palestine are filled with descriptions of the summer heat, the sandstorms, and the mosquitoes, which, when the actual fighting was over, became the soldiers' main preoccupation. Political ambiguity over the future of the Legions was demoralizing to their members. Careful not to antagonize the Arabs, the British military authorities in Palestine not only assigned marginal tasks to the Legions after the armistice, but also consistently suppressed any mention of them in the Palestinian and Egyptian press. General Allenby, in his victory speech in Cairo in December 1918, mentioned all the nationalities that had fought under his command except the Jews. As Colonel Patterson said, "Coming on top of all our persecutions, this was most remarked."[11] The diary entries written in Rafa describe moments of boredom and disenchantment relieved somewhat by the chaplain's ability to frame the experience in terms of the children of Israel wandering in the desert with the Promised Land still to be reached.

Nov. 27, 1918. Oh! This evening I knew what our forefather Jacob felt like: "During the day, I am devoured by scorching heat and ice at night."[12] It had been so hot during the day and I froze at night like a dog, because I had only one blanket. I woke up several times due to the cold and angrily looked at the shining moon that was holding back the day from coming. And during the few hours that I did sleep, I dreamt about food. Day did finally dawn and I greeted it with joy.

Yes, there is even a moving picture house here, and that is where I spent this evening. It is a tremendously large place filled with soldiers, and everyone was watching the open-air moving pictures with such interest that is impossible to conceive in civilian life. I am sure that if a stranger were brought in and his eyes covered so that he did not know that there were only soldiers here, he would be able to figure it out for himself from the cynical remarks of those watching. Whenever a woman appeared on the screen, the soldiers became as wild as animals, and they practically jumped out of their seats. It is just fortunate that there was no real woman present. She would never have gotten out of there alive. In any case, today I made myself a good bed having gotten a second blanket.

Dec. 1, 1918. At half past one I attended a meeting called by the Chaplain, which was not a success, because it was not well publicized. Nevertheless, in a few words he told us that he would organize a choir, because the [members of the] old choir were either sick or had fallen [in battle]. He would also organize lectures, classes and a Hebrew club and he would try to provide us with spiritual nourishment. He also discussed with us the question of settling in Palestine. [He said] that everything would be fine, as long as we remembered that it is only a desert. But just knowing that I am on the land of my country, which will certainly later become a good, beautiful city, makes me happy.

March 26, 1919. Somehow it seems to me that military life gets worse every day, instead of what we were expecting—that it should get better. Today, for example, the Sergeant-Major called out that we could not leave the camp, because we were on the fire brigade,* and we must be ready at any minute of the day in the event that we are called, and there will be a roll call to make sure that there are no dodgers. Then the Corporals were taken for musketry [lessons], so that they could teach it to us faster. In this way, things are getting worse instead of getting better, and my heart feels somehow sadder. I just barely made it to the end of this day.

---

* Translator's Note: In the original, Liss uses the term "fire pickets."

March 28, 1919. I am once again an escort—a damnable job. My one consolation is that it will possibly get me freed from guard duty tomorrow, and since I have done escort [duty], I have not had such a lousy job as I did yesterday. Under the burning sun, I had to go with the Turks to the former Australian camp to get the rubbish and bring it to our camp, and then do it again several times. When I got back, I thought that I was going to pass out. Nevertheless, when it was 2 o'clock, I had to go on duty . . . and once again the Turks upset me. They feel so independent here. When I gave one of them an order to do a certain task, he talked back to me, [saying] that as a sentry, I cannot tell him to do anything. I had to go grab his collar and threaten him with my bayonet. Then he did what I wanted.

Liss found satisfaction in occasional travels to the Jewish farming colonies in Palestine and provides an interesting account of Tel Aviv in its early days.

March 1, 1919. Even early in the morning in Tel Aviv it was possible to feel that it was the Sabbath, although there were very few religious symbols to be seen. That is why it appealed to me so much. Even though I am not religious, I still find it pleasant to feel the atmosphere of the Sabbath in the streets and to see the dressed up marching masses on Herzl Street. I was most amused by the little children playing and speaking my favorite language—Hebrew. And to better hear it, I actually spent a few hours with the children. When I was finished at the dentist's I took a walk to the seashore, which was very beautiful with its unusual sand. But more than anything else I was amused by two Tel Aviv girls, young high school girls, who just like me, came to spend a few pleasant hours by the sea and with whom I spent a few agreeable hours. I was enchanted by their naïve, youthful beauty as well as their education, knowledge and patriotism. In the evening I went to the Tel Aviv cinema, the only one in Jaffa, and it has nothing to be ashamed about. It is just as nice as any movie house in a large city, except that it was very disorganized. The tickets are in Hebrew, and the show is in French. After the show, "Hatikvah" was played very well, but the locals did not show it the respect that others show their hymns. When I returned to the Soldiers' Hostel at 10 in the evening, I was very disappointed to find the place locked, and I began to look for a place to spend the night. Even though Tel Aviv has more hotels than private houses, I still had to walk around for an hour going from place to place until I found one that could offer me a place to sleep. That is how busy it was all over. I had to pay one and a half shillings for a bed that was hard and had no pillows and only a thin blanket, and I got those only after pleading. This is how dearly I paid for my day's pleasure.

Liss and others in his battalion hoped to remain in Palestine after demobilization, but Patterson informed them that due to unemployment in the country, they would have to go home. The diarist, referring to the group willing to stay in Palestine as the true Maccabees, tells of the day when the dream was shattered, to the satisfaction of those who objected to the Legions remaining in the country.

> April 1, 1919. At 10 a.m. those who wanted to stay in this country were paraded before Col[onel] Patterson, dressed in belts and bayonets, thinking that we were going to be liberated soon and that our sweet dreams were going to be fulfilled. So the few who had remained in Rafa, 100 strong, marched proudly and bravely with the true Maccabees, but lightning fast, out of the clear [blue] sky, our Col[onel's] words hit us; he had been informed by the Zion Commission that there was no work in the country, and therefore, we would be demobilized, unless a person finds a job, but he is not given the opportunity, and the result is that it would be best if we would all go home, and in one minute, our sweet dreams of having no more problems and not working so hard evaporated. In the end, it turned out that [although we wanted to] be in our land—"A man will sit under his grape vine and under his fig tree"[13]—nothing became of it, and ashamed and hanging our heads we marched away under the smug glances of our enemies, the boys who always laughed at us for speaking about such nonsense, and right away, the Maccabees were unfortunately called into the co[mpany's] office. They should be written up in various places. These are the kinds of conversations of children without a land: Where are you going to? "To London," an Argentinean answers and the other one asks, "Is that your home?" And he responds that he has no home. Wherever he comes, he makes a temporary home. He has been in Argentina for 11 years, [and that is] enough.
>
> Another one travels to America, a third to Australia, a fourth to Russia and many, many more places. And these were all people who dreamed and hoped that they would eventually go home. How sad! My God, is it really right to agree with the assimilationists? The whole day was a kind of Tisha B'Av [a day of mourning] for us, except that we gathered in small groups to discuss our situation. One took "French leave"[14] and went to Jaffa. Others sent telegrams to New York. Jabotinsky eased our pain a bit with his lecture about the poet Bialik [the national poet].

The entries for the following months are indicative of the difficulty of following the military routine once the dream of settling in the Promised Land was shattered. Here are some excerpts of interest from these entries.

On Jabotinsky:

> April 2, 1919. One might have expected that Jabotinsky would not be a very stern officer, but, as it turned out, he was stricter than all the others. At the first parade, from 6–7, he drilled [us] strictly just like all the other officers, whom we call "born military men," and at the second parade, he was also terribly strict, inspecting every little thing like never before. After the inspection and the calling out of the guard in which I was included, we were still not let go but were called back for a 3rd inspection. We had to bring our kits

to the parade grounds. And if a kit inspection in the lines looks like a market, such a parade looks like a regular fair. After the 3rd parade, a 4th parade was called, but this one made everyone happy. It was a "pay parade"—at 1:30, but I was at the guard inspection parade, where the Co[mpany] Captain rebuked me for my torn things. It was a joke. My uniform is more like that of a beggar than a Tommy [British soldier] to the point that I am ashamed to wear it—and in the end, I am to blame. At 4 o'clock, I was already at guard parade and then, right away, on guard [duty]. It is good that I was camp guard. That is how I was at 3 parades. And on guard, there started the process of escorting prisoners, of which there are plenty. They have to be led to the toilet, then to get water: this one here and that one there, so that at the end, I was so tired that I was barely at my post [at all].

April 4, 1919. Early this morning we suffered from the old military condition, moving. If it had only been moving from Rafa, it would not have mattered, but this was just moving from one tent to another. The operation began at 6 o'clock in the morning. Everyone went out to the parade ground with his kit and all of his belongings, and then we began to sort ourselves out, so that the 9 men, who have to live together, should know each other. After this commotion, we had our usual breakfast: cheese, porridge and tea. At 8 o'clock, there was the 2nd parade. This time I, unknowingly, committed a crime. Just as we were being called to line up, I was in the latrine and got there late, and this made me an offender. My name and number were taken, and in the morning I was to go to the co[mpany] office. I was once again inspected very, very thoroughly by Jabotinsky. There were 15 men [there] including me. As a punishment, we had to fall out again at 11 o'clock, clean, without one stain, where Jabotinsky once again inspected us. This time, he explained to us in Yiddish, that he was doing this not because he was strict and demonstrating his power but because he wanted to see that the Jewish battalion, which was just being tried out before the world, would be a paragon of cleanliness and discipline, even though we were just as good as all the other Christian battalions.

April 5, 1919. As a result of last Saturday, when the Colonel showed up to inspect us and all we had on were our belts and bayonets, which was against King's Rules and Regulations, today we had to parade wearing our belts and [carrying] our arms, clean enough, although there was no parade to the synagogue. And because of Jabotinsky's words, I tried, today, to be a "smart soldier," and I cleaned and polished myself up as never before.

On military justice:

[April 4] At 4 o'clock we went out to stand guard on the battalion's parade ground, where the court-marshal of Shtrasburg, someone whom I knew well and who had been one of my former tent mates, was publicly read. The ceremony itself was enough to frighten the attendees. We were arrayed in the form of a U and the one charged was in the middle with 2 policemen as escorts. Behind the prisoner was the Corp[oral] of the police. When the Adjutant gave the command: "Attention! Stand!" and he began to read the private's [name] and number. (At these words, the Police Corp[oral] took his hands off the accused.) What he was accused of was trying to foment a revolution among the soldiers and not obeying the orders of his officer. He pleaded, "Not guilty," but he was found guilty on both counts and was sentenced to one year's hard labor, but, out of kindness, his sentence was reduced to 6 months. "Parade attention!" [was called], and the police escort then turned so that they stood with their faces to the guilty party. It hit us like a death blow, when we heard such a harsh sentence for something that was mostly a frame-up on the part of several sergeants, who had it in for him. The escort led the prisoner back to jail, and we were taken through the guard ceremony, even though we could barely stand on our feet after having gone through such a bad experience. But what could one do? We were in the army, held by iron chains. And we went off to do our duty as if nothing whatsoever had occurred.

On cruelty:

April 7, 1919. I saw Jewish tyranny today, when I went to see what was going on in the guard room. A Bedouin had been accused of trying to break into the ammunition dump and had been locked up in the guard room by our boys. He was sitting tied up to a tent pole and the police corp[oral] was threatening him all the while, [saying] that he would shoot him the next day and pulling his beard or running his hand over that wild person's face in a very rough manner. To tell the truth, I did not have any sympathy for this wild creature.

On soldiering culture:

April 9, 1919. Something really funny happened last night. First, I talked the Corporal into not having us stand on more than one post during the night, as we do during the day, and that came out to one hour per person. Second, we spent the whole night stealing, and fooling around. It first started with potatoes. Everyone went and stole some potatoes, and we made all kinds of potatoes: boiled, baked and fried. At night, the Corp[oral] and I took part in a real robbery—stealing bacon, and even though I myself do not like it and do not eat it, I nevertheless took it for my friends, and just like a true thief, I did my job, cut off a piece, covered it with sand and put it down, so that it would not be recognized [for what it was]. But I am, after all, not a thief and so my conscience began to bother me, and more than that I was afraid to be found out, so I hid the meat until the afternoon, and convinced them that I was certain that with this they would make some fine dishes. And afterwards, I, actually, did feel proud of my deed, because after what the boys said, it did not seem like thievery but just taking what was coming to us. And that is how the day passed. No matter how tired I was after such a long week, I still had to wash my things, and then I went to sleep breathing the sand [brought by] the big sand storm that had just started and that now covered everything.

On the celebration of Passover in a military camp:

April 13, 1919. It was a regular night before Passover in camp: busy, just like in a small, Jewish, Russian shtetl [a Jewish small town] on the eve of a holiday. At the first parade, those on guard duty were called out, and today I felt fortunate to be among them for the first time since I am in the army; first, because I will not have to do the full fatigues, which are in camp at this time, and second, this will give me the opportunity to attend the Seder, which will possibly take place tomorrow evening. It is terribly busy in camp. In one place, the suits are being given out to those who have not yet gotten them. In another place, the sheep are being slaughtered and prepared. Here a lot of huts are being pushed together for the Seder. Well, it is like a regular holiday, and I have practically forgotten about the disappointment [I felt] at not having been given leave to go visit my friend. I believe that it will be very interesting to be at the Seder in camp.

April 14, 1919. Today I was happy that I had been on guard [duty], because it seems that the closer Passover gets, the more work there is in camp, so much so that they even called those who had just gotten off guard [duty] that morning. Of course, I pretended that I did not hear anything and lay in my tent a whole day reading a book. The weather was really so bad—like never before. Just as if He wanted to remember this Passover that we spent in Rafa forever. It started with a huge sand storm that not only filled all of our belongings [with sand] but also every crevice in our bodies which sand could [possibly] get to. I had to empty sand from my ears more than a dozen times, like emptying a pot of sand, and with every breath one could feel that one was pulling masses of sand into oneself. After several hours of raging, [the sandstorm abated] and was followed by a torrential down pour, then the sand storm returned even stronger than before. There was not [much of] a Seder today. People were more interested in the [traditional dish of] matzo balls than the Hagadah [the Passover prayer book].

On the new status envisioned for Judaism:

April 15, 1919. I experienced a nice incident in the afternoon, as I escorted 4 prisoners who carried a cross from a chaplain for the tables at the front of the church, which would be used as a lectern. I happened to see the three world religions and to think about them. First, the ruling Christian religion in the form of the chaplain, who walked in front of the prisoners carrying the load; then the enslaved Moslem religion, and I and my fellow escorts [represented] the Jewish religion, which I hope, and [which I have] seen from this incident, will flourish and predominate. It seems to me that I will have to pay for my easy day, because as I was unloading my rifle, it accidentally went off, and I think that the Corporal will bring me up on charges.

An interesting encounter recorded in the diary concerns Lance-Corporal LoBagola, undoubtedly the most colorful character in the Jewish Legions. In a 1930 autobiography titled *An African Savage's Own Story*, the author, Bata Kindai Amgoza ibn LoBagola, described himself as a black Jew, descendent of the Lost Tribes of Israel, who was born in Dahomey and at a young age was rescued at sea and taken to Scotland. He ultimately made his way to the United States, where he volunteered for military service but was rejected; thus he found his way to the British recruitment office in New York, where he enlisted with the Jewish Legions.[15] Later, it was argued that the autobiography was mostly fictitious, written by Joseph Howard Lee, an African American entertainer from Baltimore, Maryland, who invented the identity of LoBagola and lived his entire life as an impostor.[16] The fact of the matter, however, is that LoBagola, whatever his real name was, did serve in the 38th Fusiliers, and some of the details he gave in the autobiography—for example, his being in charge of the battalion's library in Rafa—are confirmed in the Liss diary.

> April 28, 1919. Upon my life, it is quite nice here in the library. I have made myself a bed . . . and linen: a true paradise. I also did not get up at reveille. Of course, I am not alone but under Corporal Lobagola, the Black Jew. At 10 o'clock in the morning, I opened the store and then began to do business. It is not really such an easy thing to be in a library, where Jewish soldiers are the customers. I am over my ears in work and I am also expected to take deposits of four cents, and one has to give out books, but it is quite interesting. . . .

> May 2, 1919. There was quite a commotion in the library when a volunteer service was held in the evening and the Black Corp[oral] stopped and arrested a boy for writing during this time, and the fact that he is black aroused a racial hatred, and everyone all together asked the padre to put a white person in that place. Of course, the rabbi refused to do that, repeating his motto that a Jew remains a Jew regardless of his color. Slowly the commotion died down. After 9 o'clock in the evening, when I was closing up, the Negro, who is a very educated young man, although he has many of the attributes that come from a wild African life, which are evidenced in him at various times, began to talk with me about the scene [that took place] this evening. And walking from place to place, he told me about an injustice that exists in the civilized world, something I knew nothing about before, and something that only he suffers from. And he wanted to drag me into this. Yes, I am still quite blind in this world.

Particularly interesting are Liss's reflections on the first-year anniversary of his service in the Legions.

> April 29, 1919. Today is my first year's anniversary of army service. Yes, it has been a good year for me. I think that I will never, ever forget this year

of equal measures of joy and suffering. It seems like only yesterday that I was saying good-bye to those dearest to me. [Since then] I have been in Canada, in England and in Egypt, and now that I am already in the land of my dreams, it seems that everything that has occurred during this year is no more than one-night's dream. Nevertheless, when I leaf through my memoirs, I see many days of hunger, thirst, sleeplessness, homesickness, etc. My greatest pleasure was that I was able to see countries, customs, landscapes. Oh! How great that was. Now the calendar shows me that a year has gone by. The best thing that I observed in army life, is that one can live in equality. Yes, especially in the battalion, in our Jewish [battalion], in which people from every corner of the world, various types with various ideas, various levels of education and trades live together, sleep, eat, dress the same—a true democracy in this aspect. No vengeance. One person's suffering is everyone's and vice versa. Yes, I will always be grateful to the 39th Infantry [Battalion], which I joined.

Liss decided to stay in Palestine and made various efforts to get work there but ultimately failed to do so. When he was released from the British army, he returned to Detroit, where he completed his high school studies and then studied dentistry. He worked as a dentist in Houston, Texas, got married and had two children, and died in July 1967 while listening on the radio to news from the State of Israel, which had just won the Six-Day War.

7

The Chaplain

THE DEBATES OVER THE JEWISH LEGIONS

On December 7, 1917, Colonel Patterson requested that the Principal Chaplainry of the British Army appoint Reverend Leib Isaac Falk as the Legions' chaplain. Falk was born on January 31, 1889, in Bauska, Latvia, the son of a traveling merchant. He attended religious seminaries in Kovno and Telsch, and one of his early teachers was Rabbi Abraham Isaac Hacohen Kook. In 1911, Falk came to Scotland and served as rabbi at Dundee, where he married the daughter of a local pawnbroker. In 1915 he moved to Plymouth, where he served as clergyman in the Southern Command. "Mr. Falk is well fitted for this post," wrote Patterson, "as he is himself a Russian and a keen Zionist."[1] With the petition approved, Reverend Falk received the rank of captain and in January 1918 enlisted for two years with the Legions. He was one of thirty-five hundred military chaplains who served in the British army. After the disbanding of the Legions, Falk made an effort to remain in Palestine as part of the British military administration, but his request was refused and he returned to England. He was discharged from the army and became a minister in the Great Synagogue in Sydney, Australia. He served as chaplain of the Australian military forces during the Second World War and died in Sydney in 1957.

In this chapter, we follow Falk's 1921 memoirs, which were written in London and serialized in a Jewish journal, *The Maccabean*, in Australia in 1929.[2] We also make use of his private papers located in the Israel Defense Forces (IDF) Archives in Israel, which include drafts of Sabbath and holiday sermons he prepared in Yiddish, English, and Hebrew on pieces of paper with a variety of letterheads. Being commissioned at the age of twenty-eight to serve as chaplain of the first Jewish military formation in the modern era, Falk had to define almost single-handedly a political and ideological frame of reference that would apply to the task at hand—turning Jewish immigrants who lacked a military tradition and a clear sense of national consciousness into a vanguard of Jewish national revival. It is interesting to follow how he derived that frame of reference from both religious sources and modern notions of the Enlightenment. Falk also played an important role in the promotion of the notion of the "Promised Land," a role that became particularly crucial when disenchantment over conditions in the land had emerged.

When Falk wrote his memoirs, he was still bitter over the debate in England over the formation of the Legions, which requires some explanation. The announcement by the War Office at the end of 1917 that a Jewish regiment would be formed had not ended the controversy within the Jewish community over an independent Jewish force. The controversy in fact became even more acrimonious. The regiment was objected to both by Jewish English leaders, who feared that its distinctiveness would harm Jewish efforts to assimilate in English society, and by the masses of Jewish immigrants to England who identified neither with the British war effort nor with the Zionist cause.[3] Echoes of the resistance can be found in the English press as well as in minutes of the War Cabinet. On August 27, 1917, the London *Times* reported on protests by Jewish workers in London, led by the "Russian Council of Workmen's and Soldiers' Delegates," who issued a resolution protesting the practice of having Russian Jews serving in a distinct national unit. "We declare that we have no special Jewish interests in the present war for which we should fight under a special Jewish banner," said the resolution. "We consider the formation of special Jewish units as a restriction against us citizens of free Russia, where all national restrictions have been abolished by the Russian Revolutionary Government." The resolution labeled the formation of the Legions a "detriment . . . against the interests of the Jewish masses in England."

At the beginning of September 1917, the secretary of state for war, Edward Stanley (Lord Derby), reported to the War Cabinet that he had received an influential deputation of Jews who objected to the title "The Jewish Regiment," sanctioned by the War Office: "The deputation had urged that some 40,000 Jews had served with distinction in the British forces, and that it was not fair to them to stake the whole reputation of English Jews as fighters on the performance of this regiment."[4] A few days later, a deputation making the opposite claim met with the secretary and "asked that the original scheme announced by the Government should be maintained, and that the regiment should be Jewish by name—the Maccabees was suggested in addition to the numeral designation—with the badge of the Star of David, and that, as far as possible, kosher food should be supplied during the training in England, together with opportunities for the observation of the Jewish Sabbath."[5]

A major opponent of the ethnic distinctiveness of the Legions was the senior Jewish chaplain in the British army, the Reverend Michael Adler, who believed that English Jews were to participate in His Majesty's army as full patriots.[6] In his memoir, Falk refers to Adler with bitterness, commenting that "[l]ike a gallant soldier he went forth to give battle to the protagonists of the battalion. He sent a letter to the War Office where in strong terms he protested against the formation of the Jewish Units and even labeled the whole idea as 'irresponsible.'"[7] From the beginning of the debate, Falk was a strong supporter of a Jewish regiment. He considered an all-Jewish fighting force part of the revival of an ancient Hebrew warrior and the best way to show loyalty to England.

> Those who advocated the raising of Jewish Military Units believed that this would be the best expression of the loyalty and patriotism of the Jews in Great Britain. They believed that the Jewish Units would not only enhance Jewish prestige but will also be the best answer to the unwarranted prejudice against the Jew which was so in vogue in the early days of the war. It will (so it was argued) once and for all expose the hollowness of the untrue assertion that the Jews do not contribute their full share on the field of Battle.
>
> The spiritual as well as the religious aspects were also forwarded as arguments in favor of creating Jewish Units. Many a Jew in the early days of the War hesitated to join on account of being averse to break with life-long customs and institutions which War conditions made inevitable, whilst a special Jewish unit will be in the position to safeguard the religious requirements of the Jew.[8]

In addition to these rationales, his support stemmed from his assessment of the role of religion in the First World War. The formation of citizen armies meant that religion became an important motivational factor in the war. In *God and the British Soldier*, Michael Snape shows how chaplains were in great demand to make sense of the war and its causes, and to provide explanations for the extreme suffering. Both the officers and the troops belonged to a generation that read the Bible piously and whose motivation depended on chaplains who could anchor the war in biblical values and images. Generals sending troops to battle read biblical tales, such as the story of Israel's battle against Amalek, and interpreted their own role in the war, and the roles of their respective countries, in providential terms. Chaplains became a valuable asset and close relations often developed between chaplains and unit commanders. Chaplains ran YMCA canteens, helped soldiers with their correspondence, and conducted a variety of social welfare services. They were also functional in mobilizing churches and other religious institutions and community groups in support of the welfare and well-being of combatants.[9]

These tasks were commonly performed by non-Jewish chaplains,[10] and by Jewish chaplains in general units,[11] but Falk realized that a military unit composed almost entirely of Jewish soldiers would allow him to cater more effectively to their special needs. As he noted in his memoirs, "The safeguard of the religious requirement of the Jewish soldier proved to be a most essential factor in bracing up his spirit, driving out gloom and despair and making them forget for a short while the miseries of War conditions."[12]

Falk also felt that a distinct unit would allow him to harness Jewish welfare systems to support the needs of Jewish soldiers. His files are filled with correspondence with public and private Jewish agencies in England, Egypt, and elsewhere, ordering kosher food, urging them to cater to soldiers' well-being, making inquiries concerning the condition of soldiers' families at home, and the like. For example, on April 30, 1918, Falk wrote the following letter to the chief rabbi of Amsterdam: "Sir, I beg to approach you on behalf of a Jewish soldier, serving in the British army, who has a little daughter at present in the care of Frau van Herre, at Herzelglichen, heffgarten, Wërlitz, Germany. He has not heard from her for a considerable time, and he and myself would be very grateful to you if you would kindly communicate with the rabbiner in Dessau Auhalt, Germany, and ask him to visit the little daughter and report about her Jewish upbringing."[13]

The recruitment of Jewish immigrants of deep religious faith into an all-Jewish unit allowed these people and their families to get support they could not expect in the general army. The following letter sent by a widow to Falk, who had earlier informed her of the death of her husband, provides a moving example: "Dear Sir. I received your letter of consolation and I must thank you very much for same. I need to tell you what a blow it was to me as I had been left with a little baby who is not very strong, and at the same time it makes my life one long blank, but I suppose it was God[']s will and I have to be the sufferer. Now I must ask you to grant me a favour and tell me the name and address of the other Reverend that was present when he was getting buried because I want to write to him, about something. I received a letter from the Registration and Care of Graves, but it seems to refer to the Christian people only, because it said that crosses would be put to mark each grave, well as you know there are no crosses put on yiddisher graves so could you kindly tell me if there has been a stone put there by my poor husband."[14]

Falk performed Sabbath and holiday prayers; cared for the supply of kosher food; ordered religious artifacts such as candles on Hanukkah and matzoh on Passover from Jewish merchants in Alexandria and elsewhere; saw to it that Hebrew-speaking nurses be available to care for the wounded; established a library in Hebrew, Yiddish, and English; served as guide to the soldiers when they visited the pyramids in Egypt, the city of Jerusalem, and other locations; composed letters for soldiers; contacted their families and communities when they did not receive notice from home; and took care of a variety of other spiritual and religious needs. These tasks were often hard because of the opposition to the battalion. Falk had, for instance, great difficulty in obtaining a Torah scroll from Jewish congregations in Plymouth and London.

> Before I left Plymouth I approached the President of the Community requesting for the Battalion a Sepher-Torah [Torah book]. The community, I knew, could easily afford to spare one as they had a great number of "Sepharim" [books] not in use. I made myself responsible for its safe return. To my deep regret my request was refused. Yet, I did not bear them any grudge. I rather blamed their narrow provincial outlook. I had the utmost faith that the great London Jewish Community with all its great traditions and high prestige would surely not fail to rise to the occasion, and with ceremonial dignity and solemnity, would present the Battalion with a Sepher-Torah. I even pictured in my imagination a keen and animated rivalry between Synagogues of having the distinctive honour of presenting a Sepher-Torah to the first Jewish battalion that was leaving England to fight on the fields and mountains of Palestine.[15]

Yet the affair ended in a manner reminiscent of biblical miracles. When the 38th Fusiliers were already in the Southampton port boarding the ship to Alexandria, a miracle happened.

> Whilst I was engaged with the arrangement of my kit, a L/Cpl. walked up to me and saluting me smartly—to which I was not fully accustomed and hence felt shy—he said: "Sir! The Adjunct wishes to see you." The Adjunct, whom I knew at Crown Hill, was a Major E. Neil, D.S.O., a friendly good humoured Scotchman and a great believer in diplomacy which [is] called "tact."
>
> On my way toward a group of officers where I was told the Adjunct was to be found, I passed a group of men who were squatting near their equipment. One man, who must have really been a gifted humourist, said to his comrades: "Abe! Better say now, 'Vidui' (confession) before it is too late." To my amusement the fellow really commenced in a true Jewish traditional plaintive tune to recite the "[A]shamnu" [literally, "We transgressed"]. I rather liked the joke, which was typically Jewish. I would have liked to make friends with these two fellows, but my errand was rather pressing and so I had to give up this pleasure for the sake of duty.

"There is the Adjunct," said the Orderly to me and with a click of his heels he left me. I walked up to a group of officers who were all very busy. "Can I speak to the Adjunct," said I. "Yes," came the reply in a deep sonorous voice from an officer who appeared to me a veritable giant of splendid physique, well groomed, looking every inch of a soldier. "I am the new Adjunct, Captain Ledley," he introduced himself to me. "I sent for you," he continued, "to take over the 'Holy Book of Moses.' Which was placed in my keeping when in London."

I was astounded; a Sepher-Torah in the keeping of a non-Jewish officer! It sounded so strange. "Where is it?" I said. "You will find it somewhere on the docks," was his laconic reply; but when realizing my bewilderment he added with a smile "Do not worry, Padre! I placed a sentry over it." In full haste I departed to take possession of the Sepher-Torah, which I found lying on a blanket amidst a pile of soldiers' kit. An N.C.O., who happened to be a non-Jew was standing guard over it with fixed bayonet and with all solemnity of a well disciplined English soldier.[16]

The book, bestowed by a private donor named Captain Israel Friedman, was put first in a small wicker basket, which served as an ark before a wooden one was found. It accompanied the soldiers through the most trying circumstances, in their journeys at sea and on soil, and in the trenches. In *The Cross and the Trenches*, Richard Schweitzer tells of the "superstition, spiritualism, religious visions, and visitations" among soldiers in the First World War.[17] Here, the ark turned into a good-luck charm, as described in one soldier's memoirs.

Rev. Falk, who was our Army Chaplain, managed to get hold of an Ark for our Sepher Torah, and in a speech to the Battalion by Colonel Patterson, [we] were assured that as long as we had the Ark with us no harm would come to us. We embarked on the 25th on the "Leasoe Castle" and arrived in Alexandria on the 28th, after an uneventful voyage. It is worthy of mention that on her very next voyage the "Leasoe Castle" was torpedoed and sunk.[18]

TURNING *SCHNEIDERS* INTO MACCABEES

British officers observing the recruits, who arrived at the beginning of 1918 at the basic training camp of Crown Hill in the county of Devonshire, a few miles from the city of Plymouth, did not have a high regard for them. Major H. D. Myer, a Jewish officer, felt that the new recruits were unfit and lacked the qualities that make good soldiers. "The problem," he noted, "was not confined to the tailors, the boot makers, cabinet-makers and other typical 'East Enders.' It embraced also some of the Artists and Idealists."[19]

Falk, who arrived at the barracks in January 1918, was also worried about the quality of the recruits who were labeled *schneiders* (Yiddish for "tailors," an occupation traditionally associated with Jews). He identified among them some men (especially those who had served in the Zion Mule Corps) who had an interest in the ideals for which the battalion stood; they were, to him, "the Kalebs and Joshuas of the battalion."[20] But the majority had no such interest. They were mostly Russian-born Jews from the East End of London and the great industrial centers of Leeds, Manchester, and Glasgow who objected to the establishment of Jewish units to the very day of their mobilization. As Falk noted, "The noble conception of patriotism—that tender passion to shield one's country with life itself—that inspiring word 'my country,' which are the healthy symptoms of robust citizenship and the expression of a healthy consciousness of a normal people, did not appeal to them with the same force that it did to those Jews who were fortunate in being born in England, America, and other enlightened Western countries."[21]

Some recruits seemed to him like the "'happy-go-lucky' English type of boy."[22] Like their fellow citizens, they accepted the inevitability of those days without much fuss and tried to carry out their military duties as efficiently as any British Tommy in any other battalion. But he felt they suffered from a total ignorance of Jewish history, literature, strivings, and ideas. "Palestine, spiritual freedom, Hebraic culture, which were in those days widely discussed in the Jewish press and on Jewish platforms, were to them," he said, "practically abstract terms of subjects quite irrelevant to the existence of the Jew."[23]

Falk sought a way to serve as spiritual mentor to all categories of recruits. He did so by stressing the consistency between the goal of Jewish national revival and England's war aims, which included the conquest of Palestine. Both tasks were defined by him as providential. The camp near Plymouth became the training ground for Jewish soldiers preparing for the restoration of their ancient homeland in accordance with the prophets' vision.

> It was . . . a curious coincidence that Plymouth from whence the Pilgrim Fathers, a heroic band of idealists, sailed in 1620 in quest of a new home, where they could live in conformity with their moral precepts, should also be the training ground of the Jewish Battalion which also aimed at striking a blow for Israel's spiritual freedom and the laying of the foundation of a new life dedicated to the ideals of peace and righteousness as preached by the Jewish prophets.[24]

The ideals of peace and righteousness were attributed by Falk both to the ancient prophets and to the British Empire, which was now in charge of fulfilling them through its military's training program. Clearly, "the glorious sunshine of Devon with its fogless atmosphere was conducive to change the pale and sunken-chested 'schneiders' into robust looking fellows with expanded chests and hardened muscles."[25] Falk emphasized the development of a healthy body, praising the handful of musclemen among the troops, encouraging boxing matches with other units, and taking close interest in training and physical education. And with a healthy body came national pride:

> To see these men who only a month or two ago were sitting bent over their machines, now standing erect with their chests thrown toward "forming fours" and responding with military precision to the yelling commands of the N.C.O. and to the thundering admonitions of the all-important Sergeant Major, appeared indeed to be an achievement of the impossible.[26]

Falk was very proud when, prior to their journey to the Palestine front, four hundred Legionnaires were marched through the city of London.

> Four hundred men, the pick of the battalion, were chosen for this purpose. Special trains brought them into the metropolis and conveyed them to the tower of London where they slept overnight. The next morning the Battalion, spick and span, marched out with fixed bayonets (privilege granted only to new battalions) headed by the military band of the Cold Stream Guards. Its route was through the City of London, the Mansion House, where they were to be inspected by General Sir Francis Lloyd, G.O.C., London District, and Sir Neville Macready. The population when learning that this smart unit was the Jewish battalion, composed mostly of White Chapel boys, were greatly surprised and immensely pleased, cheering the men wholeheartedly.
>
> In the East End of London the atmosphere was full of excitement. The Union Jack and the blue and white Jewish colors made a conspicuous display. What glory! "My Yankele," "My Meishele" is a soldier! And such a soldier! God bless him! And truly the reception which the Battalion received in the heart of the Jewish Ghetto was full of pathos. Those who witnessed it, will never forget it. They were received with jubilant glamour and affection. The streets were crowded. Mothers, wives and sisters were trying to break the ranks of the marching soldiers so as to give them a loving embrace.
>
> This march through London undoubtedly filled the hearts of every Jew with joy. Even those who were unfriendly to the Battalion must have felt a certain satisfaction in witnessing the ceremony of the Lord Mayor taking the salute at the Mansion House. The old popular prejudice that the Jew cannot be a soldier was effectively killed.[27]

The march signaled to Falk that the goal of creating a soldier who combined Jewish self-consciousness with patriotism and gratitude to England was achievable. Much of his effort was devoted to establishing a connection between the Legionnaires' mundane experience and its place in Jewish and British history. He took every opportunity—during training, on the journey to the front, and in Sabbath and holiday service sermons he gave in the field—to lift up the soldiers' spirits by reminding them that they were part of a providential mission. On the occasion of handing the recruits Torah books, he said, "In the remote past the Law went forth from Zion; happy are you that take it *unto* Zion, to establish in the Sacred Land the glories of our future. Be strong and of good courage, quit yourselves like men."[28]

A special order of service written by Rabbi Shimon Bashi of Cairo to mark the moment in which the 38th Royal Fusiliers would set foot in the Promised Land was changed by Falk so as not to neglect the role of Britain in this redeeming event:

> And now Thou hast again graciously shown thy kindness to Thy people Israel. Our remembrance came before Thee for our wellbeing, to bring our sufferings and troubles to an end. And through the decree of Thy Providence, Thou didst put a Spirit of wisdom, and understanding, justice, and righteousness into the heart of our Gracious King George, and his counselors, to cause to return Thy People Israel to the land of their inheritance.[29]

In a new year service sermon he gave a year later in Palestine, Falk constructed the biblical story of Abraham as the frame of reference for Jewish military voluntarism in the First World War. When called upon to sacrifice his son Isaac, Abraham responded with the word *Hinnenieh* (Hebrew for "Here am I").

> So small a word, apparently so insignificant, but which has proved in our history—the mirror of our virtuous and faults, the barometer of our success and failures—to be the factor which saved us in critical moments from utter destruction. There were always amongst us, in each period of danger, a handful of men who were always ready to respond to the call of the people which is the call of God, with the answer of "Hinnenieh." . . . You my friends, are now those men, who a year ago were called upon by your people to make sacrifices.[30]

In a Hanukkah sermon, Falk conveyed a message that considered the redemption of Palestine from both the Jewish and British perspectives.

> I was in search of a message for an ideal to deliver to you to-day, which should be harmonious with the true and genuine spirit of Judaism, and with your duties as men of H.M. Forces, who have been called upon to shield their country and to protect their kinsfolk against misery and sufferings.[31]

He compared his listeners' role in the First World War to that of their ancient ancestors, the Maccabees, who won a religious war against

Greek forces in the second century BC. The Maccabees, he said, were endowed with a spirit that was worthy of their faith and at the same time strengthened their position among the surrounding nations. Falk defined England's role as a mighty rock and haven of refuge to the scattered and afflicted of Israel, and called upon the Legionnaires to show it gratitude and carry further the banner of righteousness and justice.

In that same sermon, Falk referenced the depiction of Jews as disloyal, pro-German, cosmopolitan cowards, while stressing the new image that was now emerging.

> The whole world were watching [and] were looking on us, but they see now the Maccabeans spirit revived, they see now that Israel is not only powerful with his voice, but he has also a mighty arm. . . . The Jewish soldier upholds now the honour of our nation. The Jewish warrior saved our national honour which was at stake. . . . A British army is standing at the gates of Gaza where our Samson performed his Herculean exploits. There are great possibilities for the Jewish people which may never occur again. Possibilities to rescue the Holy land of our fathers from the hands of a cruel oppressor who lays now waste the new settlement of Judea.[32]

Falk faced the well-known chaplain's dilemma: how can a man of religion encourage humans to kill other humans? The replacement of professional combatants by citizen-soldiers in the First World War turned this dilemma into a practical obstacle, because many of them were aware of the discrepancy between the command "Thou shalt not kill" and their involvement in killing.[33] Military chaplains were required to provide solutions to such dilemmas, as Falk found out soon after his arrival in Crown Hill. During basic training, an English Jewish NCO tried to teach the soldiers how to thrust their bayonets effectively into suspended bags, to no avail. This experience raised the question of whether a Jew was allowed to thrust a blade of cold steel into the living body of a human creature.

Falk had little religious guidance to rely on. The only book by a major rabbinical authority dealing with the rules of war was *Ma'hane Israel* (The Jewish Camp), a monograph prepared in 1881 by Rabbi Israel Meir Cohen of Radin, Poland (known as "Chafetz Chaim"), for Jews serving in non-Jewish armies.[34] But while this book is mainly concerned with the religious rituals to be maintained by Jews in a war whose aims are determined by others, fighting as part of an all-Jewish unit raised more profound questions on the nature of war and its justification.

Falk's answers to these questions differed from those of chaplains who sought a way to justify killing in the name of religion.[35] Had he tried to justify the war in reference to the prophets of Israel, he wrote, he would have encountered bitter resentment, especially from those to whom the Bible was not a sealed book and the ideals of Judaism were not an unknown quantity. He therefore searched for the justification in the instinct of self-preservation that dwells both within the individual and the nation and stated that "the brave deeds of our own heroes in time of war especially those recorded in the life and death struggle between the legions of Titus and the patriotic zealots at the siege of Jerusalem, stood before my eyes as witnesses of justification."[36] He also justified war through the need to end all wars, as he did in the above Hanukkah sermon.

> It is futile to deny or to forget the fact that by doing our duty we also shed the blood of our own brothers. This is the greatest tragedy of the war, it is the most cruel ordeal of our dispersion. But let us understand that the victory of the league of liberty over the league of darkness will make the recurrence of this tragedy an impossibility.[37]

Falk was aware of the historical precedent set by the battalion as the first all-Jewish formation in modern times and laid the foundation for military commemoration in Israel. In 1919, he ordered medals for the Jewish Legions from the Bezalel Arts and Crafts School in Jerusalem. From a letter sent to Falk by Bezalel's founder and director Boris Schatz, we learn that the chaplain considered a variety of medals, among them one carrying the icon of Matityahu Hasmonai, the high priest who launched the Maccabean revolt in the second century BC.[38]

Schatz, a sculptor, painter, and educator, opened the school in 1906 with the aim of encouraging indigenous art and design in the land of Israel. During the war, the school was closed by the Turks, but when the war was over, Schatz renewed his effort to turn Bezalel into a spiritual center, inspiring the creation of "a new Jew: a Hebrew, rooted in the land, his life influenced by Jewish values and creative achievement, and surrounded by beauty and harmony."[39] This setting appealed to Falk, who ventured to help the school, which suffered at the time from severe financial difficulties. He bought it an engraving machine to make the medals and was involved in raising funds for a Bezalel museum planned by Schatz in which one room would be devoted to the legend of the Jewish Legions, exhibiting statues of its commanders, pictures portraying the lifestyle developed in military service, and artifacts such as flags, uniforms, and the Torah scrolls.

FALK'S IDEAS ON JEWISH NATIONALISM

Falk's ideas on Jewish nationalism must be read against the background of the views expressed by his mentor, Rabbi Kook, who considered the First World War a gigantic struggle between nations, the outcome of which would bring about the redemption of the Jewish people. Kook, who lived in London during the war, linked the redemption of the world to Jewish national revival. Referring to the nations of the world, he wrote:

> They will bow down and arise full of strength, they will be renewed, invigo-rated with light and strength, legions and legions of them, with firmness of heart they will arise and cry out: A people has arisen, has begun to be a na-tion, that will release a flow of divine life to all worlds, a mighty people that has made a way in the stormy sea, that has paved an eternal pathway for the vitality of life that is distilled by attachment to God.[40]

Kook met with members of the Jewish Legions, who impressed him as endowed with a "new spirit, strong spirit and holy spirit."[41] That spirit was seen by him as the beginning of redemption, thus imposing a duty on the soldiers to construct both their own souls and that of the destroyed world. To him, the construction of the soul was, however, directly related to the fulfillment of religious rituals, which, to his disappointment, the soldiers did not follow strictly enough. In a letter he sent to Falk after his visit, he reminded him that other than in the most extreme circumstances, no military duty can justify the violation of the Sabbath. He demanded that the Jewish soldiers, who were destined to redeem the Promised Land and consequently the entire human race, follow the rabbinical rules con-cerning the shaving of beards.[42]

While the chaplain obviously could not adhere to all rabbinical rules, he was rather inspired by Kook's overall vision, and in his sermons he often stressed the need to lift national ideals above individual in-terests. In the first sermon he gave as appointed chaplain, he stressed the phrase from Exodus 19, "And you shall be unto me a Kingdom of priests and holy nation." These words, he preached, had always proved to be the unifying band that defied mighty forces and kept the Jewish spirit and intellect productive and healthy, producing thinkers and po-ets who not only pierced the darkness that enveloped the Jewish people but also cast a lustrous light over the whole world: "We are called upon once again to fulfill our mission, to be the guiding light to mankind, we [are] once again called upon to assume the guardianship of the two tables of stone."[43]

In a sermon delivered to the 38th Fusiliers in the field near Taranto, Italy, in February 1918, he discussed the biblical tale of Refidim, the lo-cation in which the Israelites walking in the desert started to complain. They began to protest, Falk said, when they could not get the full amount of bread and butter, when they found out that victory and freedom were not given but must be fought for. It was this weakening of the spirit that motivated Amalek, that watchful enemy, to attack them. As long as the Amalekites were aware of the Israelites' unity of purpose, determination, and enthusiasm to become a nation, they were afraid to attack, but as soon as they detected disorganization and lack of idealism, they did. The lesson:

> Brethren ye Warriors, ye descendants of the heroic Maccabees, you who have broken the fetter of Iron which has enchained our people over 1800 years. You who have dissipated the dark clouds, which had darkened our Sun. You who have to perform a great and sublime task, not only to rebuild your own home, but to construct a new world. Know ye, that we are not only watched by our own people and friends, but we are closely watched by Amaleck, the Common enemy, the enemy of the Country. I say therefore, unto you "never encamp in Refidim," obliterate the shameful remembrance, which brought upon us Amaleck, do not place the question of bread and water on a higher pedestal than the question of national honour, freedom and victory.[44]

Such mobilizing statements were common in the First World War. Jewish soldiers and sailors in the British forces were given booklets, issued by the office of the chief rabbi of the United Hebrew Congregations of the British Empire, reminding them of their heritage. In one such booklet, titled *History of the Jews*, Jewish history is surveyed from biblical times through the Second Temple era, the Middle Ages, and the Golden Age in Spain to the modern era of emancipation. The booklet ends by mentioning two poles in contemporary Jewish life: the idea of adaptation of individual Jews to their dominant surroundings in the countries in which they reside, and the Zionist idea calling for their concentration in Palestine. Both poles, says the booklet, pose great uncertainty for the future of the Jewish people and reinforce the conflict between the supporters of emancipation and the supporters of Zionism, a conflict that polarized the Jewish world for decades.[45]

Falk, however, did not adhere to either of these poles. To him, the Legionnaires' identity as descendents of ancient Hebrew warriors was to be linked to their identity as residents of England and the other countries in which they found refuge. Following Rabbi Kook's teachings, he believed in the opportunity the war gave to the Legionnaires to be a vanguard of the Jewish people reasserting their religious and national roots and thus gaining a place in the community of enlightened nations. In his farewell address in Plymouth, he told the soldiers they were departing from the shores of England "to add a glorious chapter to our unequalled history and the history of this noble country under whose wings we have found protection."[46]

Fighting in the Holy Land provided Falk with many opportunities to strengthen the Legionnaires' ties to their biblical past. For example, when passing through the city of Gaza, where bitter battles took place against the Turks, he reminded the soldiers of the biblical story of Samson and the continuous difficulties the Israelites had with the Philistines; when

visiting the locations of Joshua's battles, he explained the historical significance of the ancient hero's victories; and upon arrival in the village of
Beth Nuba, he was filled with biblical inspiration, in spite of the controversy among scholars over whether this is the authentic location of the
ancient priests' city of Nob.

> Our joy was greater still on learning that Beth Nuba, our resting place over
> night, is blessed with an abundance of water. The beautiful passage of Isaiah,
> "and you shall draw water with joy out of the wells of salvation," which Jews
> outside Palestine conceive as a poetic metaphor was now comprehended by
> me as a realistic description of the physical condition of the country and the
> ecstasy of its inhabitants when drawing water in abundance. To us, they re-
> ally were wells of salvation in the full sense of the word, bringing forth from
> our hearts gratefulness to God, expressed in the Old Hebrew phrase "Hodu
> L'Adonai!" [Give thanks to the Lord] . . .
>
> Whilst lying in my bivouac, under a beautiful old sheltering olive tree, the
> tragic ancient history of Nob soon began to unroll itself to me: How David
> arrived here hungry and tired, receiving hospitality and protection from the
> good-hearted High Priest, but owing to the zealous disposition of Saul the
> priesthood of Nob paid dearly for their hospitality.
>
> Was this the halting place of Nebuchadnezzar in his march on Jerusalem?
> To which Isaiah refers to in his poetic passage. "This very day shall he halt at
> Nob." (Is. X:32.) These memories of the past stood out in all their vividness.
> The divergence of opinion concerning the authenticity of Beth Nuba did not
> matter to me.[47]

CONFLICT WITH ZIONIST LEADERS

While biblical verses, such as the reference to Nob in the Book of Isaiah,
were often used by the Zionist movement to establish the right of the Jewish people to the land, Falk was more concerned with the power of the
tale of Nob, whether historically substantiated or not, to help reconstruct
the soldiers' identity. The Old Testament served him as a source of inspiration in turning the men into better soldiers. It became an almanac of
moral advice, a source of spiritual strength, a travel guide, and a general
frame of reference. When the Legionnaires were employed as guards in
prison camps, Falk took an active part, derived from his religious beliefs,
in avoiding maltreatment of the German and Turkish prisoners.[48] As we
have seen, he also played an important role in framing the Legions' unpleasant experiences in Palestine as a journey to the Promised Land that
has not yet been reached.

His creative thinking on such matters often put him in discord with
others. His call for Jews to fight under a Jewish flag as a means of enhancing their status in their respective countries of residence, for instance,

put him in opposition with Jabotinsky, who saw Jewish participation in the war as a means to support Jewish presence in Palestine. In Australia, Falk was seen as associated with Jabotinsky, but his views differed from the latter's Palestine-centered political Zionism, which left little place for Jewish national existence elsewhere. As Falk wrote, "I am not a devotee of Jabotinsky. I have, on many occasions, differed from him in some political conceptions of Zionism. Yet I believe that any difference of political opinion should not be an incentive to malign the character of an opponent."[49]

Falk's views also conflicted with those of segments of English Jewry who looked down at the new immigrants from the East and did not believe in their capability to serve as effective soldiers in His Majesty's army. Falk, on the other hand, felt that once the religious and welfare needs of the soldiers were catered to, these immigrants, representing the majority of Jews wandering the earth in the early twentieth century, would become the core of Jewish revival and a source of pride among the nations. In his farewell speech before dismissal, Falk compared the low class immigrants who joined the 38th Fusiliers to liberated slaves:

> At this great historical occasion, when a unique chapter in the glorious history of Israel is temporarily closed, to be reopened however in the near future . . . I feel that it is my duty to say to you a few words . . . that at this and only at this moment it is your duty according to the old traditional custom of our religion, to offer up now a prayer proper to the God of Israel, for having been liberated from slavery, transformed into free men and also risen from a sick bed and regained your strength and vigor.[50]

Only two years ago, he added, the slave spirit was so palpable among his listeners that he feared whether these "dry bones" would ever revive again as predicted in the Book of Ezekiel. "But thank God! You have broken the chains and cast off from you the . . . reproach of Egypt. The two years of soldiering, two years of untold suffering, have created in you a new spirit. A spirit worthy of an indestructible people." In contrast to the biblical story of the Exodus, in which a generation of slaves had to die before the Promised Land could be taken by storm by a young generation of free souls, the chaplain believed that his tailors, boot makers, and cabinet makers were those destined to fulfill the task.

This approach also led to conflict between Falk and Zionists in Palestine. The values he promoted, such as the notion of being at the forefront of the process of Jewish revival, the rhetoric stressing the strong sense of mission and fighting for ideals, and the emphasis on *re'ut* (Hebrew for "comradeship") among the soldiers, later played an important role in Israel's prestate and state military cultures, but they were associated with Israel-born soldiers rather than with Jewish immigrants from Whitechapel. Moreover, Zionists in Palestine mostly took a road to national revival devoid of religion, which Falk considered as dangerous to the future of the Jewish nation as the process of assimilation abroad.

His relations with members of the 40th Fusiliers, recruited in Palestine, were thus strained. Initially, he considered them a Jewish vanguard rooted in the soil whose strength of body and spirit would be a source of inspiration to all other Legionnaires. However, he was deeply disappointed by their endless socialist agitation and their treatment of the British military as if it were an employer to be confronted in disrespect. They filed petitions, launched rebellions, and published commentaries in labor movement magazines. In a sermon given to the 40th Fusiliers shortly before the Legions' dispersal, Falk addressed them as "heroes of Israel," recalling the enthusiasm he felt when their volunteering gave a shot of life to the exhausted Legions, who, by then, had fought for four months under the harshest conditions.

What he found, however, was a sense of despair and lack of military discipline, as well as a gap between high ideals of redemption and failure to fulfill the tasks demanded by the British army. While the Jews coming from England, the United States, Canada, and Argentina fought bravely and thus promoted the name of their people among the nations, he said, the new recruits from Palestine were preoccupied with demands for better living conditions in the army barracks. He accused them of sacrificing the honor of the nation for their trade unionist ideals. He considered their behavior a form of national betrayal, and although he did not make the connection directly, he attributed that betrayal to the Palestine recruits' abandonment of religious traditions. To him, the power of the nation, and its chances for revival, depended on recognition of the link between the tasks at hand and the long tradition going back to the biblical prophets with their insistence on justice, truth, and charity.

8

An Aristocrat of Sorts

FROM THE MUD OF FLANDERS TO CROWN HILL

In contrast to other life writings discussed in this study that have remained mainly unknown, Major Henry D. Myer's memoir *Soldiering of
Sorts*[1] has been displayed in the Imperial War Museum in London and
thus has received some scholarly attention. Mark Levene was drawn to
this memoir as "the quintessential product of Anglo-Jewish integration
and success: the Westminster public school boy who joined his father's
law firm, did soldiering in his spare time and was inducted into the hor-
rors of the Western front, in 1915, as a commissioned officer with the City
of London Rifles."[2] Considering Myer a thoroughgoing product of Anglo-
Jewry who carried an outward commitment to Jewish ritual and practice
but lacked any Jewish political ideology, Levene notes the assimilating
officer's attraction to the Palestine Zionists he encountered when he was
assigned in 1918 as second-in-command of the 40th Fusiliers: "If there are
stirrings of a specifically Jewish national consciousness here full accolades
are reserved only for the Palestinians."[3]

In this chapter, we follow letters Myer wrote to his fiancée, Louie
Solomon, between June 1918 and May 1919. At the age of eighty-seven
he annotated (and censored) the letters and incorporated them in the
above memoir. They are instructive less for Myer's observations about the
Palestine Zionists than for the developments—however slight—that can
be identified in his own Jewish consciousness. This young British officer
who belonged to the English Jewish assimilatory elite and treated displaced Jewish immigrants from Russia with snobbery becomes over time,

more than he seems to realize, part of the crowd of Israelites walking the desert road to the Promised Land.

Myer, who fought and was injured at the Western Front, reported to the Crown Hill Barracks near Plymouth on March 19, 1918, shortly after the 38th Fusiliers left for Egypt, leaving behind what he calls "something like 400 derelicts."[4] In his memoirs he all but apologizes for their appearance and behavior by claiming that all serviceable Jewish recruits had already enlisted and/or been killed or permanently disabled by then in the three years of intense fighting on the Western Front and the many other theaters of war. As he puts it, "The 38th Battalion had already taken the cream off the rather poor milk that the British Isles had yielded from the residue of the Jewish Community."[5]

Myer complained about the daily sick parade and expressed his frustration over the fact that "men, who and whose relatives owed so much to the hospitality they had enjoyed in the United Kingdom, could have refrained from showing gratitude in the form of sharing the burdens, which fell upon all Britishers."[6] These Russian immigrants, who were forced into service by the threat they would otherwise be sent back to Russia, were despised by the major, who saw his comrades die in the mud of Flanders and the Passchendaele campaign. The Jewish recruits, he wrote, "had led sedentary lives and their hearts were not in the job."[7] The British officer also saw the volunteers who arrived from America and were absorbed into the 39th Fusiliers as "a very mixed bunch, gathered from all parts of North, Central and South America, but mostly emanating via America from Eastern Europe. They had received virtually no military training and the only one with Corporal's stripes on his sleeves was a man who had worn the uniform of a convict in [jail]!"[8] Even David Ben-Gurion, who came in with this contingent, was seen from the officer's perspective as "a pain in the neck."[9]

The letters to Louie, who worked as a Red Cross volunteer in England, began on June 4, 1918, and the correspondence revealed pride in the weekly concerts given in the camp by artists and less pride in the parallel singsong performed by prisoners in the Guard Room on their own. The commander in chief of the Southern Command, Myer wrote his fiancée on June 12, 1918, was ecstatic about the soldiers' artistic performance and expressed his belief that the men are capable of anything "in the entertainment line." Myer praised the performers, but less so the American audience.

> Our Pierrot show today was quite a success—I enclose programme. But have you ever performed before an American audience? I know ours was a most intellectual one—the Staff, Surgeons, Nurses and Orderlies of a large American hospital who were being entertained by the Garrison. They say

that Englishmen are phlegmatic, but when our audience arrived I began to get the wind up. They all looked fed up and homesick, lantern jawed and for the most part be-spectacled. Oi! Oiee! As we say in this Battalion.[10]

His joy over the use of Yiddish expressions in the military barracks was a first hint of the new attitude the British officer was developing toward the recruits. On June 18, writing Louie from Southampton, where he accompanied a large group of recruits as they embarked on a ship taking them to the front, the seeds of a new viewpoint can be detected as he commented that "[t]he lads are splendid—ever so keen to go and full of good cheer. If they are led well and given a fair opportunity they ought to make a great name for the Regiment." Myer was also happy that the Legions were allowed to have a distinctive name and to wear a distinctive badge. In the same letter, he told his fiancée about an embarkation officer who came up to him and asked why the men had the Star of David as an emblem—Myer explained that they were Jews. The officer, he wrote, almost refused to believe it: "It is extraordinary how few people know any but the hook-nosed, bejewelled type, which I am sure does not really predominate."

This sentiment reflects a duality that has characterized the thinking of a large segment of modern Jewry. While proud of their heritage, many Jews had internalized anti-Semitic stereotypes they were persistently exposed to. The letters indicate a strong urge by the major to prove these stereotypes wrong. He expressed, on June 21, 1918, for instance, pride in the soldiers' boxing skill, as if the image of the Jew as weakling was based on reality. "Boxing and music," he said, "seem to be our fortes at present, but we are beginning to show a great improvement in other directions as well." Myer also noted a constant improvement in the men's soldiering skills and by June 25 could comment that "the new arrivals are splendid material and if you are feeling pessimistic about things in Palestine, just come and have a look at them."

Myer's letters describe routine army life in a Jewish battalion, as when he groused on June 29 about the extra work he had to do as mess president: "My serenity of mind was rudely shaken today when I was told I must take over the duties of Mess President and that without a moment's delay from an officer going away immediately. I loathe and abominate the job and I hope to pass it on to someone else as soon as I can." The Jewish British officer seemed, however, to enjoy his military service in a Jewish environment, as indicated by his occasional humorous comments: "The best name is always that which one uses when one thinks of a person. That's why the Jewish Regiment would be the best name for us. We are nearly always referred to as that—except, of course, officially—and few people connect us with the Royal Fusiliers; only with the Jewsiliers."[11] As time passed, his confidence in the soldiers under his command became more apparent. He wrote on July 6, 1918, that the battalion would do "creditably whatever it is called upon to do." When training a group of recruits from America, he admitted that he had to be tough with them because he required a high standard but generally felt very proud of the men.

THE CALL OF THE PAST

In mid-August 1918, Myer and two companies under his command began their journey to Palestine. They sailed from Southampton to France on the SS *Caesarea*, which he saw as symbolic because the ship was named after a historic place in the land of Israel. They were then transported by train through France and Italy. For security reasons, he was careful not to mention the route they passed but told of the beautiful scenery and the comfort he enjoyed in the officers' compartment, especially since none of the other officers snored. In Taranto, they switched ships and sailed to Port Said, taking an indirect course to avoid German submarines. Myer was lucky to have a toppings cabin, because the heat was unbearable; he spent the days reading a guidebook to the Holy Land. From then on, the scenery was always described in relation to its history, beginning with the muddy port. On August 28, for example, he wrote that "[s]ince early morning the water has been a thick, muddy colour. I understand that the water in this neighbourhood has been this extraordinary colour since the very earliest ages and many travelers have noted it."

After disembarkation, the troops were brought in awful summer heat to the Tel El-Kabir camp, where no appropriate housing was available. Myer found shade in a small structure made of plaited reed and wooden uprights that he called Succah, the biblical tabernacle erected by the Israelites in the desert during the biblical exodus. He was also reminded of the ancient past when he observed the local Egyptian population, and he wrote to Louie on August 31:

> As you probably know, the women wear black robes and either black or white yashmaks. The men, apart from the higher classes and Government employees, usually wear a sort of long nighty made of cotton of any colour, opened in front to show a sort of embroidered false waistcoat. The garment is drawn in at the waist slightly and if the wearer is engaged in agriculture the skirt is rather shorter than usual. Their appearance is much the same as in "British Museum" days and one wonders how it was, unless it was due to numerical superiority and made jealousy, that they have enslaved the Israelites.

Serving in the Egyptian desert during the Jewish High Holidays made Myer particularly conscious of what he called "the call of the past," as reflected in his letter of September 6, 1918.

Since the transport has arrived I have been able to get at the flag ornamented by you. The Colonel likes it very much and insisted that it should fly outside the Orderly Room. I accordingly had a special flag-staff made for it and it certainly looks fine. The Magen David [Star of David] glitters in the sunshine and the effect against the blue sky is most striking.

I was rather impressed at hearing the man who is going to blow the Shophar[12] for us, practicing in the desert. These things cause quite a peculiar sensation to pass through one and one can't help feeling the call of the past. I experienced the same sensation when I saw the fellaheen working in the fields in the same sort of way as they have since before history and in the same sort of dress as they are portrayed in the earliest pictorial records, also, when I saw the pyramids which our ancestors are credited with building for the Gyppies in ancient times.

Praying Kol Nidrei in the Egyptian desert was also noteworthy. On September 15, Myer wrote, "It is Yom Kippur. We have just had the Kol Nidrei service under the stars on the sand of the Desert. It was most impressive . . . a really solemn Yom Kippur, grand in its simplicity."

Myer anticipated the arrival of the recruits from Palestine with some anxiety, which he shared with Louie on September 18, 1918.

Our Palestinians join us in our camp tomorrow, in large numbers. . . . They are said to be a stalwart lot but, as the Colonel says, the real site of the Tower of Babel was Tel El-Kabir. They speak all languages from Spanish to Babylonian and they are of every hue—except, I believe, copper. Aren't the Jews a marvelous race? . . . The 38th Battalion, as by now you know, I suppose, have won two Military Medals already and another man has been strongly recommended. The Jew Boy can fight alright! And we're training like the Devil! Up at 4:30 a.m. when a narrow little band on the horizon proclaims the coming of dawn and, with a break for [breakfast], it's parade work until the weather gets too hot at 11 a.m. and from 3:30 p.m. until dusk. It makes a long day for all, but we seem to be standing the strain well.

When the volunteers from Palestine did arrive, Myer was impressed by their physical attributes, which on September 21 he contrasted to his idea of the stereotypical Jew.

On Thursday night the Palestinians came here. They are a fine body of men. The only difficulty in training them is that of language. However, most of their officers have quite a fair knowledge of Hebrew and the men are beginning to learn English. As a whole their physique is remarkably good, they are lithe and wiry and their facial features are clear cut and almost of an ascetic type. Noses are straight and narrow, lips not too thick and complexion, except that of the Yemenites and Egyptians, fair. There are quite a large number of ex-Turkish officers and soldiers in their ranks, who have been captured at various times since the beginning of the War. These are well disciplined and, apparently, extraordinary keen. One of them acted as Chazan [cantor] today. He had a beautiful voice.

On September 22, Myer had some good news from the front for his fiancée. The main Turkish force in Palestine had been cut up and was not expected to make another stand. He raised the question of what would happen if the Turks were defeated without his unit's assistance, which shows his awareness that the Jewish Legions could serve as a lever for Zionist political gains in Palestine after its occupation. He wrote that the news they got in camp about the conquest of the city of Haifa meant a great deal to the Palestinian recruits not only because their homes would now be freed from the Turks but because "channels will soon be opened for commercial activity and there will be markets for their products." Myer showed an ongoing interest in and admiration for the Palestinian Jews.

I'd like to see something of Palestine. . . . Parts must be pretty good otherwise they would not have produced the splendid types that are to be found among the Palestinian Detachment here. They compare favourably with the average Anglicised–East End–Jews and vastly excel the Cairenes and Alexandrines who are not of a very high order of intelligence or physical development. The agricultural life of the Colonists has made them hardy and strong and much more amenable to discipline than other Jews with whom I have been brought into contact. . . . I think they are worthy representatives of the race.[13]

REFLECTIONS ON THE FUTURE OF PALESTINE

Myer often expressed his hope for the success of the Zionist project in Palestine. After a meeting with Edwin Samuel, son of Herbert Samuel (soon to be appointed high commissioner for Palestine), he wrote on October 4 that "[a]pparently both father and son are keen Zionists and from what I can gather the schemes for the regeneration of Palestine are not to be allowed to fail." At the same time, he remained an outsider to that project. His letters reflect not the Zionist discourse of the time but the European traveler's fascination with the Orient: "I am just crossing the Nile, the river of antiquity. It has looked the same for thousands of years. Along its banks from time immemorial the camels and donkeys have carried their burdens, ridden or driven by people attired in the same style as today. Similar sailing craft have passed year after year and day by day beyond the memory of man."[14]

Moreover, while the future leaders of the Palestinian Jews, many of whom served under Myer's command in the 40th Fusiliers, were preoccupied with practical issues concerning the future of Palestine, the major preoccupied himself with very different kinds of questions. On October 10, he wrote the following:

> I forgot whether I told you that among other duties I am Mess President. It's the most loathsome job imaginable. In most Battalions the lot of fulfilling this duty usually falls to the Jew or, if more than one, to the Senior Jew. Presumably this is due to the Epicurean tendencies and organizing abilities that distinguish the race. We are therefore like the gathering of Masons in our Mess. All are past Mess-Presidents or else aspirants and suggestions and criticism are not lacking. Suitable functionaries for the more menial duties, such as waiting and washing up are not easy to find—so in keeping with the Jewish temperament.

Myer's criticism of the Jews' disorderly conduct during mess can be read against this military officer's attraction to any sign of order and discipline.

> On Saturday morning we had a pleasant service and the greater part of Sunday morning we spent in a visit to the Prisoners of War Camp, which a detachment of our men are guarding. There are now over 15,000 of them, more are constantly coming in. They all seem contented with their lot and with good reason too, as they are being better treated than they have been before for some time.
>
> I can't understand how or why the Huns could have treated our prisoners so damnably, except that the Hun is such a swine. One's natural feeling is one of pity for the men inside the cage and I found myself asking all sorts of questions as to their comfort etc. as though I loved them instead of hated them. The Huns have a separate portion of the Camp all to themselves. They are well disciplined and soldierly and mostly belong to technical branches of the Service. As Huns go, they are of a good type.[15]

Myer attended Hebrew lessons and realized the importance of the language to national integration but did not find it easy, as he explained in a November 6 letter.

> I have just had my second Hebrew lesson. It was very short and sweet, but I am afraid I shall not pick up the language easily. I wish there were an easy road to becoming a good linguist. It is so useful to be able to speak several languages well. I think there is sufficient impetus behind the Zionist movement to make it worth while learning the language whether one intends to reside in Palestine or not. It is almost certain to become a center of Jewish learning, both religious and unsectarian and men of all faiths and races will go there for inspiration and knowledge. At home one does not appreciate the

strong nationalist tendency of the modern Zionists and it is when a people is most conscious of its national character that it produces its best master-pieces in literature and art.

As the above words indicate, Myer was exposed to the ideas floating among the soldiers under his command, who established a debating club and spent long hours in the Egyptian desert arguing over the various Zionist plans for postwar Palestine. He always remained, however, a bystander, and thought, "Our Palestinians are widely enthusiastic Zionists and some to my mind, overdo it a bit, but it is an interesting experience serving with them and one has to be very tactful in handling them properly. I haven't had a lesson for a week and I'm afraid I've gone backwards instead of forwards."[16]

When three hundred men were sent to join the 39th Battalion and the tone of the departure seemed to him too affectionate, the major treated them with all the snobbery he had developed as a veteran of the Western Front. He wrote of his opinion to Louie on November 28, 1918.

> Jews are an extraordinarily affectionate race. To an outsider the partings between the drafts that have left us lately and the men staying behind have been a most tragic affair. To me they have been rather humorous, because they will be seeing one another again in a few days' time and yet there has been so much shaking of hands, saying farewells, serenading, cheering.

And yet, once the order came to leave for Palestine, Myer could not hide his own affiliation with the "affectionate race." He wrote his fiancée on the second day of December about his departure to "the Promised Land" and on December 9 called Colonel Patterson "a second Moses," believing that "Jews all the World over and for many generations to come will owe him a great debt of gratitude." The major, whose letters are dominated by descriptions of football matches and other rituals conducted in British military barracks and filled with details on the lizards, mice, goats, tortoises, guinea pigs, and other creatures he and his fellow animal-loving officers adopted in the Orient's deserts, now perceived a greater meaning in the places he visited and the work he did.

When he arrived on a very stormy night in Ludd, on the Jaffa-Jerusalem road, and had to erect tents in the mud, the historical significance of the event was not lost on him. "Since the earliest times Ludd has been noted for its mud—the ancient historians remark on it," he wrote on December 7. When the rain stopped two days later, he indulged in the wonderful panorama of the country—"fruit and olive groves in the foreground and the mountains of Judea in the distance and a mottled sky overhead, villages perched on the sides and even on the tops of the mountains and here and there towers and minarets and domes." While still distancing himself from his fellow Jews by comparing the scenery to that of Italy, he nevertheless endowed it with a certain sacredness and commented to Louie on December 9 that "[s]ome day I should like you to see this Country. It may be that it looks particularly fascinating now, after the rain. . . . The stars seem so bright at night and so near to one that one can understand people regarding this land as being nearer Heaven than any other."

The descriptions of places he visited in the land of Israel are filled with love for the country. After a ride to the city of Jaffa, Myer wrote that he was impressed by the beauty of the scenery and the wealth of color: "In particular one notices the blue of the Mediterranean, the cream-coloured buildings with their red-tiled roofs and the palm trees dotted here and there." He noted that in Jaffa itself, the only signs of progress are Jewish while the Arab quarter "is still mediaeval and squalid." Of the return journey, he wrote, "nearly all the way, I had before me a wonderful panorama of the mountains of Judea."[17]

After a march through two Jewish agricultural settlements, Myer commented on December 14 that he found the settlements up to his expectations from an agricultural point of view, although "in other respects they are both very much like any village in England, except that the trees and foliage are rather different." In other words, Myer did not share his colonel's fascination with the Jewish settlements in Palestine as the beginning of messianic redemption. He observed them very much as a tourist would, talking from some distance about the land's produce: "The orange crop seems to me to be excellent this year. The oranges are delicious and comparatively cheap, costing from a penny upwards—rather different from London prices I expect." What he returned to again and again, however, was the new breed of Jews he felt was developing in the country: "The Jews are of a sturdy type and judging by their fresh complexions and clear skins, their environments and climate agrees with them well."

An interesting ambivalence can be detected here. Myer constantly contrasted the sturdy pioneers he observed in Palestine to the stereotype of the dysfunctional Jew he was obsessed with. A striking example can be found in a December 24 letter in which he praised the Palestine Jews of his battalion at the expense of the East End Jews who were enlisted in the 38th Battalion or conscripted into the 39th, whom he mocked as tailors. "The Jews of this Battalion are far preferable to the 'schneiderim,' if I may coin a word, of London or Leeds," he stated. "They are people with ideas and ideals of things besides mere money making, and the soil of Palestine is suited to such. They are well developed mentally and physically and they are men."

At the same time, he did not feel comfortable with the ideas propounded by the Palestine Jews. On December 21, he told Louie of the contentment he found during service from the soothing Book of

Ecclesiastes, explaining it by the fact that "[i]n the midst of people with big ideas and high ideals, it is comforting to think that one can also serve by merely putting one's back into doing the concrete tasks that lie before one." The Zionist ideas debated endlessly in the 40th Battalion remained foreign to the major, who was more concerned with the practical problems facing the land. On the first day of 1919, he reflected as follows:

> The after-war politics of Palestine are very obscure and there are many problems that will require very delicate handling. The relations between Jews and Arabs are not good and it will be a difficult matter to improve these. The Arabs are at present adopting a dog in the manger attitude and as they seem to be opposed to progress of any kind it will not be easy to avoid friction with them.

Myer was aware of the difficulties ahead for the British government, which needed to create a balance so as not to offend the Muslims—which would endanger the whole empire—or the Jews—which would raise difficulties throughout the world. He believed that a strong British administration was necessary until the Jewish population outnumbered the Arab population and that it would be premature to discuss local autonomy until then. "Whether the ardent Zionists will be patient until that time," wrote the officer, who knew all too well the soldiers under his command, on January 1, 1919, "remains to be seen." As much as he admired the Palestine Jews and shared their disdain for the Orthodox community in Jerusalem and elsewhere, he did not intend to share in their fate and was not even interested in staying in the country and serving in the British administration when offered the opportunity. When demobilization of the Legions began in early 1919, he explicitly estranged himself from the Zionists, however sympathetic he might have been to their cause.

> Time is not yet ripe for the garrison of Palestine to be specifically Jewish or Arab or even partially so. For some years Non-Jewish and Non-Arab administration and troops are necessary and then it will be possible to say what the destiny of the country should be. We have now no role and so the sooner we are demobilized the better. I don't think hot-headed Zionists realize this, but though I am only a sympathizer with their aspirations and not an active Zionist, I am sure that my views are sound.[18]

In his letters from that period, the British officer seemed to identify more readily with the British administration than with his fellow Zionists. It was General Allenby, the British war commander, who became Myer's hero. He told Louie on January 25, 1919, that "while out with the Colonel I saw Allenby riding on the sands. He is a handsome fellow—quite a model hero and a first-rate specimen of British manhood."

Myer had no sympathy for the Zionist demand to keep part of the Legions mobilized. "I am still convinced," he wrote to his fiancée on February 2, 1919, "that the interests of Zionism would best be served by returning the members of the Battalion to useful constructive work in Palestine." In his encounters with Zionist activists, he continued to take an outsider's position. Upon visiting a Jewish farming cooperative whose members objected to Jewish landowners employing Arab labor and insisted that Jews cultivate the land themselves, he concluded that while their tenets were "mild Bolshevism," the result appeared so far to be "eminently satisfactory." He was unable, however, to consider such projects a way to achieve Jewish independence in Palestine: "I'm a little cynical about the state of affairs in the future—say ten years ahead."[19]

He saw great economic opportunities for the country but believed its political affairs could only be handled by the British administration. This stance became a source of ambivalence when that administration marginalized the Legions, which Myer saw as an outgrowth of anti-Semitism. "Really one is now face to face with anti-semitism in a form that I have never met it before," he wrote on March 14. "Whether the Authorities know that they are countenancing it or not, I am not clear, but the situation gives me food for thought." He felt, however, it would be a mistake to engage in open conflict with the British authorities. "I insisted that we had to be careful not to give unnecessary trouble to the Authorities just at present, as the Arabs are doing their best to ensure that we should with a view to our making ourselves unpopular," he said four days later. Like many travelers to the Orient, Myer looked at the Arabs with a degree of romanticism (even venturing to learn Arabic before his demobilization), but he also used harsh words to describe Arab attitudes. "The real trouble with the Arabs," he said, "is that they have never had enough time to convert their swords into plough shares."[20]

Myer's last letters to his fiancée reflect the duality that accompanied him all along. He had a deep interest in Palestine and had proven to be a sharp-eyed observer of the political situation there. However, his main pride lay in wearing the British military uniform as a way to assert a different Jewish identity from that envisioned in the stereotypical view of the Jew. While this attitude made him seem more an observer than a participant in the Zionist endeavor, it may be concluded that this attitude also had its place in the journey to the Promised Land.

9

Memory and Identity

MEMORIES

In this chapter, we discuss a memoir written in 1968 in English by a veteran of the Jewish Legions, Benjamin Bronstein of Lynn, Massachusetts, who served in the 40th Royal Fusiliers and was later an active war veteran in the United States.[1] As mentioned before, obvious differences exist between memoirs written half a century after the war and war diaries. As a rule, the former may be treated as less reliable due to failures of memory, exaggerations, and the tendency to apply to past events perspectives gained later. Memoirs provide no valid account of changes in soldiers' consciousness over time as they are written ex post facto, and they often suffer from a didactic approach, with the memoirists trying to disseminate norms gained during their military service to future generations. Memoirs often represent more of the veterans' reflections than their authentic experience. These reflections, however, are not without historical value. While the Bronstein memoirs discussed in this chapter were written half a century after the events, they shed light on the way the war experience shaped the writer's consciousness. These memoirs seem to follow notes written during the war quite closely, but their main value lies in their depiction of the effects of the veteran's service in the Jewish Legions on his later thoughts and experiences.

Bronstein's journey to the Promised Land began on April 11, 1918. He was part of a group of five hundred volunteers who left Boston for Windsor, Nova Scotia. He describes the commotion accompanying the departure of the volunteers, chaos that did not end in Boston. Since America had not declared war on Turkey, only nonaliens could be recruited, and thus most American Legionnaires were volunteers encouraged to join the Legions by the Labor Zionist movement Poaley Zion, headed by Ben-Gurion and Ben-Zvi, who took the opportunity to establish a Jewish fighting force in Palestine. The volunteers were greeted with enthusiasm by supporters of the Zionist cause.

On that day Boston Zionist organizations arranged a big reception for this group with a dinner at Ruggles Hall in Roxbury. A parade with a band of music led by the representatives of the many Zionist organizations and a police escort marched through the center of Boston past City Hall and the State House where we were greeted by the then Mayor and Governor. Both the City Hall and the State House displayed the Zionist flag of white and blue with the Mogen David. About 7:30 that evening we gathered at North Station where a special train waited to take us to our preliminary station in Canada.

The special Legion train pulled out of Boston's North Station at 8:00 p.m. The Legionnaires, tired from the events of the day, began to doze off in their seats and fell asleep, not minding the terrible noise a fast moving train makes. Suddenly, I heard a knocking on the window near my seat, and someone calling that we were in Portland, Maine. Around 11 p.m. as I looked out, I recognized the faces of two young men that had lived in our City of Lynn, and had moved to Portland a few years back. They were two brothers from the Cushing family and ardent Poaley Zionists. As I stepped out to greet them, they handed me boxes of oranges, apples, candy and cigarettes for all the boys, and told me that all the Zionist groups of the Portland area arranged the greeting of our train and provided the goodies for all of us, and again we shared a mutual inspiration. The train did not stay too long in this station, and by 11:30 p.m. we were on our way, and most of us dozed off again.

The next awakening came when all of a sudden we began to hear the strains of music coming from a band. It was about 2:00 . . . in the morning on April 12th. The train was pulling into the Bangor, Maine Station. When we popped our heads out the car windows, we beheld an amazing sight. There was a band of musicians, led by a detail of Police, and followed as it seemed by the whole Jewish community of Bangor. Fathers carrying youngsters in their arms, and mothers holding on to the older children. As the train stopped, the band played "Hatikvah," and again gifts of fruit, cigarettes, and candy were distributed to all the boys. The enthusiasm was great. Fathers lifted their young daughters to kiss the boys goodbye and wish them well. Until this day, I cherish and remember the inspiring sight at the Bangor Station that brought tears of exaltation to many of the Legionnaires and maybe to those that greeted us.

When the train arrived in St. John, Canada, it was greeted by representatives of the small Jewish community there who planned to invite the soldiers to Friday night service in the synagogue, after which they would be hosted by the Jewish families in town. The plan had to be changed, however, because the Canadian military authorities did not allow the soldiers, who were still in civilian clothes, to scatter into the town.

As it happened St. John, being a small city, did not have a place big enough to accommodate 500 men at one sitting. The only place that could hold half of the number was a Chinese restaurant, and it was therefore necessary to take it.

About 5:00 P.M. the president of the Shul [synagogue] and his committee appeared at our barracks dressed in full dress suits and stove pipe hats, and together with the military personnel led us in a march from the barracks through the city streets to the Shul. As I said before, the Jewish community being small in number had a small Shul and could only accommodate about 300 or 350 people, and with 500 of us, you can imagine how much space was left for us. The Shul was full when we got there, for it seemed that every Jewish man and woman and child turned out to greet us, but somehow we managed to squeeze in. I believe that all of us, who are still among the living, and those of St John's community, have never forgotten that wonderful, Orthodox Cantorial *Kaboles Shabos* [Friday night prayer] performed by one of our Legionnaires. He was a member of a chorus who sang with many a prominent Cantor of those days.

After the services, we left there for the Chinese restaurant, and we ate in two shifts. It was about 9:00 P.M. when we left the restaurant, and marched over to the biggest theater in the city for entertainment. The whole orchestra was reserved for us, and the balconies were full of people, and many wounded Canadian soldiers who came back from the fighting fronts of Europe. As we entered the theater the orchestra played "The Yanks are Coming," the whole orchestra stood up and cheered. When we were all in the theater and ready to be seated, the orchestra played the British and American National anthems. They also played "Hatikvah." It was about 12:00 midnight when we parted from our hosts and marched off to our barracks.

The appearance of the Jewish Legion volunteers on the American scene has greatly improved the Patriotic image of the American Jew. No matter what city or town the volunteers came from, the local press had fully covered the events of the farewell parties, and send offs given their volunteers. This helped a great deal to remove the label of *slacker* given to many of our Jewish boys. The American public did not take into consideration the fact that many of our Jewish young men of military age were not yet American citizens, and as such had a right to claim exemption.

The receptions in London's East End were less warm. Bronstein tells of the group's arrival in Whitechapel, where the commanding officer, Frederic Samuel, made the soldiers aware of the resentment felt there toward American soldiers with Zionist ideals.

He pointed out that previous groups of American Legionnaires who went to London on their own encountered opposition from the English Jewish soldiers. Especially when they visited Whitechapel, there were a few street brawls. Perhaps this was because the Jewish girls favored the American Legionnaires. In order to stop these unpleasant incidents, the community appointed a special committee to handle the American and Canadian Jewish volunteers, who began to come into London every month by the hundreds.

The committee headed by Major Shonfield took good care of the soldiers during their ten-day vacation in London. They were housed at the battalion's headquarters on Cheney Street and on Saturday were invited to join services in the city's synagogues.

In the morning, at our first Shabbos [Saturday] breakfast, Major Shonfield announced that no one should leave the place, since he received requests from practically every Jewish Congregation in the city, Orthodox and Reform, for Legionnaires to be their guests at Services and Kiddush [blessing]. In order to satisfy everyone Major Shonfield, knowing the size of the different Shuls and Congregations, allotted them groups of 5, 10, 15, and 20 or more.

The service [in the Reform synagogue I went to] was not too long, accompanied by a choir and organ. The Rabbi greeted us, and what he said I do not remember. When Major Shonfield came up on the *Oamed Platform* [reader's desk] to thank the Congregation for their hospitality, he mentioned with a voice full of emotion. You American Volunteers of the Jewish Legion, if you have not done anything yet as soldiers, as volunteers you have accomplished something of great value to our Jewish people. You have awakened the spirit of Judaism and support for the cause of Zionism. If some of my friends would have told me two months ago that this Temple would display the Zionist flag, together with all allied flags, he continued to say, and that the organ would play the strains of "Hatikvah," I would not have believed it. But today, it is a fact, you see it, you've heard it, and this was made possible by your display of courage and zeal to volunteer by the hundreds and leave the United States to come here to join the Jewish Battalions to fight for the liberation of Palestine in the hope of establishing a homeland for our Jewish people. Your presence here has greatly contributed to the Reformation of this Reformed Congregation. After the services we returned to a dining hall, where a chicken dinner was served. The seating arrangements were a lady escort for each Legionnaire. After the dinner was over, many individuals extended private invitations to many of the boys to be their guest at home, and took them to a movie and then to tea. It was an inspiring Shabbos for all that participated.

The memoirs also note the excitement felt by non-Jews over the presence of uniformed Jewish soldiers in the streets of London.

The carfare on buses and subways were half price for soldiers in uniform. We surely took advantage of it and would board a bus and travel to its last stop, and then board another going in a different direction. This was being done by many of the visiting groups and it gave the impression to the traveling public that we were in great numbers. Many travelers were being attracted by new uniforms, especially the *Mogen David Patch* on our shoulder sleeve. They began to talk to us and ask questions. We explained to them that we were American Jewish volunteers who joined the Jewish Battalions to fight for Palestine. They were very much impressed by our statements. The English people, being believers in the Old Testament, remarked that maybe it is the beginning of the fulfillment of the prophecy of your prophets that the Children of Israel will sometime return to Zion, and would wish us success.

The memoirs then tell of the training in Plymouth and the travel of the 40th Fusiliers to Southampton, where they boarded the *Caesarea*, which took them across the English Channel to Cherbourg, France, where they went on freight trains to Taranto, Italy. In Taranto they boarded another ship to Port Said and ended up in a camp in the Egyptian desert. The memoirist tells of the Yom Kippur prayer of 1918 in the Egyptian desert.

We arrived in camp late in the evening, turned in our passes to the Battalion Orderly room, and joined our company. We learned that the 39 Battalion R.F. had been sent up to the front lines to join the 38 R.F., which participated in the liberation of the Jerusalem area in the early part of 1918. Our battalion, the 40th, was ordered from general headquarters in Cairo to remain in our camp to complete our training for desert warfare acclimation. Most of the men in the Battalion were disappointed, for we all wanted to go to Palestine. Colonel Samuel put us all at ease and told us that we would have time to be killed a few months later.

Our training consisted of marches in battle dress in the day time and some during the night. We had lectures on how to take care of ourselves in sand storms, to avoid mirages, and how to use water from our water bottle, which was part of our battle equipment, and many other subjects. We were not used to the hot climate and the intensive workout that we were getting, so we welcomed the announcement that we would have no training on Yom Kippur day. Every man not on duty would have to present himself for Shul Parade and Service, and all company kitchens would be closed from sundown the day before, to sundown of the day of Yom Kippur, and no food would be issued to anyone after we had our meal before sundown the day before Yom Kippur. We had plenty of men who could chant and perform any kind of religious service so the Chaplain had no trouble in getting a *chasen* [cantor].

Our Shul had no walls and no roof as it was in the open desert in back of our camp. The blue sky, the moon, and stars were our roof. A table covered with a white cloth was the [reader's desk], and a wooden box housing a little Torah served as the *Oren Hakodesh* (or the Ark). Indeed it was awesome and inspiring. Here were 1500 Jewish soldiers who volunteered to fight for liberation of the promised land, stand assembled under the open sky to listen to the age old chant of *Kol Nidre* on the most revered night of our calendar.

We were thousands of miles away from home and our families, having in mind what we may confront in the future, we were overwhelmed with sadness when the *chasen* began chanting the Kol Nidre service, there was not a dry eye in the assembly.

Another experience concerned Bronstein's meeting with Jewish Turkish prisoners of war who had joined the Jewish Legions.

Our Battalion camp was spread out under the famous biblical Mount Carmel which in normal Palestinian weather makes a beautiful sight. I presented myself to the Battalion orderly room and was sent back to my original company. Since most of my comrades of the original 40th were transferred to the 38th and 39th, I found myself assigned to tent with new comrades with whom I was not able to converse. They could not speak Yiddish or English. After a while I found out that they were Turkish soldiers and prisoners of war. While in prison camp they applied to the British military authorities for permission to join with the Jewish Battalions, and that permission was granted to them. They were a hard working group of about 200 men and were attached to our Battalion. My first night with them at camp a strong wind of storm proportion hit our camp and leveled every tent, including ours. We remained standing in the rain with nothing but our under clothing. These men started to immediately put our tent up again. They did not let me do anything. They gave me a blanket and motioned to me to wrap myself in it and stay aside until the tent was back in position.

After a few weeks we learned to understand each other by using a few words of Hebrew and English, which they began to learn.

There are also descriptions of a visit to Jerusalem, which demonstrate the effect of that visit on the memoirist, who came to realize that the Promised Land was not just the abstract concept taught for two thousand years in Hebrew schools.

Walking through the streets of the old city I was entranced, because I could not believe that I was in Jerusalem. When I was a youngster and went to *Chader* (Hebrew School) in Russia, and began to learn the Bible, and later the prophets, I never believed that the land of Israel and the places mentioned in the Scriptures were still existing on this earth. My *Rabi* (teacher) used to translate the Hebrew into Yiddish, the same way his *Rabi* taught him. He had no maps to show us where the land of Israel was located, therefore, most of the youngsters had to accept facts as they were told. As I grew older and began to attend the Russian public school and then high school, I began to learn Ancient History and Geography. I never realized that there was a Jewish nation and a Jewish government in Israel that played a great role in ancient years amongst the nations of the world.

It was natural for us Legionnaires 50 years ago, as it is for the Jewish soldiers of the six day war in 1967, to first visit at the *Kotel Hamarovi* (the Wailing Wall). This wall was the monument left of the greatness of our nation and the Holy Temple built by King Solomon as the House of Worship to God. I cannot describe the emotion and the feeling I experienced at the moment I approached . . . the wall. I stood trembling with awe and reverence. I felt as if I were a part of that generation of my people that built the Holy Temple thousands of years ago, and that it left an everlasting religious mark on mankind. It was natural for me as a Jew to be overwhelmed with emotion at the sight of this Holy monument, but when I looked around me, I noticed two general staff officers standing not far from me. It looked to me as if they too were overwhelmed with awe. The expression on their faces, and the way they stood at attention, it was probably the way they would stand in the presence of their King of England.

The Promised Land, and the memoirist's role as its liberator, became particularly real for him during the Passover seder (ritual meal) in Kibbutz Dgania in the spring of 1919.

We were invited for the seder by the settlement of Dgania. Our Captain Harvey accepted the invitation. This seder left an everlasting impression on the memory of all of us who had the privilege of being there that seder night. Leaving a group to guard the camp, the rest of the company was assembled on the parade ground and ordered to take their rifles and ammunition with them. It is not a Jewish way to observe a seder, but the unrest among the Arabs forced us to be ready. About 8:00 . . . in the evening, we marched off to Dgania. Arriving there, we stacked our rifles on the side of the big dining hall and everyone was seated at both sides of long tables, with our officers at the head. Kiddush was sung by one of the older settlers, and the questions were asked by one of the youngsters from the settlement children.[2] We all participated in singing from the Hagodah [the story of the Exodus read at the Passover seder] and drank the four cups of wine and more. I must say that due to the fact that the settlement was liberated from the Turks about 8 or 9 months before the holiday, the spirit was good even though their supply of meat was low, and our meat cutlets had to be beefed up with vegetables. We realized that this Pesach [Passover] we not only celebrated the freeing of our ancestors from Egypt, but also of freeing our brothers and sisters who have settled in Palestine from the Turkish yoke.

As the night went on, a few more cups of wine were consumed by the men and officers. The singing became louder, the tables and benches were pushed aside, and the dancing began. The Hora [an Israeli dance] and Chasidic dances were performed by the men and some of the officers participated. The prize of the evening went to one of our young Jewish officers who was born in England. When he performed the *Russian Kozatchke*, a dancer from the Russian Ballet could not have danced it better than our officer.

It was midnight when we took leave from our host. The air was warm, the moon shone bright, our spirits high, we began our march back to camp. We sang marching songs. We wanted the echo of our singing to resound wide and far into the hills and valleys of upper and lower Galilee and bring them the message that we came to Palestine to help in the resettlement of our people in the ancient home land, and live again as an independent nation.

REFLECTIONS

The feelings of many North American volunteers that they had come to Palestine to fulfill a Zionist goal did not prevent tensions with Jewish ideologues in Palestine, many of whom enlisted with the 40th Fusiliers. To the latter, the Yiddish- and English-speaking Jews who came from abroad were not genuine Zionists, in spite of their devotion to the cause and their bravery in the war against the Turks (the 40th Fusiliers were enlisted after the fighting was over). The Palestine-centered ideology considered true Zionism to consist of settling the land—preferably in an agricultural settlement—and speaking Hebrew. Soon after their enlistment, the Palestine recruits engaged in strikes and walkouts, in the best socialist tradition, against the British military authorities. It is interesting to follow the story of the 40th Fusiliers from the perspective of Bronstein, who in 1919 served for a while as a clerk of the sergeant major's office in the 40th Fusiliers and, though a devout Zionist, became quite ambivalent toward the Palestinian Jews.

The ambivalence is not obvious because, according to this memoir, the Palestinian Jews saw the volunteers from abroad as allies in their socialist struggle against the "bourgeoisie"—namely, settlers who came a few years before them, established private farms, and often preferred cheaper Arab labor on their farms. According to Bronstein, at the end of the war, about twenty-five hundred Legionnaires wished to remain in Palestine, but only four hundred were permitted to stay after the discharge. He claimed that rumor had it at the time that the British refusal to allow more to stay was the result of pressure by the early settlers, supported by the Zionist leadership in Palestine, who were afraid that thousands of Legionnaires would boost the ranks of the Union of Jewish Workers, which fought fiercely for Jewish labor. Whether or not the rumor was true, it indicates that a certain bond existed between the Palestinian Jews and the Zionist volunteers from abroad, but the memoir also demonstrates resentment over the Palestine-centered demand that the Hebrew language be exclusively used in public performances in the army camp.

The American and English boys of our 40th had been told that they may have to wait about 6 months before their discharge papers will come through. One day our battalion received a request from General Headquarters in Cairo for English speaking volunteers to go for a few months of duty to the Island of

Cyprus. Many of our American boys were sick of laying around in the desert, signed up figuring that in a few days they would be called to leave, but that did not happen right away . . . the colonel granted permission for the Palestinian comrades, who in civilian life were the leaders of the Histadrut (the Jewish Workers Union) and whose membership was almost entirely in the ranks of the 40th Battalion to bring into our camp their library and musical instruments from their orchestra.

A special big tent was put up to house the library and the orchestra with a stage for entertainment. All the speaking, singing, or reading portions of the program were performed in the spoken modern Hebrew tongue, which the American and English boys did not understand, and they vigorously protested. They demanded that the programs should include Yiddish and some English numbers, but the fanatic Hebraists of the Palestinians would not give in, although 95 per cent of the Palestinians could speak and understand some Yiddish and English. This attitude of the Palestinians irked the American and English boys and they began to create obstructions at these programs and would not let them go on. Our non-commissioned officers, who by now were mostly Palestinians, realized that they have to do something before it will come to violence.

One day Sergeant Major of my B company [Dov Hoz] called me into his company office and asked me why the Americans and English so vigorously objected to the programs. Knowing my background that I was an active Zionist in the States, he thought that I could persuade the objectors and let the program go on. I told him on the contrary that I am one of the supporters of the objectors for the simple reason that we volunteer[ed] for and came five thousand miles to fight for Palestine and we are entitled to recreation programs in the language that we speak and understand. Furthermore what have the Palestinians done in the 6 to 7 months we have been with you in the Battalion to arrange and give us instructions on how to read, write, and speak Hebrew. There were many leisure hours, and many capable men amongst you who could do that, but you people have not done that, and you expect us to sit around [like] dumb bells at these programs and enjoy them.

Apparently, the arguments were convincing, as was the threat that the American and English boys would not let the programs go on. Future performances were given in all three languages: Hebrew, Yiddish, and English. Had the conflict not been managed, Bronstein believes, it would have led to fistfights, which would not have looked good in the eyes of the Gentile superior officers.

Although Bronstein served in the 40th Battalion side by side with many of Israel's future leaders—Labor leader Berl Katznelson, Prime Minister Levi Eshkol, Chief of Staff Yaakov Dori, and others—he was less impressed by his encounters with them than by events related to his Jewish heritage, such as a wedding he attended or the celebration of Jewish holidays during his service. This may be one indication of the chasm between the hard-core socialists in Palestine and the foreign volunteers, which led to the relative neglect of the Jewish Legions in Israel's history books, which were largely inspired by the former.

HOMECOMING

As is often the case, soldiers returning from the battlefields are surprised and frustrated when they find out that civilian life, however disrupted by the war, goes on as usual and concerns other than cherishing the war veterans are on people's minds. The last pages of the memoir include references to the soldier's realization, which was probably reinforced by many years of activity in war veterans' associations, that his and his comrades' contribution was only partially appreciated. Compare the following description of a visit to a synagogue when the writer was hospitalized with malaria in a Port Said hospital in fall 1919 to his descriptions of similar visits a year earlier.

> I soon realized that the High Holiday season was at hand, and it must be about *Rosh Hashanah* time. I got permission from the Doctor to leave the hospital to go into the city. I do not remember how it came about that I located a small Congregation in the foreign quarters of the city. Our European Jews were having religious Services in a regular house, which served them as a *Shul*. I must say I was very disappointed, as my presence there the first day of *Rosh Hashanah* was hardly noticed. No one approached me to ask who I was or where I came from, and how I happened to be at the Service. This was not the custom of our European Jews for no matter where they live they always arranged a place and someone to greet a stranger and give him a meal if he needed it, a *Hachnosas Orchim* [hospitality]. But, at this group of Jewish *Polacos*, as they called them in Egypt, no one cared. As a Jew my pride was hurt, but it did not matter, as far as a meal was concerned I did not need it for I went back to the hospital and had my meal there.
>   This was Rosh Hashanah of 1919.

The anger over the congregation's lack of hospitality, noted fifty years after the fact, is not confined to that congregation or to non-European Jews. Similar experiences can be detected on other occasions; the individuals and crowds the soldier meets in his journey back from the Promised Land are not remembered as being equally cheerful as those greeting him on the journey to the battlefields. In Marseilles, for instance, he had the following experience:

> The last week of our stay in Marseilles included the week [of] Succoth (the holiday of Tabernacles) and last day of Simcha[t] Torah. I visited the French Jewish Temple with a few of my comrades, but we were not impressed. We could not understand their French *devenen* (praying). They could not speak

Yiddish and we could not speak French so we could not communicate. When we left the Temple we were disappointed, but we found out that there was a small community of our Eastern European Jews with a *Shul* on a street near the waterfront. We decided to visit the Shul on Simcha[t] Torah Day (The Jubilant Day of the Torah). We found the Shul located on the second floor of a tenement house. We went into a large room which served as the main praying room, and were greeted by the menfolk who occupied the front part of the room. The womenfolk sat in the back. We were honored by being called up to the reading of the Torah. When the services were over, and some of the people began to leave, a surprising thing happened. An intelligent looking young man got up and blocked the exit and began to speak in French. I understood some French, and by his tone of voice I realized he was chastising the Congregation for letting the Legionnaires, who were their guests, leave without serving them refreshments, especially since it was Simcha[t] Torah. It did not take long before we were surrounded by the womenfolk and some young girls who made us stay. In about 15 minutes a table was set with the traditional food of the holiday; shnaps, honeycak, kichel, and herring. The young man who spoke up greeted us and apologized for the Congregation. All was well that ended well.

When the Legionnaires arrived in the demobilization camp for American soldiers in Winchester, they were treated differently than they were on the way to the front. Bronstein noted, "There was no committee to greet us, and no arrangements for a special place to stay while we were on leave. It was different from the first ten days leave we had when we came from the U.S.A." The mood improved, however, when the repatriated Legionnaires arrived at the docks of Liverpool.

We were directed to the berth where the ship was anchored, and found a gathering of people from the Jewish community of Liverpool. The bow of the ship was decorated with the British, American, and Jewish flags. The ship's orchestra was playing "Hatikvah," and a committee distributed cigarettes, candy and fruit. As we boarded the ship they all cheered us and wished us Bon Voyage. As soon as we got aboard, the ship's siren began to blast the signal that the ship was ready to sail.

As the ship was a first-class liner, it arrived in New York harbor in no time and the Legionnaires were dispersed, but not before they were given a last opportunity to celebrate their journey to—and from—the Promised Land.

It was close to midnight when all of us were ready to leave the pier a free man. Those whose homes were in New York City went home, but those who had to travel were taken over by representatives of the Zionist office and the Red Mogen David [the Jewish emergency assistance service]. We were asked to be their guests for the night, and since we had no place to go we accepted their invitation. They took our group to the Famous Libby's Turkish Russian Baths. We refreshed ourselves and stayed over night. In the morning they provided us with breakfast and then took us to the office of the Zionist organization of America, where each of the Legionnaires received twenty five dollars as a gratuity from the Zionist[s] of America for our great service we had rendered to the cause of Zionism by our volunteering to serve in the first organized Jewish Armed Forces since the destruction of the Second Temple in Jerusalem.

Each one of us went on our way to begin to find a path back to the life we [were] accustomed to before we became Legionnaires.

10

A Soldier Left Behind

DISPLACED ONCE AGAIN

As most of the Legionnaires returned home and began to find their way in civilian life, some stayed behind. The story of soldiers' disorientation when wars are over is a relatively neglected part of military history but comes up in individual life writing. The letters discussed in this chapter were written in Yiddish by a Legionnaire named B. Zilberman, who wandered in Egypt and Palestine after the demobilization. The letters were written to his former comrade Yehoshua Davidzon, who was born in Warsaw in 1898 and migrated with his parents to New York in 1912. Davidzon's parents died within the year and he worked as a shipping clerk during the day and went to school at night. He joined the Legions in April 1918, served in the 39th Fusiliers, and was honorably discharged in December 1919. He settled in New York, where he was self-employed in the textile business, married in 1922, and had a daughter and a son. He was involved in Israel-related activities and had, as we shall see, a strong urge to settle in Israel. Even late in life, during a visit to the Legions House in 1958, he wrote in a short biographical note that his hope was to settle in Israel in the near future, a dream that never materialized.

While Davidzon began to settle down in the United States after the war, Zilberman found himself displaced with no money and little hope. This condition apparently was chronic because when the veterans were asked by the Legions House in the 1960s to submit their pictures and short biographical notes, all that Zilberman wrote under his picture was a phrase in Yiddish, noting it was the picture of a Jew who has *gevalt* served as a

Jewish soldier. The Yiddish word *gevalt* defies translation but is similar to "Oh my gosh!" in its combination of shock and irony. The desperate Zilberman did not even write down his full first name or any biographical details. His letters, however, written in Yiddish and probably donated by Davidzon to the Legions House, are important historical documents not only because they reflect the thoughts and feelings of a displaced Legionnaire but also because they shed light on life in Palestine during the first years of British rule in the country.

The first letter, here in its entirety, shows the difficulty of finding work in Palestine. At the beginning of 1919, when the demobilization process in the British army had begun, about twelve hundred North American soldiers expressed their wish to settle in the land of Israel. The World Zionist Organization, whose Zionist Commission (which became the Palestine Zionist Executive in 1921) oversaw all matters concerning the Jews in the land and negotiated with the British authorities, realized that these demobilized soldiers would have no land to settle on and no means by which to sustain themselves. This realization delayed the process of demobilization and caused much turmoil among the soldiers. Moreover, Ze'ev Jabotinsky, founder of the Legions, believed that the Legionnaires' continued service in the British army as part of the occupation force in the Middle East would be of political value to the Zionist cause. The British military and civilian authorities, for their part, were unhappy about both options: allowing Jewish soldiers to play a role in the occupation force, which would cause trouble with the Arabs, or demobilizing a large group of Jewish soldiers who would become a burden on the limited resources in the land. Thus, while demobilization proceeded for the Legionnaires from Great Britain, who generally expressed no interest in staying in Palestine, the North Americans went through a more difficult demobilization process and, as the letter indicates, some continued to encounter problems after their release.

Alexandria Egypt May 2, [19]20
My Dear Friend Yehoshua Davidzon,
    I duly received your postcard of the 17th of March. As you can see from my writing, I am, thank God, in Egypt, and you are surely curious to know what I am doing in Egypt and how I came to be in Egypt, so I will tell you the whole story. After I spent some time in Palestine and saw that I could not get any work in Palestine and realized that I was superfluous in Palestine and still having several pounds in my pocket, I mulled it over and thought that perhaps it would be a good plan to return to America. [After all] what good could I do the Jewish people and how could Palestine benefit if I remained in Palestine and starved, doing nothing? I came to the conclusion that the plan was a good one. Since my traveling to America meant going through Alexandria or through Saudi [Arabia] and since I still had enough for a ticket

(albeit 4th class)—the British government refused to send me back—so I decided to take things into my own hands, and I packed my things and that is how I came to be in Alexandria. Once in Alexandria, however, I found out about another difficulty, namely that in order to travel to America, I need permission from the American consulate, and since I am not an American citizen, the American consulate refused to grant me permission [to travel]. If I had documents to prove that I was from some other country, I might still have gotten this permit [to travel], but I had no documents at all showing that I belonged to any country, so I could, under no circumstances, get any kind of permit. The British government also refused to grant me this permit, since I was not British, and my having been a soldier meant nothing to them. Since I had just been demobilized, I was no better than anyone else. That is what they said, and once they say something it is final! I write this to you as a kindred soul. But the writing of it is easier than getting it done. It took a long time until I found out that I could not travel, and in the meantime the few pounds I had were spent and there I was stuck in Alexandria—lost either way: not in Palestine but suffering nonetheless. What could I do and what would happen? Oh, only God in heaven knows what the end will be. In the meantime, I am suffering. If you think that you can do something for me, do it as soon as possible. It is most important that you answer me the same day that you receive my letter, because I feel very much alone here.

I wrote the same thing to a friend of mine named Moyshe Grossman. He lives at 168 Monroe St. New York. So, if you want to do something, get in touch with Grossman. If he has already done [something], then you do not need to do anything. It is essential that something be done quickly, since I am suffering terribly here.

You have certainly heard what a joy Palestine was: first about the Galilee where 2 male and 2 female comrades were killed. The 2 males were, unfortunately, from our division. You certainly knew one of them. [He] was together with us [when we left] Canada; I believe he was in A. Co[mpany]. I think his name was Sharf.[1]

The second one was named Toker, but that was not our Toker. Our Toker was in C. Co[mpany], and I do not think that you knew him, but I knew him very well. And the 2nd joy of this wonderful Passover that the Jews had in Jerusalem is something that I cannot write about in more detail, because I do not know more than you do. About the latest news that we read in the newspaper that the San Remo Conference decided that Palestine belongs to Jews. I hope that brings us true joy . . . even though I do not have much faith in that.

Write me an answer immediately. Your friend, who wishes to see you soon,

B. Zilberman

P. S. If you are about to get married any time soon, I ask you to wait until I can come. Give my sincere regards to Mendelson and all the friends whom you still meet. Warmest regards to your brother and his family and to everyone who is dear to you. Write to me at this address:

Mr. B. Silverman

c/o Carmel Oriental Alexandria Egypt

The reference to the two joyous events is made sarcastically. The first event was the fall of Tel Hai and other Jewish settlements in the Upper Galilee, the northern region of Palestine. In spring 1920, the Upper Galilee had been evacuated by the British military as part of the Sykes-Picot Agreement of 1916, in which the British and French governments secretly divided among them the land to be taken from the Turks. With the British leaving before the French military stepped in, Arab bands besieged the few isolated Jewish settlements in the area. Joseph Trumpeldor, the Jewish Russian officer who in 1915 formed the Zion Mule Corps with Jabotinsky and served as Patterson's deputy in Gallipoli, gathered a small group of young Jews, including several ex-Legionnaires, and went with them to defend the settlements. In the battle that erupted on March 1, 1920, Trumpeldor and seven others were killed and the settlements were evacuated.

The "wonderful Passover" refers to the Easter riots in Jerusalem in April 1920. Following the British government's reconfirmation of the Balfour Declaration earlier that year, Muslim Arabs participating in the festival of Nebi Musa, involving a pilgrimage from Jerusalem to Jericho, where Moses is believed to be buried, attacked Jews in Jerusalem, killing six and injuring over two hundred.[2] These riots, launching the continuing religious war between Muslims and Jews in Palestine, marked the failure of the Jewish Legions to become a Jewish defense force, because the Legionnaires were confined by the British authorities to their Serafend camp. Jabotinsky, whose hope to turn the Legions into such a force was shattered, was involved at the time in the organization of an illegal Jewish defense force, Haganah (Hebrew for "defense"). And although the Haganah had little effect in these riots, Jabotinsky was arrested along with another nineteen Haganah members and sentenced to fifteen years of hard labor, of which he served three. Shortly after, riots erupted in other parts of Palestine, with the hands of the Jewish Legionnaires tied by the British military headquarters.

The above letter also refers to the conference at San Remo on the Italian Riviera in late April 1920 in which the Allied powers discussed the future of the former territories of the Ottoman Empire and decided to grant Great Britain and France a League of Nations mandate to rule these territories. Such historic events continue to appear in Zilberman's letters, which mostly expressed pessimism over them, interwoven with pessimism over the writer's own financial and personal conditions.

Alexandria June 20, [19]20

My Dear Davidzon,

It has been almost 2 months since I wrote you a letter and have not yet received a response. Why does it have to be like this? Is it because I wrote

you about my bad situation? Is this possible? No, I do not want to believe this. I believe that our Legion friendship stands higher than such trivialities. So, comrade Davidzon, please, as soon as you receive this letter write me an answer right away. With me the situation is like this: now I could receive a travel pass, but I no longer have any reason to travel. I need to have at least 200 dollars in order to travel and I do not even have one *prute* [cent]. So, listen, my friend Davidzon. It is possible that several of my friends there will lend me the sum [necessary], then I could come straightaway and would repay them with gratitude. And the main thing is that it should happen as soon as possible, because I am suffering greatly here. You simply cannot imagine it. So I ask you once again to discuss this with several of your friends and I believe that they will do this, but the main thing is that it should be done with dispatch and write me an answer right away. I do not even feel like taking pen in hand [to write] about the situation in Palestine, because all the Jews in the world were so overjoyed with the San Remo Conference Treaty, but now things have changed; now the whole world says, "Jews you are fools and you have nothing to be happy about." Practically every day I read letters that arrive from Palestine [saying] that today they are expecting a pogrom in Haifa, [and] tomorrow in Jaffa and a third one somewhere else. Is it possible that in lieu of protests [they now make pogroms]? Is this Balfour's Declaration? They hold conferences and decide to thank [themselves] for the great kindnesses that they are doing for the Jewish people. Instead of the pogroms that they had before only in the cities of Kishinev and Sedlitz and other such cities, now they have added another lovely name—the holy city of Jerusalem, and the Jewish people are holding conferences.[3] Oh, what a situation we have come to that we do not feel the blows that we are being dealt today. Go write something about this. Go explain this to the whole world. Don't be happy! Instead protest! Make some noise! I will probably remain the fool. That is why it is better to remain silent. Please, I ask you once again to write me back right away. Your friend, B. Zilberman
Mr. B. Silverman
c/o Carmel Oriental
Alexandria, Egypt

The personal problems facing the writer were shared, as shown in the following letter, by other residents of Palestine at the time.

Alexandria July 3 [1920]
My Dear Friend, Yehoshua Davidzon,
    I duly received your letter dated the 2nd of June. In your letter, you say that you wrote me again after the post card, but I did not receive it. That is not because the address was wrong, since you had written to me previously at this address of the Zionist Commission and you yourself know what wonderful letters there are in the Zionist Commission. The first thing that I want to write to you is about myself, my own situation.
    I got stuck here in Alexandria and cannot make a move. Before I had some money but could not get a passport. Now I could get a passport, but

I do not have a piaster, and I do practically no work at all. I think you can understand how good it is to be in Alexandria and not earn anything and not have any money. Well, my situation is very bad. I would like to escape from Alexandria as much as a person wants to live, but how? I wrote you a letter two weeks ago and you have certainly received it. There I wrote you that you should get together with several of our [mutual] friends and borrow at least $200 dollars for me, so that I can escape from here. Let me be rid of this Egyptian hell. Oh, it has already gotten to my bones. I am asking you the same thing again but it is important to do it quickly, because every day is like a year to me. My friend Grossman sent me articles from newspapers [describing] how happy they are there in America with the San Remo Conference Treaty. People are congratulating each other in the streets. It is a joyous occasion . . . not simply a personal happy occasion but a national victory, which is much, much more significant than a personal event. I also read here in New York Jewish newspapers that in Palestine, the treaty [signed] at this conference is already recognized. They are already reaping the fruit of two thousand years of plowing and planting. Well, now Jews have gotten upset. Actually, two of my friends from the Legion came yesterday: Maruszon (from your B. Company) and the other, Shokhat, from Palestine. Oh my, the things that they reported. Oh, how awful it is there. Inflation is terrible. There is no place to earn [anything], unless you are ready to compete with the dirty Arab, or if you have a lot [of money] and can get into the Zionist Commission and crunch along with everyone else. But when I just go down to the street and see new faces and say hello [and ask] "Where do you come from?" [the answer is] "From Palestine." "And where are you going?" One person answers, "To America," another "To Russia," and quite a few "To Belgium." (I think that Belgium will now become a large Jewish center, because so many Jews are now going there, because there no one talks and no one writes, but it is actually being built up.) And if I am foolish enough to ask, "Why?" Oh, what stories they tell. So I ask you, whom should I believe? Should I believe the writer, who sits on the third floor on East Broadway and is well paid to write propaganda for Capitalistic Zionism and knows as much about Palestine and its situation as I know what is now going on in Moscow? Or should I rather believe the eyewitnesses with their sunken faces and their bloody facts, who arrived from Palestine just yesterday?

I write you this, because in your letter you express such surprise that I was so discouraged by Palestine, and you shout so loudly: "From you, from you." I only wish that everything were a lie, but unfortunately, it is all true. When I was still in Jerusalem, and saw the suffering of my poor brothers and sisters and especially the suffering of my brothers in the Legion, several of whom came to me to borrow a shilling simply to buy a piece of bread. At that time, I used to come to the Zionist Commission, or as the Jerusalemites call it the Office of Troubles* and watch how they treated the poor people. The

---

* Translator's Note: Here he is punning on the similarity between Vaad HaTsirim (the Zionist Commission) and Vaad HaYisurim (meaning "suffering").

bureaucrat sits there in his softly upholstered [arm]chair and the pauper asks him for something, not, God forbid, money but a favor of some kind, and he refuses him in an ugly, boorish way. At the same time, his servant brings him a good glass of tea in a nice pot, and he asks also for some marmalade. You understand that a good glass of tea was insufficient after having had a good lunch. He still needed marmalade [to top things off]. And the poor, unfortunate person is standing to the side, and has, most likely, not seen such a glass of tea for a very long time. And unbidden this thought came to me. In the last few years we have produced 2 important Jews: one is Trotsky and the other is called Weizmann. Both have expressed great ideas concerning the worker.

Capitalistic newspapers add that under Trotsky's leadership, neither he nor his staff live any better than the people do. If there is not enough bread, the people do not have it and his staff doesn't have it and neither does he. And the question arises: Who is in a better position?

No. You hear? I must tell you up front that I am not a Bolshevik. I have never been close to Bolshevism, have not suffered anything for it, and have nothing to do with it. On the other hand, I am for Zionism with all my heart and soul and have ruined myself for it both emotionally and physically and am ready at any minute to give up my life [for it], but when one's stomach is empty bad thoughts come into one's mind. Oh these negative thoughts; how does one drive them away? And it is all the fault of one's stomach. It wants to be filled. Oh, what does one do with it? Don't you think that it would, perhaps, be better to have a Trotsky-like Weizmann? What do you think? I read [about] your personal situation with great interest. Of course, your physical suffering comes from your having changed climates, but you changed not only your climate but your whole way of life, and of course if one changes one's way of life other things also change, and it will take a bit of time before everything will straighten itself out. But you are suffering emotionally and that is worse than physical suffering.

NOSTALGIA AND DESPAIR

As the obsessive writing in this long letter goes on, Zilberman falls into a sentimental mood regarding his service in the Legions, reminding his former comrade of the great experience they had and the idealism they shared, which is now gone and will never return.

Despite all of our hatred and fighting, there was also idealism. Take, for example, our famous friend, Tageblat, who was really an animal in human form, but I can mention many more who weren't any smarter than he was, and we did not hate them. Why then did we hate him so much? It was simply because he was a contrast to our lives. He did not possess what we had. He was a totally physical being without a scrap of soul, and we were, if I can use the expression, special. Before we came to Palestine, [we were] completely soul. That is why he was so alien to us. He could never mix with us. You remember . . . the last few weeks before we left for Palestine? We were about to leave and the sun shone for us, and then we were not going and everyone was upset. You remember how we hated the "slackers" as we called them. Those were the ones who did not want to go to Palestine. I think today you are in New York with so many people and none of them want to go to Palestine, and it never occurs to you to hate someone who does not want to go to Palestine. Why is that? Because then you were completely soul, outside of the whole foolish world and totally involved in a new life that diametrically was different than the foolish world. Then suddenly you were out of this completely good world and back in the world of lies. Oh, what a terrible exchange it was. But it had to be. It is over now. That is how life is and that is how life must continue. And my advice is—continue with your life's work; earn money and be ambitious in your life and also for your ideals. Save some money. In time, the situation in Palestine will improve and then perhaps? I wish that it were so. Perhaps the dream of every Jew will be fulfilled. But under no circumstances should you ever get it into your head to join in a legion, if such a thing would be formed. You would never have the joy, the emotional pleasure that you previously had from the Legion. That was the kind of happiness that you could only have once, and you could have it only when you had never experienced it before. You can never again experience this same pleasure.

Listen to me and get rid of this thought, and you will be the better for it. Be ambitious in this world of falsehood and you will certainly be a success, and then, then . . . may I only live to see it . . . Palestine will, perhaps, be reestablished and—would that it were so—we should actually, joyously, be in a Jewish Palestine and not a British Palestine.

I started this letter on July 3rd and finished it on the 4th of July precisely at the time that America is celebrating its Declaration of Independence. As I am sitting and writing, a young man, who just arrived from Palestine, came into the house and brought me very good news from Palestine. He told me especially a lot about Herbert Samuel, who is doing a lot, may it only be true. In a few days, I will write you another letter, and, hopefully, with good news. Hopefully, we will also have a Declaration of Independence . . . on a smaller scale, but at least something.

I am closing my letter, and ask the same thing, that you answer my letter as soon as you receive it.

Your friend, who hopes to see you soon in America,

B. Zilberman

Sincere regards to your brother and sister and your fiancée and everyone else dear to you. Give all of our friends whom you meet regards from me.

B. Silverman c/o Carmel Oriental

Alexandria Egypt

Herbert Samuel, the Jewish British liberal politician, was nominated as high commissioner for Palestine in 1920. Due to his favorable view of Zionism, Samuel's nomination raised high hopes at first among Palestine Jews, who were soon disappointed when he implemented policies that were unfavorable to the Zionist cause, as when he suspended Jewish immigration to Palestine following Arab riots in 1921 and asserted that Palestine would not be converted to a Jewish national home.[4] Subsequent letters reflected Zilberman's growing disappointment.

Quantara August 4, [19]20
Esteemed, Dear Friend Yehoshua Davidzon,
    As you see, I am already, thank God, in Quantara. I did not come to Quantara for pleasure. As you know Quantara is not a resort. One does not travel there for pleasure. I was forced to sell myself for a piece of bread, and although you told me to have patience and especially as a Legionnaire one should and one must have patience, but my damned stomach does not want to know if it is a Legionnaire or not; it wants to eat. In such [a state of] poverty I came to Quantara, because I could not find anything to do in Alexandra [sic]. I am now working for the government in Quantara, and you know the kind of wages the government pays civilians. But I did one good thing: they wanted me to sign a contract and I refused. As soon as I receive some money from you, which should come any day, I will go either to Alexandra or to Jerusalem, get my passport and I am off to America.
    Practically every day I see people going to Palestine and people coming from Palestine, and as usual, those who are traveling to Palestine are going full of hope. Just the opposite, those who are coming from Palestine are disappointed, and if one asks them something, the smarter ones do not want to respond, and this means more than if they had spoken. Those who are not very bright tell stories. Of course, [they are] the old stories about the colonists who look in vain for work and that the Employment Council does not want to do anything for them. The newspapers write that Herbert Samuel is now rolling up his sleeves, and others write that he had rolled up his sleeves long ago and has been working, [but] one doesn't see much going on at all. What is going on where you are? How is your health? Was being in the country good for your health? I do not put much faith in the American countryside. It seems to me that one can only get sunburned there. Write me an answer right away and write to the old address in Alexandria. Give my regards to all my friends and to all your loved ones as well.
    Your friend, B. Zilberman
    B. Silverman c/o Carmel Oriental
    Alexandria Egypt

Zilberman's continuous pleading did lead to a fundraising effort to get the Legionnaire left behind back to America, which resulted in the following letter.

August 17, [19]20 Quantara
My Dear Friend, Yehoshua Davidzon,
    Today I duly received your letter dated July 15th and I am hurrying to answer you the very same day. First about myself personally: it is true that

I am having grave difficulties and I would very much like to be rid of my problems already and this exile in Egypt as well. Oh, how awful things are for me here. You cannot imagine it. Not only would I like to be rid [of Egypt], I would give a chunk of my life to be rid of it and to escape to America. Nevertheless, I ask you as a friend and as a comrade immediately to stop the collections. Under no circumstances should charity be collected for my sake. I am still strong and healthy enough to make my way through [this] on my own without accepting any charity. I thought when I was writing you about my situation and asked you to do whatever you could for me, I had in mind that 4 wealthy comrades should help me out with 50 dollars apiece, and I would, with great appreciation, have paid each one back. But if there were, unfortunately, no wealthy people among my friends, "Salvation will come for the Jews from a different place."[5] God will probably help, and under no circumstances will I permit charity to be collected for my sake. I thank you very much for your efforts. I cannot even express the extent of my appreciation. I am mindful of how much you sympathize with me; that is really true friendship and more precious than gold. I also thank those friends who have contributed and most likely generously to the Zilberman Fund. (You probably already gave it this name, because there in America everything has a name.) Thank God, however, I am not yet at that point. My pride as a human being has not yet sunk so low as to beg for charity. So, friend Davidzon, once again, please, in the name of our genuine friendship, on the same day that you receive this letter send everyone back their donation in my name with my greatest gratitude.

You wrote that when you were writing to me you were in a bad mood and if you had not mentioned it to me, I would have been able to discern it for myself in between the lines. I cannot remember the preaching letter I must have written to upset you so and to insult your feelings. I simply cannot remember it, but if, unwittingly, such a bad thing did come from my pen, I beg your forgiveness.

What kind of trouble are you having there? Somehow I read so many doubts in your letters, so much disappointment. Why do you not write to me about all this? Why don't you write to me about your fiancée in every letter? Is this perhaps the reason for my pessimism? In any case, treat me as a true friend and write to me about everything.

Please write me an answer right away.

Your true friend, B. Zilberman

Sincere regards to all my friends as well as to all your loved ones.

Still the same address:

B. Silverman

c/o Carmel Oriental

Alexandria, Egypt

At that time, negotiations were held over the allocation of land to veterans of the Jewish Legions in the Lower Galilee. These prolonged negotiations led nowhere (the Legionnaires' settlement of Aviha'il in central

Israel was only formed in 1932). The disenchanted Zilberman warned his friend not to join the project.

Quantara Feb. 6, [19]21
My Dear Friend and Comrade, Yehoshua Davidzon,
 I duly received your letter dated the 10th of January, and you will excuse me if today's letter will be brief. This is because I, somehow, don't feel like writing today. I feel a little depressed. I simply want to respond to the question you asked me—if the rumor that is circulating is true that the English government is willing to give the veteran Jewish soldiers 300 dunams[6] of land for 99 years for someone who has 1,000 pounds cash and is willing to put it in the ground. This means if a veteran soldier has 1,000 pounds and is willing to invest it in cultivating the 300 dunam of land, he can get the land right away. That is the rumor, but I have not yet heard of anyone who has gotten any land; first of all, because what veteran soldier has a thousand pounds, and second, if there was one who had a thousand pounds, he is not so anxious to put it into the land. Third, the place where the land is being offered is surrounded on all sides by Bedouins. There are only a few [other] people there and it is a horrible place to live. In such place, large groups are needed and it has to be a group where everyone wants to invest 1,000 pounds. So far, this is not to be found in Palestine. You write that there in America it is just about a sure thing, here in Palestine there are a lot of things that are still on shaky legs, while there it is a certainty. And concerning what is being said there [in America], that money is also being given to the land that is completely false. Let me ask you personally: who is going to give this money, if the rich aunt (America) has stopped giving the money?
 Concerning me personally—there is no news. Things are very bad for me. I am suffering greatly. I am sick and tired of being among these Gentiles. Oh, how awful it is to be with these damned, English Gentiles.

In another letter, written in the British army camp of Quantara on March 11, 1921, Zilberman reminded his friend that, as their common experience in the Legions had taught them, British promises could not be trusted for "the orders given today are rescinded tomorrow" and that Davidzon should therefore get the idea of settling in Palestine out of his head. The letter is indicative of the discourse that had taken place in many American households between Zionists who felt an urge to settle the land and those who considered the prevailing conditions there too hard to endure.

You were in Palestine and know very well that building up Palestine will take more than human efforts. I think that you also know the Palestine community somewhat. So how can you speak such foolishness?
 Listen Davidzon, I have already written to you several times and asked you, just like a father asks his own child, to put Palestine out of your mind, at least for a while, because this is a scourge that will ruin you physically

and emotionally. But from what I can see this is already so deeply rooted in you that you cannot get it out of your head. In that case, I would advise you not to make a mistake and not bother anyone with this [matter], not even your fiancée, because what do you have against her, a nice girl, a good child. Why should she suffer from your madness? Pack up and come to Palestine. You will enter a colony. You will spend 2 days working in the colony, then 2 days on the railroad and on the roads and suffer starvation and fevers and not have a penny in your pocket. Then you will write to friends in America [asking them] to send you money to come back. Your friends will send you the money and I hope that you will return healthy and cured and you will not suffer, and then you can tell others not to bother their heads with this.

That, I think, is the best cure for your disease. My friend Davidzon, I rolled up my sleeves [in preparation] to write you a long letter and discuss the question of your group and convince you of how foolish it is and you would be cured, but the problem is different. Your disease is, after all, not the land scourge, it is the Palestine scourge. So I would rather not speak about your group at all. Do as I wrote you, and then you will be cured.

The letter expressed the frustration felt by many Zionists over their own need to rely on financial aid from abroad, just like the unproductive Jews who lived in the holy sites before the advent of Zionism. At the same time, it reflected the tendency of many American Zionists to contribute to the settlement effort in Palestine by sending money so that others could settle there.

I am in complete agreement with the American Zionists, who have stopped giving money to those in Palestine, because if I am giving money, I want to know what the money is for. But I hope that the messengers [collectors], who have just left for America, will straighten out these questions and America will once again begin to give money. I am, however, certain of one thing that if, through good management, American dollars will build Palestine, I am more than certain that it will not be the American Jew who builds Palestine. The American dollar yes; the American Jew no way! The American dollar and the Polish, Russian and Galician Jew, that is a good combination. It will provide clothes for the Palestinian [Jews] and that will build Palestine, but when? . . . When the American Jew will come here and with the hands of a tailor or a doctor build Palestine?

Zilberman explained that while Russian or Polish Jews who came from oppressive regimes could adapt to the conditions prevailing in Palestine, American Jews, used to living in a free society, would not.

And when an American young man comes to Palestine and says that he wants to build Palestine with his tailor's hands and American freedom and American equality in his head, then he will not only be ruined himself but he will ruin the settlement. This is the reason that I am always writing you to get Palestine out of your head. It is a lost cause. Once you have tasted America and soaked up the ideas of freedom, then I must discourage you from coming to Palestine to work. Oh, but if you want to come to Palestine with a lot of money and start a business here in the American way, well, that you see is something different. But that requires a lot of money. So would it not be better for you to give up the idea of Palestine now and put your energies into making money? Then you will be a blessing for this land.

He was glad that former members of the Legion who were in New York were getting together and reminiscing about the good times they had in the Legion. Citing a Hebrew song based on Psalms 133, "Behold, how good and how pleasant it is for brethren to dwell together in unity," he wrote, "Oh how I would love to be there with you," and talked as if he was himself at a veterans' get-together.

Has Yoysef Mendelson gotten more mature? I hope so. The proof is that he has become a father. Tell him mazal tov [good luck] from me, but a sincere, heartfelt mazal tov, and may he merit to raise him [the child] to Torah, the wedding canopy, and good deeds. Heartfelt regards to Asher Suskind, to Shayn, to Beskind and to all the guys, whoever you run into. Sincere regards to your sister and brother and their families as well as your dear fiancée and all of your loved ones and friends, your comrade, B. Zilberman.

No wonder the writer felt a certain despondency. With the era of soldierly comradeship over, even the landscape no longer seemed filled with biblical images.

Quantara March 17, [19]21
My Dear Friend, Yehoshua Davidzon,
    Sitting now in the tent, a thin rain is falling outside but there is a lot of wind. It is a dark night and my heart and soul are melancholy. [I am] far from friends and feel abandoned somewhere in the desert, actually the same desert where Jews sanctified themselves and prepared to receive Holiness itself. Actually, here in this desert, Jews received all of Judaism, the Torah, but, nevertheless, I am sitting here alone today. There are no Jews [here]. Everyone around is Gentile, just Gentile. There is not a trace of those former Jews: not a trace of that former Judaism.

Instead of the Legions' songs that had warmed his heart just two years earlier, the former soldier was now listening to songs sung by drunken soldiers in a nearby military canteen or to the sad, heartrending selections of longing by an Egyptian in the distance (believed to be "enslaved to the damned English"). As the following paragraph indicates, Zilberman's misfortunes were largely the result of his own making.

I have already been here for 7 months, suffering in all ways. For what? So that I can save up for a ticket to America. Not, God forbid, so that I can actually travel to America, God forbid, but so that I can with a lighter heart go to work on the roads in Palestine. And I almost had the money saved up, but the devil got mixed up in this swindle: a Ford automobile that I bought with a partner. I had thought to make several pounds on this [deal]. In short, now it looks like I will, God forbid, lose all the money I invested. I close my letter with the hope that my next letter will be a happier one.

Your friend and comrade, B. Zilberman

Sincere regards to all my friends. Tell all of my friends that I do not mention anyone's name, not because he is, God forbid, not important but because all of them are very important to me, and I send all of them regards from the depths of my heart.

On May Day of 1921, another round of riots broke out in the Middle East. Following a skirmish between an unauthorized demonstration of Bolshevik Jews in Tel Aviv and an authorized demonstration of a more moderate Jewish socialist faction, the Achdut Ha'avoda (United Labor Party), Arabs from the neighboring city of Jaffa attacked Jewish shops and homes and a conflict of great violence between Arabs and Jews erupted. During these riots, which lasted for a week, Legionnaires stationed in Serafend defied an order to stay idle in the camp and intervened, an event which led to the dismissal of their commander Eliezer Margolin from the British army and to the final dispersal of the Jewish Legions. The riots spread to five Jewish settlements, including Peta'h Tikva and Re'hovot.[7] Later in the month, anti-European riots erupted in the Egyptian towns of Cairo and Alexandria, violence that Zilberman himself witnessed.

May 23, [19]21

My Dear Friend Yehoshua Davidzon,

It has been quite a while since I wrote to you, and now that I am writing to you, I write at a time when I am very upset. You will certainly very soon read in the newspapers about the disturbances in Egypt in general and in Alexandria in particular. . . . Well, this house is made of brick and we have barricaded ourselves with boards and with stones. A guard has to sit by the door. The guard changes every hour. I have just come off guard duty—holding my soul and my life in my hands. So I write you this letter. You might think that the pogrom was specifically directed at Jews, God forbid. It is not like that at all. Here the British are not wanted and along with the British come the Europeans, so they are fighting us as Europeans. I am struggling to discover the difference between being beaten in Jaffa for being Jewish and being beaten here for being European. It seems to me that the blows are the same and hurt equally. But that is the way things are and we are being beaten. I am sitting here and writing and every minute there is crashing and shooting. Oh, how awful it is. The number of dead just since last night is around 100 and so many wounded on both sides. Today, with my own eyes I saw a European beaten to death with a stick. Oh, how horrible!

Well, what do you expect after the "joys" of Jaffa? You have also surely read about the "joys" of Peta'h Tikva and Re'hovot. You have certainly read what the cause of all this is. But we are being kept out of Palestine and we have been promised better times. Well, isn't Zionism the same as our old beliefs? Our old faith keeps promising us that the future will be good: we will eat the great ox and the leviathan and all kinds of good things. Zionism and the Jewish government of Palestine also assure us that the future will be good. It seems that we have exchanged one thing for something not so different. What am I doing in Alexandria? Well, I myself do not know. But you can soon expect me in America! Right now, I am very upset, that is why I am ending my letter. Continue to write to me at the Jerusalem address. I hope that we will see each other soon.

Your friend and comrade, B. Zilberman

The months went by and the hapless Zilberman returned to Palestine with no money and no prospects.

Aug. 21, [19]21 Jaffa
Worthy Friend and Comrade, Yehoshua Davidzon,

As you see, I am already, thank God, in the land of Israel. I turned my hat around and returned. I traded America for the land of Israel. Idealistically speaking, it is not a bad trade, but practically speaking one does not compare to the other. I think that you are entitled to a clear explanation as to why I took this step.

On the 28th of June, I sent you a telegram asking you to send me 20 pounds. On the 15th of July a ship left that was going directly from Alexandria to New York. The boat ticket was very inexpensive. If you had sent the money out right away, as I thought [you would], I would have been in America long ago. But since I only received the money 5 weeks later, while I waited and ate, a large part of the few pounds that I had [was spent]. In addition there was also no longer an inexpensive ship [leaving] and since I could not get work in Egypt, there was nothing else I could do but go to Palestine!

I still have 20 pounds. Hopefully I will not have to touch that money, and just as soon as I get settled here, I hope to send it back to you! Right now I have been here for a week already and have not found anything. Since after the pogrom, things have been very bad here, but we hope that after the Carlsbad Congress things will improve.

I have a lot to write to you about, but somehow right now I do not feel like writing. I will write more in the next letter. Please forgive me.

Peace. Your friend B. Zilberman.
Sincere regards to all my friends, also to your brother and sister, your fiancée and your love.

The Carlsbad Congress Zilberman referred to was the twelfth congress of the World Zionist Organization, during which a resolution was adopted welcoming the British mandate over Palestine and calling for peaceful coexistence between Jews and Arabs in Palestine. Such a coexistence proved elusive, and the following letter, written after yet another flare-up of violence on November 2 (the fourth anniversary of the Balfour Declaration), expressed deep despair over the tense relationship between Arabs and Jews in the land.

> B. Silverman Tel Aviv-Jaffa Palestine
> Monday Nov. 7, [19]21
> My Dear Comrade and Friend, Yehoshua Davidzon,
>   I received your letter a long time ago and answered it a long time ago. Your New Year's greeting card . . . I received only several days ago, and I thank you very much. I actually do not have anything to write to you about right now, although my heart is heavy and I would like to unburden myself a bit, then perhaps I will feel a little better. It is not about my own personal problems that I want to talk to you about now, although there are more than enough of them. I want to talk a bit about the events that occurred in Jerusalem on the 2nd of November.

The letter first revisits the Easter riots of April 1920, referring to the British chief administrative officer at the time, General Louis Bols, who was warned beforehand that riots would erupt but dismissed the warning. It then mentions the messianic hopes accompanying Herbert Samuel's nomination as high commissioner for Palestine, and finally the disappointment in him following the May Day riots.

> During the first pogrom that occurred in Jerusalem about 18 months ago, when people asked if this was government [sanctioned], they were told that it was just a novelty, something new, because such a thing had never happened here before. That was why such a thing could not have been predicted and not prevented. . . . We later found out that General Bols, who was then the overseer of all Palestine including the civilians, was a rabid anti-Semite. We kept hoping that if a good Gentile would come, such a thing would not happen. (We never even dreamed that a Jew would take his place.) God helped, and instead of that flagrant anti-Semite, we got a Jew, and what a Jew! A Jew . . . who attends synagogue whenever he has the opportunity. A Jew . . . who when spoken to in Hebrew, answers in Hebrew right away. A Jew, who had a son in the army . . . in the Jewish Battalion, in the 40th division. (Do you remember that when we had just arrived in Quantara, a young officer spoke to us in Hebrew? That was his son.)[8] And all of Palestine rejoiced. This was nothing to sneeze at. The rabbis did not know what to do with him. Some compared him to Samuel the Prophet and others likened him to Nehemiah. The main point was that everyone was wild with joy. The Jews of the whole region were delighted, they were going out of their minds. One Jewish man shouted that he deserves all the credit for Samuel being sent to become High Commissioner.

This went on for so long, until God helped and it was the first of May 1921 and everyone was disappointed. What did this mean? A Jew sits on a bench and such a thing happens? Besides hurting so many Jews and making this pogrom. What will the world say? What will the Jewish capitalists say, those who want to come and invest money in Palestine in order to build it up? Who would dream of coming at this time, when a Jew's life is not certain and a Jew's property is up for grabs? The United Labor Party, they told the world that a bad element of Russian Jews had come to Palestine: Bolsheviks. And when they went out to demonstrate for the first time with red flags, the Arabs got all upset, and it led to a clash between the peaceful Arabs and the Bolsheviks. But we all know here that the conflict has just begun. It is 12 o'clock here, but in another part of the city, Jews were already being beaten an hour ago. The rest of the world does not know this or has glossed over this. And immediately afterwards, instead of punishing the real murderers with heavy penalties, so that they would know not to do it again, they picked on the Bolsheviks and sent them out of Palestine. And now is there peace in Palestine? What do they want now? What will the real murderers say now? It is not the mouse that stole but the person.

Zilberman's shock over the violence he witnessed on November 2 is clearly apparent in his writing.

Why did the old beadle from the synagogue deserve to be killed? Whom had he harmed? Whom did the 19 year old from Galicia harm? He came here to build Palestine and worked hard all day in construction. At night he did not even go to sleep but worked for Amdurski in the hotel, so that he could send something back to his elderly parents in Galicia. On the 2nd of November he was sure of his life, but there was an old woman, one of Amdurski's cleaning people, wanted to go home to her children but was afraid [to walk alone], so he walked with her. Why did this young man, only 19 years old, deserve to be murdered? Whom did this completely pure soul harm? The same for the other three. Why did the old rabbi, who was just walking in the street, deserve to be stabbed three times with a knife? What did they have against the little children? Why did they toss three bombs in the Talmud Torah [religious school]?

Making a comparison between the riots and the light-handed British approach to the rioters and the pogroms suffered by Jews, most recently during the civil war in the Ukraine, the writer cast doubt on the chances of the entire Zionist project.

Who knows? Who knows what reason they will yet think up to rationalize this pogrom too? My dear friend, it is very difficult to live here. Who knows if it is even worth it. Who knows if we are only suffering here for the Arabs' sakes, or in the best case, for the Evil Kingdom.[9] We are worthless here. Our lives are up for grabs. The sentence has been passed. The worst punishment was 1 year in jail. . . . One Arab was only fined a few pounds and he left the court like a royal minister. It cost me a few pounds, but the spectacle was worth it. Arabs still walk around in the streets today singing, "Palestine is Our Land." And the Jews are in their hands. It has become a kind of folk song for them.

Last night, when the train rode through Tel Aviv, rocks were thrown out at the Jews standing around looking, and nothing could be done. We have no one to defend us, and we are not permitted to defend ourselves. One of my friends, who works in a government office, said to me: "Oh, if you only knew what kind of orders the Army was getting in relation to the Jews. [It is] terrible, terrible!" And our great Jew sits in his palace on Mt. Scopus,[10] watches all this and pretends he knows anything about it. And when he gets tired of sitting, he either pops into the synagogue, where he is given all kinds of honors, or he goes for a stroll to visit the Arab sheiks, where he gets a royal payment. This is his pay for letting Jews be murdered. It is horrendous. How much longer must we wait? For how much longer will our lives be up for grabs in our national home? There is more that I could write, but let this be enough for now. I can do no more now!

My personal situation has still not improved. I am still not working. Oh, if only I could return to America. But how can I?

Write me about everything that is going on there. Some news. Have you gotten married yet? Your friend and comrade, who wishes you all the best. B. Zilberman

Sincere regards to all my friends, your fiancée, your sister and brothers and their families.

B. Silverman c/o Shmeril Ashkenazy
Shaare Zedeck Jerusalem Palestine

Winter was approaching and even the temporary jobs were disappearing. Zilberman was afraid of the coming winter and kept writing about his desire to travel to America, a dream that became more and more remote. The farther the fulfillment of the dream, the more sentimental his letters were. He longed for all his friends from the Legions who were back in America. When the year 1921 ended and 1922 set in, he realized he lacked the powers to cope with the problems he faced. He told Davidzon at length about an unpleasant experience he had believing he might get a job as vendor in the canteen wagon on a train but not getting it, accusing the British Mandate authorities for the faux pas. On December 12, 1921, he wrote, "Oh, my friend Davidzon, how bitter is the Evil Kingdom England. Wherever I go I am treated unjustly. What is being perpetrated against us Jews? It really looks like they are trying to take revenge on us. Oh brother, it is bad. The situation for us Jews is very bad in Palestine. What will be the end of my story? Who knows?" When Davidzon announced his marriage to his fiancée, Zilberman sent him, on January 19, 1922, warmest greetings and, realizing he would not be present when the former Legionnaires gathered for the wedding, made a last request: "Sincere regards to all friends . . . and when they will drink at your wedding, let them have a drink for me."

11

Existential Zionism

In 1918, the word spread in the small Jewish community in Palestine, devastated by four years of war, that a massive force of Jews led by Jabotinsky was making its way to liberate the Promised Land. In spite of the fear of retaliation by the Turks, who still controlled large parts of northern Palestine when Allenby entered Jerusalem in December 1917, the elated community began to enlist volunteers to the British army. In March 1918, Jabotinsky arrived with the 38th Fusiliers at the port of Alexandria and went to Tel Aviv, where he was welcomed by the political leaders of the community with enthusiasm that soon, however, turned into disappointment. While he spoke of the Jewish Legions as a political force intended to make a difference in a coming peace conference, which required that Jews joining the British army turn into disciplined soldiers who fulfill their military duties with devotion, they referred to the volunteer movement in terms derived from a socialist jargon he could not identify with, such as "self-fulfillment."[1]

This was the beginning of a strained relationship. When the Legionnaires from abroad began to show up in Jewish settlements in Palestine or were met by the volunteers from Palestine, most of whom served in the 40th Fusiliers, in the training camp in Tel El-Kabir, they were often treated with a sense of estrangement. To the Palestinian Jews, especially the socialists among them, the Yiddish-speaking Legionnaires did not seem to match the ideal of the "new Jew,"[2] who is expected to speak Hebrew and abandon old Jewish traditions for the sake of a new form of productive life allowing the formation of a just society. To them, the ultimate product of Zionism, the Jewish national movement, was the pioneer holding a scythe in one hand, and a gun in the other. This image of the free and muscular farmer-soldier through which they portrayed themselves can be found in the annals of many national movements, especially those developing their cultural identities while settling new geographic frontiers.

The educational system and popular culture in frontier states have always preferred the lone hero to the diverse public plodding along. This is why the South American gaucho and the North American cowboy with their "rugged individualism, unbending principle, frontier spirit, and manly courage"[3] have been mythologized. Various studies have shown how the romanticized image of the illiterate horse- and cattle-raising gauchos of the Argentine prairies served Argentina's national elites at times when urban immigrant masses came up with demands for socialism, electoral reform, and workers' rights.[4] North American popular culture has similarly nurtured the image of the lone cowboy riding west.[5] In his study of the myth of the frontier in twentieth-century America, Richard Slotkin shows how the violence attributed to the cowboy has functioned in the formation of American national identity. The violent cowboy helped shape the identity of those who have freed themselves both from the "savage" of the American wilderness and the metropolitan regime of authoritarian politics and class privilege.

The Zionist movement took a similar path, although the pioneer symbol required quite an adjustment due to the difficulty of ignoring the historical image of the "wandering Jew," aligned not with a lone hero but with the ordinary Jewish family, whose men, women, elders, and children are moving from exile to exile with packs containing few belongings on their backs. A great intellectual effort was needed to devise the symbolism of the "new Jew," who would resemble the gaucho or the cowboy more than the ordinary Jewish family. Such an effort was made wherever Jews were involved in settlement of land. In 1910, writer Albert Gerchunoff represented the Jewish settlement in Argentina in his novel *The Jewish Gauchos of the Pampas*, while Jewish rural settlement in the United States produced such works as Isaac Raboy's Yiddish novel *The Jewish Cowboy*, describing the author's experiences as a settler in North Dakota at the beginning of the twentieth century.[6]

While these literary works kept a balance between old Jewish traditions and the pioneering experience, Jewish settlers in Palestine mostly stripped the new experience of its traditional roots. They considered themselves avant-garde while seeing Jews in the Diaspora as landless, living a life of exile, dependent on the mercy of strangers, and engaged in traditional occupations (such as tailoring) unworthy of independent people living in their own land and controlling their own destiny.[7]

Historian Shmuel Almog explains the ambivalence toward Diaspora Jews by the mixed feelings of the pioneers toward them. Although on one hand, the pioneers were proud to have left home, on the other hand, the difficulties awaiting them in the new land—scarcity, unemployment, and skirmishes with local Arabs—endowed the life back home with a certain appeal. The way these young people coped with this ambivalence, Almog suggests, was by stressing their own self-sacrifice in striving to build a new society and a new race of man, as opposed to people back home, like their parents, who were preoccupied with the petty matters of raising families and pursuing petit bourgeois hopes.[8]

A similar attitude was applied to the Jewish Legionnaires from abroad, in spite of the fact that they came to fight for the land of Israel and could also be seen as an avant-garde. It was inconceivable that Yiddish-speaking Jews who held on to their language and religious tradition could also perceive themselves as descendents of the Maccabees and Simon Bar Kokhba.

Signs of the estrangement felt by Labor Zionists toward the Jewish soldiers from abroad (which, incidentally, was also directed at recruits from the Orthodox and Sephardi communities in Jerusalem and Alexandria) can be detected in a column called "Bagdudim" (In the Battalions) appearing in the Labor Party's weekly, *Kuntres*. The column was devoted to short pieces written by comrades who served in the Jewish Legions, who often complained about the spiritual void they felt in the British military barracks. A way to overcome that spiritual void was to teach the Legionnaires from abroad Hebrew, thus turning them into worthy pioneers. As one soldier writes, "the Hebrew lessons that were arranged attracted many soldiers and introduced an opportunity for the 'better ones' to influence the 'lesser ones.'" He tells of the commotion in the barracks when the "better ones" prepared for a ceremony commemorating Theodor Herzl, founder of the Zionist movement, on the day of his death: "We decorated the hall, arranged for ribbons and tickets, a choir, and even produced a written booklet whose importance lay not in its literary value but in representing the social spirit of our company." He notes that during the ceremony, everybody's eyes were tearing, and even the commanders admitted they had never experienced such an emotional event in their military careers. He writes that such moments in which Ashkenazi (European-born), Sephardi (Middle East–born), American, and English Jews share in a common sentiment of hope, trust, and confidence are of great importance to both sides: those committed to teaching the labor movement's values and those expected to acquire them.[9]

The notion that the soldiers belonging to the Jewish labor movement in Palestine were endowed with the mission to bequeath the movement's values to all others is reflected in another letter sent to *Kuntres* during the dismantling of the 40th Battalion in 1920. The writer admits that he and his comrades failed in making their service in the British army a lever for the construction of a Hebrew military force. They should have been more insistent, for example, in their demand that the Hebrew language be used in the barracks and replace English military expressions like "cookhouse" and "bugle." And he adds:

> Pass by the tents in the evenings and listen: fellows speaking in their tents Hebrew, jargon [probably referring to Yiddish], Spanish, Arabic, English, Turkish, Russian, etc. As if all of these have not become obscure . . . in the last two years. Our hope is that the Hebrew military camp becomes the first school in which the volunteer who comes from the Diaspora would learn the language, the [conditions of the] country, our ways of life and aspirations . . . for how will the mass of newcomers who will arrive in the Land from different places, with different ideas and opinions, with different customs and habits, be molded into the new type—the young Hebrew?

Another soldier writes about the need to care for the families of former Jewish Turkish prisoners who ended up serving in the Legions. As he expresses his concern for their families, he notes the gap between the soldiers from Turkey and the pioneers from Palestine in terms of language, customs, and ways of thought. He admits that these Turkish Jews possess strong, genuine national feelings but considers these feelings to be incomplete because they are solely rooted in religious faith. He reports with satisfaction that when these foreigners met the pioneers from Palestine, they became familiar with Hebrew as a spoken language, not just as the language of the prayer book, and with the land of Israel as a reality, not just a religious dream. He is also glad to report that they had begun to show interest in "important things,"[10] apparently referring to the long speeches by Labor Party leaders.

Particularly instructive is a *Kuntres* item written by D. Gogol, who served with the soldiers from abroad in the 38th Fusiliers stationed in the desert towns of Rafa and El Arish. He refers to that battalion as the "stepson" of the Jewish settlers in the land of Israel and blames the negative attitude toward it on, among other factors, the "human element" composing the battalion, which, he admits, is unattractive to the "workers' cultural forces." He accepts what seems to be a common contention—that the activities conducted by the 38th may not be conducive to "our national affairs"—but claims that the activities are important. The battalion was stationed along a 220-kilometer line from Quantara to Gaza; protected water-pumping stations; guarded trains going to Damascus, Cairo, and Beer Sheva; and engaged in hard tasks, such as the loading and unloading of trains, that no "white" English soldiers were asked to perform. Gogol writes that although the "poor creature" manning the 38th Battalion does not share the ideals propounded (but not always fulfilled) by the Zionist leaders, he came from afar to save the nation's honor and should therefore be treated more decently. At the time of his writing, the battalion's soldiers had difficulty in obtaining books for their library or getting local lecturers to come and speak to them. Even the public concerts given by their musicians were not attended by the local population.[11]

These examples suffice to illustrate the attitude of many Palestinian Jews, especially those belonging to the labor movement, who defined themselves as Zionists and considered the foreign Legionnaires as non-Zionists. As we have seen in the introduction, that distinction was prevalent in writings about the Legions. The life-writing perspective we took in this study, however, makes one question the distinction between Zionists and non-Zionists among the Legionnaires. Following the thoughts and feelings of young, often displaced immigrants who were drafted into the British army, we uncovered the development of a form of consciousness that may be called existential Zionism: that is, identification with the cause of the redemption of Zion that is more related to religious sources than to ideological formulations.

The Jewish Legions in the British army never became poster heroes of the Zionist movement. Even the founder of the Legions, Jabotinsky, who recognized their courage in the battles of 1918, was never able to reconcile the fantasy he had about a Jewish force that would conquer Canaan by storm with the tailors and shoemakers he managed to mobilize as members of that force. In their memoirs, Legionnaires showed awareness of the little recognition they received from the Zionist movement, especially in the 1930s when the Palestine-centered socialist wing of the movement took control of the World Zionist Organization and both Jabotinsky and the British government fell out of favor.

The life-writing material discussed here, however, provides strong evidence of the development of an authentic, existential Zionist consciousness among the Legionnaires. When Miguel Krel of Warsaw, Chaim Baruch Berezin of Mohileff-Podolsk, and Ira Jacob Liss of Russia came to the New World to find refuge from persecution, they were not necessarily versed in the Zionist writings of Max Nordau, Theodor Herzl, and Ahad Ha'am. But when recruiters for the British army called upon them to liberate the Promised Land and they did, in their own eyes they turned into descendants of Old Testament judges and kings and of mythological figures like the Maccabees and Bar Kokhba. Whatever the degree of their religiosity, this transformation did not involve dismissal of their former religious heritage, nor did they acquire any persona promoted by the Zionist movement or its socialist wing in Palestine. On the contrary, they negotiated the soldiering culture they were exposed to and the national mission they were endowed with within the parameters of their personalities and upbringings.

The Legionnaires needed little help from Zionist ideologues to frame their soldiering experience as a journey to the Promised Land, as this paradigm was consistent with their heritage. The anonymous soldier whose travelogue is discussed in chapter 3 naturally attributes to his passing through the Strait of Gibraltar on the way to Palestine a more sacred meaning than it had when he passed through it as a refugee from Russia. His wish to stay in the land of Israel stemmed not from grand ideas debated in Zionist congresses but from the refreshing feeling he got when a cool, mild breeze was blowing and he looked "at the long mountain range, at the lovely valley and at the clear blue sky covered with small, white clouds." Ira Jacob Liss, whose diary is presented in chapter 6, related his walk in the Egyptian desert to the frame of reference he grew up with as the son of a teacher of religion, feeling that the dry and sandy land on which he walked under a sun that beat down mercilessly was the same land his ancestors walked during the Exodus. His parade to the synagogue among fifteen hundred Jewish boys dressed in khaki drill suits, wearing helmets with blue Stars of David and carrying bayonets on their belts, made him envision himself and his comrades in the most genuine sense as "heroes of Israel." And the war widow who asked Reverend Falk, in the letter we included in chapter 7, whether a stone has been put on her poor husband's grave did so not out of concern for national emblems but as a religious woman demanding proper burial for her husband.

The "existential Zionism" of the Legionnaires, marked by such authenticity, stood in contrast to the common rhetoric of Zionism, which imagined the Jewish state as one of renewal rather than of tradition. In *The Jewish State*, Theodor Herzl wrote that "a wondrous generation of Jews will spring into existence," which would demand, among other things, that they "give up using those miserable stunted jargons, those Ghetto languages which we still employ, for these were the stealthy tongues of prisoners."[12]

The Legionnaires, however, did not give up the Yiddish jargon as they reflected on their journey to the Promised Land and absorbed their experiences—military life, encounters with soldiers of other nations, visits to faraway lands—within their own folklore and tradition. In doing so, they provided a unique viewpoint on modern Jewish nationalism. Zionism, calling upon Jews to live in the land of Israel, has been called "an authentic response to the existential situation of the modern Jew,"[13] but it developed a purified and idealized model of the pioneer who was to make the journey, while the Legionnaires' response to the notion of the Promised Land stood out for its authenticity. It was consistent with the original biblical tale of the Exodus—the prototype of liberation from house of bondage to Promised Land.[14] In that tale, it is not a selected avant-garde of pioneers that is endowed with the mission but, as Moses says to Pharaoh, "we will go with our young and with our old, with our sons and with our daughters, with our flocks and with our herds will we go" (Exodus 10:9). The varied group of Legionnaires from London, New York, Montreal, and Buenos Aires did not resemble the icons cherished by modern national movements, not even in their own perception, but they drew in their life writing a rich and colorful picture of the journey to the Promised Land in which everyone takes part: the displaced immigrant, the travelling singer, the perceptive young man, the British aristocrat, the chaplain, the brave combatant, and the soldier left behind.

We would like to conclude by stating that our focus in this study on identity formation on the individual level seems to be in line with the way the Legionnaires themselves perceived their experience. In December 1949, a group of veterans of the Jewish Legions met in Aviha'il, the rural settlement in central Israel where some of them settled after the war, and decided to build a Legions House that would serve as a museum and an academy for military studies. Being aware that their contribution was less acknowledged than that of Israel's prestate military formations associated with the symbol of the "new Jew," they decided to emphasize the individual dimension of their service in the Legions. They collected personal memoirs, diaries, newspaper clippings, and photos to be housed in the museum. The true tales of the Legions, they said, are buried at the back of drawers in the houses of an old farmer in Britain, a scientist in New York, or a settler in Israel.

At the Legions' fiftieth-anniversary celebrations, Dov (Bernard) Joseph of the 39th Fusiliers declared:

> The Jewish Legion was a living symbol of the will and fervent aspiration of the Jews to national revival. The very idea of establishment [of] a Jewish Legion to redeem Palestine was in the nature of a revolution in the life of the Jewish people dispersed as it was among the nations of the world, a nation not yet recognized by the world as such, a nation many of whose sons refused to consider it a nation. The recruitment and actual existence of such a Jewish Legion was decisive proof of the existence of a Jewish People, since it entailed, in a measure, the normalization of the people.[15]

It is interesting that Joseph, a Canadian Zionist youth leader who became a prominent cabinet minister in Israel, did not refer to the Legions' contribution to the establishment of the state. Joseph, like many veterans, realized that the Legions were first and foremost a locus for the development of a military culture and national identity among individuals. And while the consciousness of individual soldiers has always received less attention in history than the actions and rhetoric of the prominent leaders and generals who sent them to war, our focus on identity formation among the nonprominent may be seen, in some way, as partial fulfillment of the Legionnaires' own wish to be remembered.

Notes

CHAPTER 1

1. Yitzhak Ben-Zvi, *The Jewish Legion: Letters* [in Hebrew] (Jerusalem: Yad Ben Zvi, 1967).

2. Roman Freulich, *Soldiers in Judea: Stories and Vignettes of the Jewish Legion* (New York: Herzl Press, 1964), 31.

3. Freulich, *Soldiers in Judea*, 33.

4. David Todis, "From Riga to Lawrence of Arabia," file no. 39, document 2, Legions House, Aviha'il, Israel.

5. Baruch Gurevitz, "Extraordinary Encounters," 40th Legion, file 4b, Legions House.

6. Eric J. Leed, *No Man's Land: Combat and Identity in World War I* (Cambridge: Cambridge University Press, 1979), 204.

7. Edgar Wallace, *Kitchener's Army and the Territorial Forces* (London: George Newnes, undated).

8. Ian F. W. Beckett, *The Great War 1914–1918* (Harlow, UK: Longman, 2007), 295.

9. Todd M. Endelman, *Jews of Modern Britain, 1656–2000* (Berkeley: University of California Press, 2002), 185.

10. Michael Berkowitz, *Western Jewry and the Zionist Project, 1914–1933* (Cambridge: Cambridge University Press, 1997), 11.

11. Christopher M. Sterba, *Good Americans: Italian and Jewish Immigrants during the First World War* (New York: Oxford University Press, 2003), 54.

12. Sterba, *Good Americans*, 29.

13. Berkowitz, *Western Jewry and the Zionist Project*, 20.

14. Cecilia Elizabeth O'Leary, *To Die For: The Paradox of American Patriotism* (Princeton, NJ: Princeton University Press, 1999), 237.

15. Peter Simkins, *Kitchner's Army: The Raising of the New Armies, 1914–16* (Manchester, UK: Manchester University Press, 1988).

16. Stuart A. Cohen, *English Zionists and British Jews: The Communal Politics of Anglo-Jewry, 1895–1920* (Princeton, NJ: Princeton University Press, 1982), 216.

17. *Jewish Chronicle*, December 25, 1914.

18. Martin Watts, *The Jewish Legions and the First World War* (New York: Macmillan, 2004); Igal Elam, *Hagdudim Ha'ivri'im Bemilhemet Ha'olam Harishona* [The Jewish Legions in the First World War] (Tel Aviv: Ma'arachot, 1984); Ze'ev Jabotinsky, *Megilat Hagdud* [The story of the battalion] (Tel Aviv: Ministry of Defense, 1991).

19. John Henry Patterson, *With the Judeans in the Palestine Campaign* (New York: Macmillan, 1922); Denis Brian, *The Seven Lives of Colonel Patterson: How an Irish Lion Hunter Led the Jewish Legion to Victory* (Syracuse, NY: Syracuse University Press, 2008).

20. Brian Porter, "Britain and the Middle East in the Great War," in *Home Fires and Foreign Fields: British Social and Military Experience in the First World War*, ed. Peter Liddle (London: Pergamon, 1985), 159–74.

21. See David R. Woodward, *Hell in the Holy Land: World War I in the Middle East* (Lexington: University of Kentucky Press, 2006).

22. Brian, *The Seven Lives of Colonel Patterson*, 122.

23. Arthur Hertzberg, *The Jews in America* (New York: Simon & Schuster, 1989), 232.

24. See Cate Haste, *Keep the Home Fires Burning: Propaganda in the First World War* (London: Allen Lane, 1977); Troy R. E. Paddock, ed., *A Call to Arms: Propaganda, Public Opinion, and Newspapers in the Great War* (Westport, CT: Praeger, 2004).

25. Elam, *Hagdudim Ha'ivri'im*, 153.

26. King James Bible, Lamentations 1:6.

27. Christian Classics, www.ccel.org/ccel/bunyan/pilgrim.titlepage.html.

28. Paul Fussell, *The Great War and Modern Memory* (London: Oxford University Press, 1975), 138–39.

29. Quoted ibid., 139.

30. Quoted in Elias Gilner, *War and Hope: A History of the Jewish Legion* (New York: Herzl Press, 1969), 177.

31. *Toronto Globe*, April 30, 1918.

32. *Toronto Globe*, May 30, 1918.

33. Undated clip, general file 8b, document 37, Legions House.

34. Yehuda Slutzsky, "Diary of the Life of Yehuda Slutzsky," 39th Legion file, document 3, Legions House.

35. Deborah Dash Moore, *GI Jews: How World War II Changed a Generation* (Cambridge, MA: Harvard University Press, 2004), 84.

36. Moore, *GI Jews*, 54.

37. See David Taylor, "From Fighting the War to Writing the War: From Glory to Guilt?" *Contemporary British History* 23, no. 3 (September 2009): 293–313.

38. Edna Lomsky Feder, "The Meaning of War through Veterans' Eyes: A Phenomenological Analysis of Life Stories," *International Sociology* 10, no. 4 (December 1995): 463–82.

39. Leed, *No Man's Land*.
40. Leo Braudy, *From Chivalry to Terrorism* (New York: Vintage, 2005).

CHAPTER 2

1. Albert Lichtblau and Michael John, "Jewries in Galicia and Bukovina, in Lemberg and Czernowitz: Two Divergent Examples of Jewish Communities in the Far East of the Austro-Hungarian Monarchy," Universität Salzburg, January 14, 2009, www.sbg.ac.at/ges/people/lichtblau/cape.html.

CHAPTER 3

1. William R. Taylor, *The Twentieth Century World: An International History* (New York: Oxford University Press, 1984).
2. See J. Glenn Gray, *The Warriors: Reflections on Men in Battle* (New York: Harper & Row, 1970).
3. Woodward, *Hell in the Holy Land*, 43.

CHAPTER 4

1. Colonel Fred Samuel, a Jewish British officer, was commander of the Crown Hill training camp and later of the 40th Battalion.
2. The diarist is probably referring to Chaim Broytman, a barrel maker in the Rishon Lezion winery, and his second wife, Hanna (his first wife died in 1917).
3. Cyril Falls, *Military Operations: Egypt and Palestine from June 1917 to the End of the War* (London: HM Stationary Office, 1930), 423.
4. While the number of casualties in the Jewish Legions is unknown, it is estimated that malaria affected as many as 80 percent of the soldiers who served in the Jordan Valley. See Watts, *The Jewish Legions*, 187.
5. Gilner, *War and Hope*, 251.
6. This is probably a reference to David Levitan, an artist and member of Hashomer, an organization offering guard services, who was killed near Re'hovot in August 1913.
7. Gilner, *War and Hope*, 254.

CHAPTER 5

1. Jabotinsky, *Megilat Hagdud*.
2. Watts, *The Jewish Legions*, 130–31.
3. Exodus 13:21.

CHAPTER 6

1. This is a reference to Exodus 18:21 and 25.
2. "Khantshe in America" is a Yiddish operetta composed in Russia in 1913.
3. The Shema is a prayer beginning with the words "Hear, O Israel! The Lord is our God! The Lord is One!"
4. Menorah, meaning lamp, refers here to the seven-branched candelabrum used in the Temple in Jerusalem. This menorah became a major Jewish emblem.
5. Woodward, *Hell in the Holy Land*, 199.
6. Gilner, *War and Hope*, 247.
7. Eran Dolev, *Allenby's Military Medicine: Life and Death in World War I Palestine* (New York: I. B. Tauris, 2007), 162.
8. Woodward, *Hell in the Holy Land*, 199.
9. Liss is probably referring here to recruits from Alexandria.
10. The diarist is likely referring to the battle of Tel El-Kabir, the last major battle in the Anglo-Egyptian war of 1882.
11. Patterson, *With the Judeans*, 180.
12. This quote is from Genesis 31:40.
13. This quote is from Micah 4:4 and Kings 1:5.
14. A "French leave" is a quick departure or absence without explanation, announcement, or permission.
15. Bata LoBagola, *An African Savage's Own Story* (London: Knopf, 1930).
16. David Killingray and Willie Henderson, "Bata Kindai Amgoza Ibn LoBagola and the Making of *An African Savage's Own Story*," in *Africans on Stage: Studies in Ethnological Show Business*, ed. Bernth Lindfors (Bloomington: Indiana University Press, 1999), 228–65.

CHAPTER 7

1. J. H. Patterson, letter to Colonel John Wynne of December 7, 1917, Falk Private Papers, IDF Archive, Tel HaShomer, Israel.
2. L. I. Falk, "With the Jewish Battalions in Palestine: Memoirs of a Jewish Chaplain," *The Maccabean*, memoirs serialized from February 15, 1929, to November 15, 1929.
3. Patterson, *With the Judeans*.
4. War Cabinet Extracts 227 from September 3, 1917, Letters and Memos, file 6–26, Jabotinsky Archive, Tel Aviv.
5. *Evening Standard*, September 12, 1917.
6. Jonathan Hyman, *Jews in Britain during the Great War*, Department of History Working Paper 51 (University of Manchester, UK, October 2001).
7. *The Maccabean*, February 15, 1929.
8. *The Maccabean*, February 15, 1929.
9. Michael Snape, *God and the British Soldier: Religion and the British Army in the First and Second World Wars* (London: Routledge, 2005).
10. Doris L. Bergen, *The Sword of the Lord: Military Chaplains from the First to the Twenty-First Century* (Notre Dame, IN: University of Notre Dame Press, 2004);

Duff Crerar, *Padres in No Man's Land: Canadian Chaplains and the Great War* (Montreal: McGill-Queen's University Press, 1995).

11. On Jewish chaplains in the British army, see Michael Adler, ed., *British Jewry Book of Honour* (London: Caxton, 1922). On Jewish chaplains in the American army, see Albert Isaac Slomovitz, *The Fighting Rabbis: Jewish Military Chaplains and American History* (New York: New York University Press, 1999).

12. *The Maccabean*, February 15, 1929.

13. L. I. Falk Private Papers, IDF Archive.

14. Letter by Mrs. Malkin, L. I. Falk Private Papers, IDF Archive.

15. *The Maccabean*, May 3, 1929.

16. Ibid.

17. Richard Schweitzer, *The Cross and the Trenches: Religious Faith and Doubt among British and American Great War Soldiers* (Westport, CT: Praeger, 2003), 47.

18. Robinson memoirs, 38th Legion, file 2b, document 3, Legions House (see chapter 5).

19. H. D. Myer, *Excerpts from Letters* [of] *H. D. Myer 1918–1919*, Legions House Library, 98.

20. *The Maccabean*, March 22, 1929.

21. *The Maccabean*, March 8, 1929.

22. *The Maccabean*, March 22, 1929.

23. Ibid.

24. *The Maccabean*, April 5, 1929.

25. Ibid.

26. Ibid.

27. *The Maccabean*, April 26, 1929.

28. Falk Private Papers, IDF Archive.

29. Ibid.

30. Ibid.

31. Ibid.

32. Ibid.

33. Fussell, *The Great War*.

34. Israel Meir Cohen, *Ma'hane Israel*, www.hebrewbooks.org/33289.

35. Clarence L. Abercrombie, *The Military Chaplain* (Beverly Hills, CA: Sage, 1977).

36. *The Maccabean*, April 5, 1929.

37. Falk Private Papers, IDF Archive.

38. Professor Boris Schatz to Rabbi Falk in spring 1919, Falk Private Papers, IDF Archive.

39. "A Temple in the Wilderness: Bezalel in Jerusalem," Israel Museum, January 25, 2009, www.imj.org.il/eng/exhibitions/2006/schatz/bezalel_jerusalem .html.

40. Abraham Isaac Kook, "The Significance of the Revival," in *Abraham Isaac Kook: The Lights of Penitence, the Moral Principles, Lights of Holiness, Essays, Letters, and Poems*, trans. Ben Zion Bokser (New York: Paulist Press, 1978), 286.

41. Zvi Yaron, *Mishnato Shel Harav Kook* [The philosophy of Rabbi Kook] (Jerusalem: Jewish Agency, 1974), 280.

42. *Igrot Ha'raih* [Rabbi Kook's collected letters], volume 3 (Jerusalem: Mossad Harav Kook, 1965), 136–38.

43. Falk Private Papers, IDF Archive.

44. Ibid.

45. Paul Goodman, *History of the Jews: Soldiers' and Sailors' Edition* (London: The Office of the Chief Rabbi, 1917).

46. Falk Private Papers, IDF Archive.

47. *The Maccabean*, November 15, 1929.

48. Jabotinsky, *Megilat Hagdud*, 133.

49. *The Maccabean*, February 22, 1929, 12.

50. Falk Private Papers, IDF Archive.

CHAPTER 8

1. Henry D. Myer, "Soldiering of Sorts," general folder, file 10, Legions House.

2. Mark Levene, "Going against the Grain: Two Jewish Memoirs of War and Anti-War, 1914–18," in *Forging Modern Jewish Identities: Public Faces and Private Struggles*, ed. Michael Berkowitz, Susan L. Tananbaum, and Sam W. Bloom (London: Vallentine Mitchell, 2003), 84.

3. Levene, "Going against the Grain," 105.

4. Myer, "Soldiering of Sorts," 98.

5. Ibid.

6. Ibid.

7. Ibid.

8. Ibid., 100.

9. Ibid., 101.

10. Ibid., 103–4. June 15, 1918.

11. Ibid., 106. July 3, 1918.

12. The *shophar* is a horn blown as part of the ritual of the Jewish High Holidays in the autumn. In his annotation, Myer wrote that "[t]he Shophar is the ancient ram's horn, which from the time of Moses, and later Joshua, was blown much as a bugle is blown in the infantry and Marines." Ibid., 118.

13. Ibid., 125. September 26, 1918.

14. Ibid., 127. October 7, 1918.

15. Ibid., 129. October 15, 1918.

16. Ibid., 140. November 18, 1918.

17. Ibid., 147. December 11, 1918.

18. Ibid., 159. January 16, 1919.

19. Ibid., 170. March 9, 1919.

20. Ibid., 176. March 30, 1919.

CHAPTER 9

1. Benjamin Bronstein, "Memoirs," 40th Fusiliers, file 4b, Legions House. This document has no successive page numbers. Therefore, the quotations in this chapter are given without additional referencing.

2. That youngster, incidentally, was Moshe Dayan, who later became Israel's chief of staff and minister of defense.

CHAPTER 10

1. The two Legionnaires who fell with Trumpeldor in Tel Hai were Ze'ev Scharf and Yaakov Toker.

2. See Naomi Shepherd, *Ploughing Sand: British Rule in Palestine, 1917–1948* (London: John Murray, 1999) and Martin Kolinsky, *Law, Order and Riots in Mandatory Palestine, 1928–1935* (London: St. Martin's Press, 1993).

3. Zilberman was probably referring here to the World Zionist Organization meeting called for July 1920 in London.

4. See Michael J. Cohen, *Palestine to Israel: From Mandate to Independence* (London: Cass, 1988).

5. This quotation comes from the biblical book of Esther. Mordecai tells Esther that if she will not help the Jews, help will come from elsewhere.

6. This refers to a measure of land—one *dunam* equals one thousand square meters.

7. See Albert M. Hyamson, *Palestine under the Mandate, 1920–1948* (Westport, CT: Greenwood, 1950).

8. Edwin Samuel, Herbert Samuel's son, served in the Royal Field Artillery and was part of Allenby's Egyptian Expeditionary Force. In August 1918, he volunteered to serve as a training officer for the 40th Fusiliers, and after the armistice, he returned to the British military headquarters.

9. This is a reference to Great Britain.

10. This is a reference to the high commissioner's residence in Jerusalem.

CHAPTER 11

1. See Ahuvia Malkin, *Eliahu Golomb: Biography* [in Hebrew] (Tel Aviv: Am-Oved, 2007), 186.

2. See George L. Mosse, "Max Nordau, Liberalism and the New Jew," *Journal of Contemporary History* 27 (October 1992): 565–81.

3. Richard Slatta, *Cowboys of the Americas* (New Haven, CT: Yale University Press, 1990), 91.

4. Donald S. Castro, "The Gaucho Revival in Argentina in the 1930s and 1940s," *Studies in Latin American Popular Culture* 14 (1995): 171–89.

5. Tom R. Sullivan, *Cowboys and Caudillos: Frontier Ideology of the Americas* (Bowling Green, OH: Bowling Green State University Press, 1990).

6. Debra Shein, "Isaac Raboy's *Der Yiddisher Cowboy* and Rachel Calof's *My Story*: The Role of the Western Frontier in Shaping Jewish American Identity," *Western American Literature* 36 (Winter 2002): 359–80.

7. Michael Keren, "National Icons and Personal Identities in Three Israeli Autobiographies," *Biography* 27 (Spring 2004): 357–83.

8. Shmuel Almog, *"He'halutz Hametaphori* Mul Hazikna Hagalutit"* [The metaphorical pioneer against "diaspora-driven old age"], in *Idan Hazionut* [The era of Zionism], ed. Anita Shapira et al., 91–108 (Jerusalem: Shazar Center, 2000).

9. A., "Bagdudim" [In the Legions], *Kuntres* 10 (1918): 27.

10. D. H., "Lemazav Anshei Hagdud Miturkia Umishpa'hotei'hem" [The condition of the Turkish members of the battalion and their families], *Kuntres* 7 (1918): 37.

11. D. Gogol, "Haben Ha'horeg" [The stepson], *Kuntres* 2 (1918): 35–37.

12. Theodor Herzl, *The Jewish State*, 1896, Jewish Virtual Library, www.jewish virtuallibrary.org/jsource/Zionism/herzl2.html.

13. Paul R. Mendes-Flohr, "Between Existentialism and Zionism," *Journal of the American Academy of Religion* 47 (1979): 429–40.

14. Michael Walzer, *Exodus and Revolution* (New York: Basic Books, 1984).

15. File 8d, document 50, Legions House.

Bibliography

Abercrombie, Clarence L. *The Military Chaplain*. Beverly Hills, CA: Sage, 1977.

Abramson, Glenda. *Hebrew Writing of the First World War*. London: Vallentine Mitchell, 2008.

Adler, Michael, ed. *British Jewry Book of Honour*. London: Caxton, 1922.

Auerbach, Sascha. "Negotiating Nationalism: Jewish Conscription and Russian Repatriation in London's East End, 1916–1918." *Journal of British Studies* 46 (July 2007): 594–620.

Bar-Yosef, Eitan. *The Holy Land in English Culture 1799–1917: Palestine and the Question of Orientalism*. New York: Oxford University Press, 2005.

Beckett, Ian F. W. *The Great War 1914–1918*. Harlow, UK: Longman, 2007.

Ben-Gurion, David. *Letters to Paula*. Translated by Aubrey Hodes. London: Vallentine Mitchell, 1971.

Ben-Hur, Raphaella Bilski. *Every Individual, A King: The Social and Political Thought of Ze'ev Vladimir Jabotinsky*. Washington, DC: B'nai B'rith Books, 1993.

Ben-Zvi, Yitzhak. *The Jewish Legion: Letters* [in Hebrew]. Jerusalem: Yad Ben Zvi, 1967.

Bergen, Doris L. *The Sword of the Lord: Military Chaplains from the First to the Twenty-First Century*. Notre Dame, IN: University of Notre Dame Press, 2004.

Berkowitz, Michael. *Western Jewry and the Zionist Project, 1914–1933*. Cambridge: Cambridge University Press, 1997.

———. *Zionist Culture and West European Jewry before the First World War*. New York: Cambridge University Press, 1993.

Braudy, Leo. *From Chivalry to Terrorism*. New York: Vintage, 2005.

Brian, Denis. *The Seven Lives of Colonel Patterson: How an Irish Lion Hunter Led the Jewish Legion to Victory*. Syracuse, NY: Syracuse University Press, 2008.

181

Brown, Malcolm, ed. *The Imperial War Museum Book of the First World War: A Great Conflict Recalled in Previously Unpublished Letters, Diaries, Documents and Memoirs*. London: Sidgwick & Jackson, 1991.

Cesarani, David. "An Embattled Minority: The Jews in Britain during the First World War." In *The Politics of Marginality: Race, the Radical Right and Minorities in Twentieth Century Britain*, edited by Tony Kushner and Kenneth Lunn, 61–81. London: Cass, 1990.

Cohen, Michael J. *Palestine to Israel: From Mandate to Independence*. London: Cass, 1988.

Cohen, Stuart A. *English Zionists and British Jews: The Communal Politics of Anglo-Jewry, 1895–1920*. Princeton, NJ: Princeton University Press, 1982.

Crerar, Duff. *Padres in No Man's Land: Canadian Chaplains and the Great War*. Montreal, QC: McGill-Queen's University Press, 1995.

Das, Santanu. *Touch and Intimacy in First World War Literature*. Cambridge: Cambridge University Press, 2005.

Dolev, Eran. *Allenby's Military Medicine: Life and Death in World War I Palestine*. New York: I. B. Tauris, 2007.

Egan, Susanna. *Mirror Talk: Genres of Crisis in Contemporary Autobiography*. Chapel Hill: University of North Carolina Press, 1999.

Elam, Igal. *Hagdudim Ha'ivri'im Bemilhemet Ha'olam Harishona* [The Jewish Legions in the First World War]. Tel Aviv: Ma'arachot, 1984.

Endelman, Todd M. *Jews of Modern Britain, 1656–2000*. Berkeley: University of California Press, 2002.

Falk, L. I. "With the Jewish Battalions in Palestine: Memoirs of a Jewish Chaplain." *The Maccabean*. Serialized from February 15, 1929, to November 15, 1929.

Falls, Cyril. *Military Operations: Egypt and Palestine from June 1917 to the End of the War*. London: HM Stationary Office, 1930.

Feder, Edna Lomsky. "The Meaning of War through Veterans' Eyes: A Phenomenological Analysis of Life Stories." *International Sociology* 10, no. 4 (December 1995): 463–82.

Freulich, Roman. *Soldiers in Judea: Stories and Vignettes of the Jewish Legion*. New York: Herzl Press, 1964.

Fromkin, David. *A Peace to End All Peace: The Fall of the Ottoman Empire and the Creation of the Modern Middle East*. New York: Henry Holt, 1989.

Fussell, Paul. *The Great War and Modern Memory*. London: Oxford University Press, 1975.

Gilbert, Martin. *The First World War: A Complete History*. New York: Henry Holt, 1994.

Gilner, Elias. *War and Hope: A History of the Jewish Legion*. New York: Herzl Press, 1969.

Goodman, Paul. *History of the Jews: Soldiers' and Sailors' Edition*. London: Office of the Chief Rabbi, 1917.

Gray, J. Glenn. *The Warriors: Reflections on Men in Battle*. New York: Harper & Row, 1970.

Grescoe, Audrey, and Paul Grescoe. *The Book of War Letters*. Toronto: McClelland & Stewart, 2003.

Gouttman, Rodney. *An Anzac Zionist Hero: The Life of Lieutenant-Colonel Eliazar Margolin*. Portland, OR: Vallentine Mitchell, 2006.

Haste, Cate. *Keep the Home Fires Burning: Propaganda in the First World War*. London: Allen Lane, 1977.

Herzl, Theodor. *The Jewish State*. New York: Dover, 1988.

Hertzberg, Arthur. *The Jews in America*. New York: Simon & Schuster, 1989.

Holmes, Richard. *Acts of War: Behavior of Men in Battle*. New York: Free Press, 1989.

Howard, Michael. "Introduction," in *A Part of History: Aspects of the British Experience of the First World War*. London: Continuum Publishing Group, 2008.

Howard, Michael Eliot. *The First World War: A Very Short Introduction*. Oxford: Oxford University Press, 2007.

Hyamson, Albert M. *Palestine under the Mandate, 1920–1948*. Westport, CT: Greenwood, 1950.

Hyman, Jonathan. "Jews in Britain during the Great War." Department of History Working Paper 51, University of Manchester, UK, October 2001.

Jabotinsky, Ze'ev. *Megilat Hagdud* [The story of the battalion]. Tel Aviv: Ministry of Defense, 1991.

Joseph, Bernard. *British Rule in Palestine*. Washington, DC: Public Affairs Press, 1948.

Katz, Jonathan. "Constructing a Jewish Legion for Canadians." *Dorot* 9 (2007): 117–28.

Katz, Shmuel. *Lone Wolf: A Biography of Vladimir (Ze'ev) Jabotinsky*. Fort Lee, NJ: Barricade Books, 1996.

Kay, Zachariah. "A Note on Canada and the Formation of the Jewish Legion." *Jewish Social Studies* 29 (July 1967): 171–77.

Keegan, John, and Richard Holmes. *Soldiers: A History of Men in Battle*. New York: Viking, 1985.

Keren, Michael. "Commemoration and National Identity: A Comparison between the Making of the Anzac and Palmach Legends." *Israel Studies Forum* 19 (November 2004): 9–27.

———. "National Icons and Personal Identities in Three Israeli Autobiographies." *Biography* 27 (Spring 2004): 357–83.

Kolinsky, Martin. *Law, Order and Riots in Mandatory Palestine, 1928–1935*. London: St. Martin's Press, 1993.

Kook, Abraham Isaac. "The Significance of the Revival." In *Abraham Isaac Kook: The Lights of Penitence, the Moral Principles, Lights of Holiness, Essays, Letters, and Poems*. Translated by Ben Zion Bokser. New York: Paulist Press, 1978.

Larson, Thomas. *The Memoir and the Memoirist: Reading and Writing Personal Narrative*. Athens: Ohio University Press, 2007.

Lasswell, Harold D. *Propaganda Technique in World War I*. Cambridge, MA: MIT Press, 1971.

Leed, Eric J. *No Man's Land: Combat and Identity in World War I*. Cambridge: Cambridge University Press, 1979.

Levene, Mark. "Going against the Grain: Two Jewish Memoirs of War and Anti-War, 1914–18." In *Forging Modern Jewish Identities: Public Faces and Private Strug-*

gles, edited by Michael Berkowitz, Susan L. Tananbaum, and Sam W. Bloom. London: Vallentine Mitchell, 2003.

Liddle, Peter H., ed. *Home Fires and Foreign Fields: British Social and Military Experience in the First World War*. London: Pergamon, 1985.

Liebman, Charles S., and Eliezer Don-Yehiya. *Civil Religion in Israel: Traditional Judaism and Political Culture in the Jewish State*. Berkeley: University of California Press, 1983.

LoBagola, Bata. *An African Savage's Own Story*. London: Knopf, 1930.

Mendes-Flohr, Paul R. "Between Existentialism and Zionism." *Journal of the American Academy of Religion* 47 (1979): 429–40.

Moore, Deborah Dash. *GI Jews: How World War II Changed a Generation*. Cambridge, MA: Harvard University Press, 2004.

Mosse, George L. "Max Nordau, Liberalism and the New Jew." *Journal of Contemporary History* 27 (October 1992): 565–81.

——. "Two World Wars and the Myth of the War Experience." *Journal of Contemporary History* 21 (1986): 491–513.

O'Leary, Cecilia Elizabeth. *To Die For: The Paradox of American Patriotism*. Princeton, NJ: Princeton University Press, 1999.

O'Neill, Robert, ed. *I Am Soldier: War Stories from the Ancient World to the Twentieth Century*. Oxford: Osprey, 2009.

Paddock, Troy R. E., ed. *A Call to Arms: Propaganda, Public Opinion, and Newspapers in the Great War*. Westport, CT: Praeger, 2004.

Patterson, John Henry. *The Man Eaters of Tsavo and Other East African Adventures*. London: Macmillan, 1907.

——. *With the Judeans in the Palestine Campaign*. New York: Macmillan, 1922.

——. *With the Zionists at Gallipoli*. London: Hutchinson, 1916.

Roberts, Brian. *Biographical Research*. Buckingham, UK: Open University Press, 2002.

Schweitzer, Richard. *The Cross and the Trenches: Religious Faith and Doubt among British and American Great War Soldiers*. Westport, CT: Praeger, 2003.

Shepherd, Naomi. *Ploughing Sand: British Rule in Palestine, 1917–1948*. London: John Murray, 1999.

Simkins, Peter. *Kitchner's Army: The Raising of the New Armies, 1914–16*. Manchester, UK: Manchester University Press, 1988.

Slomovitz, Albert Isaac. *The Fighting Rabbis: Jewish Military Chaplains and American History*. New York: New York University Press, 1999.

Snape, Michael. *God and the British Soldier: Religion and the British Army in the First and Second World Wars*. London: Routledge, 2005.

Solomon, Norman. "Judaism and the Ethics of War." *International Review of the Red Cross* 87 (June 2005): 295–309.

Sterba, Christopher M. *Good Americans: Italian and Jewish Immigrants during the First World War*. New York: Oxford University Press, 2003.

Streeter, Patrick. *Mad for Zion: A Biography of Colonel J. H. Patterson*. Harlow, UK: The Matching Press, 2004.

Taylor, David. "From Fighting the War to Writing the War: From Glory to Guilt?" *Contemporary British History* 23 (September 2009): 293–313.

Taylor, William R. *The Twentieth Century World: An International History.* New York: Oxford University Press, 1984.

Tulchinsky, Gerald. *Taking Root: The Origins of the Canadian Jewish Community.* Toronto: Lester Publishing, 1992.

Walzer, Michael. *Exodus and Revolution.* New York: Basic Books, 1984.

Watts, Martin. *The Jewish Legions and the First World War.* New York: Macmillan, 2004.

Winter, Jay M. *Sites of Memory, Sites of Mourning: The Great War in European Cultural History.* New York: Cambridge University Press, 1995.

Woodward, David R. *Hell in the Holy Land: World War I in the Middle East.* Lexington: University of Kentucky Press, 2006.

Yaron, Zvi. *Mishnato Shel Harav Kook* [The philosophy of Rabbi Kook]. Jerusalem: Jewish Agency, 1974.

Index

Breinigsville, PA USA
08 August 2010
243122BV00002B/1/P